# ABOUT
# FACES

# ABOUT FACES

## Terry Landau

ANCHOR BOOKS
DOUBLEDAY
*New York   London   Toronto   Sydney   Auckland*

*For Richard and Marika*

AN ANCHOR BOOK

*Published by Bantam Doubleday Dell Publishing Group, Inc.*
*666 Fifth Avenue, New York, New York 10103*

ANCHOR *and the portrayal of an anchor*
*are trademarks of Doubleday, a division*
*of Bantam Doubleday Dell Publishing Group, Inc.*

*Library of Congress Cataloging-in-Publication Data*

*Landau, Terry.*
  *About faces.*

  *Bibliography: p.*
  *Includes index.*
  *1. Face—Miscellanea.   2. Physiognomy.   I. Title.*
*QM535.L36   1989   573'.692   88-28532*
ISBN *0-385-24981-0* (pbk.)

DESIGNED BY MARYSARAH QUINN
AND CLAIRE M. NAYLON

FIRST EDITION
WAK

# Contents

## DIVERSITY

*It is the common wonder of all men, how among so many millions of faces there should be none alike.*

SIR THOMAS BROWNE

# 1

# The
# Evolutionary
# Perspective

The human face is one of the most fascinating of all images: powerful, purposeful, personal. At the same time, it is a highly specialized part of the body and the most convincing proof of an individual's identity. How did the face come to be so important? Evolution emphasizes the role of the environment in shaping the face's form. The modern scientific theory of evolution by natural selection, first proposed by Charles Darwin in 1859, enables us to understand why each species is adapted to its particular environment and why its face looks and behaves the way it does.

It was Darwin who first noticed that individuals vary in their anatomical and behavioral characteristics. Some seemed more suited to survival than others. Darwin also observed that species over-reproduce: those best adapted to the environment are more likely to survive and reproduce offspring. In this way, he believed, some characteristics are weeded out and others are favored and preserved for the important reason that they enhance the individual's prospects of survival and progeny. Darwin called this evolutionary mechanism natural selection because nature "selects" for survival those who are best adapted.

Change is the raw material for the selection process. For Darwin, change meant greater adaptability. Adaptability enabled an animal to survive in a particular environment, as well as to venture successfully into new environments in the never ending search for food. Certain changes increased the individual's chance for survival and reproduction. These would be preserved within the population through the laws of heredity. (The principles of heredity guarantee that the parents' characteristics are passed along to the offspring in the form of biochemical units called genes—more about genes later.) Those changes that decreased the individual's chances for survival were eliminated quickly, as there were simply no children to perpetuate them. Evolution, then, by natural selection is the sum of adaptation. It is the reason that our faces look and behave the way they do today.

The continuity of the fossil record demonstrates that every human face on earth today arose out of simpler animals by a succession of minute improvements in design that contributed to survival over hundreds of millions of years. No mutants arose suddenly—rather, it was imperceptible changes over a very long time that fashioned new faces out of old.

In terms of natural selection, the story of your face begins about 350 million years ago, when an adventurous variety of fish called *Crossopterygia* mi-

CHARLES DARWIN
Born February 12, 1809. Died April 19, 1882.

*I have called this principle, by which each slight variation, if useful, is preserved, by the term natural selection.*

CHARLES DARWIN

grated to dry land, perhaps because of drought. According to the internationally known scientist Robert Jastrow, *Crossopterygia* was well equipped for such an adventure because this salmonlike fish possessed two advantageous traits: powerful muscular fins, capable of propelling it across the land, and lungs as well as gills. In time, the descendants of *Crossopterygia* established themselves on the banks of rivers and streams until, gradually, under nature's pruning action, the crossopterygian stock changed. The brain improved somewhat. Lungs evolved into a new kind of breathing apparatus. Gills began to disappear— or, rather, to change into something else. Bones of the gills arched and evolved slowly into jawbones. Then the gill muscles, originally used for pumping water, transformed into a new kind of muscular veil that was eventually to become the human face—the face you see in the mirror. Almost all of your skull bones can be traced back, bone by bone, to these stumpy-finned adventurers who set out to explore life on dry land 350 million years ago.

The fossil record shows that it took another 25 million generations for a transitional form of animal to come into being. This creature, the amphibian

FISH TO HUMAN
The fossil record is evidence of evolution. It reveals that every face on the land today can trace its ancestry back to a fish called *Crossopterygia*. Evolution does not travel a narrow and determined path—rather, there are many dead ends and new beginnings.

ancestor of today's frogs and toads, lived part time in the water and part time on dry land.

Another 50 million generations passed and the reptiles appeared on earth. That was about 300 million years ago. These animals mastered the land for a time and ultimately gave issue to many different evolutionary lines, including the mammals (the class to which we humans belong), before losing their predominance. The appearance of the mammals marked a great step in the evolution of a sentient, responsive face.

Mammals derive their name from and are characterized by the fact that they suckle their young with milk produced by the mammary glands of the mother. Mammals possess a four-chambered heart. They breathe air reoxygenated in the lungs and have a growth of hair over the body. Much that we consider human about ourselves is attributable to our mammalian characteristics, including our capacity for learning.

The existence of our early mammalian predecessors is revealed to us through a few fossilized teeth and bone fragments. These tell us they were insectivores, who ferreted about the forest floor for food. The most obvious things about their faces were their long olfactory snouts and sensitive "antennae," which took the form of long whiskers or vibrissae, which provided their faces with an acute sense of touch. (Today, in the higher primates, such as monkeys, apes, and human beings, the tactile functions of vibrissae have been transferred to the lips and hands.) Their skulls reveal something else: they had relatively larger brains, were more intelligent than any other animal that had come before, and possessed a keen sense of hearing. These basic mammals evolved simultaneously into horses, pigs, whales, elephants, and other modern mammals during a period of some 30 million years. Changes in the face's design developed in the direction of increased efficiency as these various mammals moved into all the environmental niches, on the land, in the sea, and in the air.

The fossil record shows that at some point between 60 and 70 million years ago an inquisitive band of forest mammals left the forest floor and climbed up into the trees, where arboreal life offered special rewards, including new foods and protection from predators. This move was decisive and launched the primate order (the order to which we humans belong); it embraces the lemurs, monkeys, and apes. Natural selection went to work on this small band of venturesome individuals and adapted their faces and bodies to suit their life in the trees. Judging distance, for example, is fundamental to survival in the trees, but it requires eyes that point straight ahead and produce overlapping fields of vision (which is the basis for three-dimensional stereoscopic vision).

How did the primate eye adapt to this need? The answer lies in the slight variations in position that occurred from one individual to another in the population over a long time as the eye sockets in the skulls of the early primates gradually moved around to the front of the head, until in the monkey and the ape they came to face directly forward. By random mutation and natural selection over an immense period of time, a new strain of tree-adapted animals evolved. The fossil record demonstrates that this movement of the eye sockets took approximately 20 million years, that it also involved the transformation of the paw into a hand and contributed to a general enlargement of the brain in the monkey and ape, and that it ultimately produced the kind of vision that enabled a creature to, as Robert Jastrow has so poetically put it, "caress an object with its eyes."

At the same time, sensitivity to color was adding another dimension to vision and more circuits to the brain. Color made it possible to spot fruit at the end of a branch. Color sped up recognition of danger. In the world of the trees, color became a matter of life and death.

Tree living redesigned the face in other ways too. When early primates adapted to an arboreal habitat, their diet changed. They became herbivorous. This shift created major changes in the anatomy of the face and in the function of the teeth. The molar teeth, for example, lost their piercing and slicing ability and became grinding and milling devices instead.

About this time, too, primate faces first began to communicate and function as signaling organs. The first primates—the prosimians, who took to the trees about 65 million years ago—did not have the proper equipment to display an array of emotions on the face. Their facial muscles consisted mainly of broad bands of fibers, which tended to contract all together and produce gross movements. It happens that lemurs (today's surviving prosimians) are capable of only a single clear-cut facial expression: the drawing back of the lips to bare the teeth for biting. This is a signal of fear or anger. It is the original primate expression.

The next recognizable stage in the fossil record is about 30 million years ago when these arboreal primates gave issue to the monkeys and apes in whose faces we can recognize much that is familiar. But while the monkey face did not change very much from then until now, the ape line continued to evolve in many different directions and produced a variety of distinctive faces, including our own.

The great apes and humankind belong to a superfamily of primates called the Hominoidea, meaning "humanlike." This superfamily has two branches. The Pongidae branch of the family includes the orangutan, the gorilla, and the chimpanzee, while all living and extinct forms of human beings belong to the family Hominidae. It is convenient to refer to all these sorts as hominids.

Although it is not certain that we have identified the earliest ancestral hominid, there is something to be said for a species found in East Africa by Mary Leakey. Her discovery was given the name *Proconsul africanus*. Dating revealed it to be a 20-million-year-old ancestor. In *Proconsul* the eyes are fully forward and produce stereoscopic vision. The brain is markedly larger than anything that had come before, but the teeth show the creature to be very apelike because the big canines are locked in a way that is definitely not humanlike.

Tracing the changes in the face from *Proconsul* (ancestral to both apes and humans) to our modern face leads next to *Ramapithecus*, who many experts believe may be the first representative of the human family—a true hominid. *Ramapithecus*'s face was significantly different from *Proconsul*'s, having been reshaped by a changing climate. One of the consequences of this change in climate was the spread of grasslands at the expense of forest. Grasslands, sometimes called savannas, offered new evolutionary opportunities to a wide variety of mammals, including the primates.

Reacting swiftly to the challenge of the changing environment, a few primate stocks, including *Ramapithecus*, opened new horizons and lived in India, Kenya, and possibly also China and Greece. Ramapithecines left evidence of their existence in the form of jaw fragments and other bones.

Paleoanthropologists also deduce from the evidence that Ramapithecines moved about freely and were quite capable of dealing with a variety of circumstances. Though potassium-argon dating of a *Ramapithecus* jaw uncovered by Louis and Mary Leakey confirmed the fossil jaw to be 14 million years old, it had distinctive human characteristics: the teeth were all about the same size and there was an unmistakable humanlike sweep of the upper teeth.

Teeth are often the only fossils an anthropologist has to work with, and they can be of enormous help in classification. Canines, incisors, premolars, and molars differ widely in number, shape, and size among primates. Often a single tooth can indicate whether the owner was a monkey, an ape, or a human. In *Ramapithecus* the dental arcade is rounded,

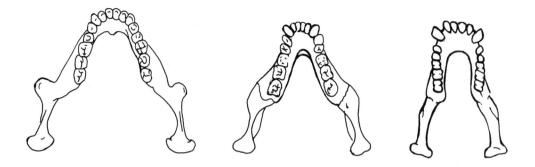

## TEETH AND PALATES

Open your mouth wide and look into a mirror. You will notice two things about your upper jaw; both are hominid features. The first is that it has a hard palate (roof) and is arched. The second is that your teeth go back on each side in a broad, elegant, parabolic curve, with the widest part of the curve at the very back. By contrast, the hard palate of an ape is flat and its jaws are U-shaped. *Ramapithecus* can be identified as leading in a human direction by the nature of the teeth and part of a palate which reveal that the premolars are evenly proportioned as they are in humans and the palate is arched and curves outward toward the back, the way ours does.

the canines are small, and the molar teeth do not increase in size from front to back as they do in the apes. (It has been suggested that the shortening canines in the transmutation of ape to human can be closely associated with the manual use of weapons and tools.)

Though we know very little about *Ramapithecus*, we do know that a dramatic thing happened to this prehuman creature that paved the way for the first face-to-face encounters: they learned to walk upright. This straightening up of the body had enormous impact on social relationships and forever changed the face, redefining its job.

The period between 8 and 4 million years ago is a fossil void. But since evolution occurs by a process of repeated branching, most scientists suspect that the hominid line branched and the line to man separated from the line to modern apes so that the next recognizable stage in the human lineage started about 4 million years ago when the record introduces us to a two-legged prehuman creature, belonging to the genus *Australopithecus*. *Australopithecus* stood upright, walked on two legs, constructed base camps, and became dependent upon a division of labor between the sexes. This is the oldest hominid species yet found and it may or may not be ancestral to all other forms of humans.

*Australopithecus* lived in South as well as East Africa. Most fossils of *Australopithecus africanus*, another branch of the *Australopithecus* line, have come from South African caves. Of these, the most legendary specimen is the Taung baby skull, which was recognized by the neuroanatomist Raymond Dart as being something other than that of an ape. Dart drew bold conclusions from the skull. He believed that he had found the distant ancestor of the human line and declared that the Taung specimen represented a creature that was advanced beyond the apes in two distinctly human characteristics: its teeth and the improved quality of its brain. The teeth and facial elements were not those of an ape, Dart insisted. He thought the position of the foramen magnum, the aperture through which the spinal cord leaves the brain case, implied that the creature had walked on two legs, not four. This provoked a widespread controversy. But in the end Dart had identified a new ancestral line which he called *Australopithecus*, meaning the "Southern ape." (*Pithecus* is the Greek word for "ape.")

Dart's discovery changed the course of paleoanthropological research. From then on, experts looked to Africa as the birthplace of the human face. Indeed, in the course of the last sixty years numerous *Australopithecus* bones and teeth have been recovered and it is clear they represent a prehuman phase of hominid evolution in which considerable advance was made in the development of bipedalism, changing teeth to accommodate a changing diet, and brain expansion.

Among the Australopithecines appeared a momentous development in human evolution: the habit and tradition of tool making. Both males and females used tools for protection, for plant gathering and preparation, and perhaps for hunting. There is every reason to believe that tool making and use marked a quantum leap in the advance of human intelligence and that it profoundly impacted the face's form and function. There is no question but that tool making played a key role in fostering social relationships and encouraging face-to-face communication as males

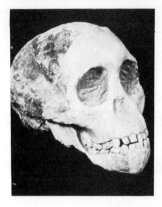

THE TAUNG SKULL

*I stood in the shade, holding the brain as greedily as any miser hugs his gold . . . here, I was certain, was one of the most significant finds ever made in the history of anthropology.*

RAYMOND DART

and females used tools and attempted to pass on knowledge about them. It is also clear that tool making was an evolutionary breakthrough that conferred immense survival benefits on its practitioners—male and female—by enhancing their ability to manipulate the environment.

*Australopithecus* is what zoologists call a genus— a classification that can include several different species. It seems that after about 2 million years the genus *Australopithecus* divided into two species, the gracile *africanus* and the heavily built *robustus*. *Robustus*'s huge cheeks, teeth, and massive musculature of cranium and jaw were adapted to a fibrous vegetarian diet. *Africanus* was a hunter and scavenger of small game. A fascinating conjecture is that these two species—*Australopithecus africanus* and *Australopithecus robustus*—lived side by side in the Olduvai Gorge for hundreds of thousands of years, but that eventually hunting sharpened the wits of *africanus*, making it a more successful competitor—bigger, stronger, and more dangerous to others. But though *Australopithecus* seems to be humanlike, it is not the direct link to us, as this hominid line became extinct about a million years ago.

In 1961, Louis Leakey unearthed a momentous find in Tanzania's Olduvai Gorge that would change our notions about just how old the human face is. This find he classified in the zoological genus *Homo*, and eventually it came to be named *Homo habilis*, meaning "skilled man" or "handy man." There is much controversy about this classification. (Some investigators, such as anthropologist Nancy Makepeace Tanner, classify this find and others similar to it as *Australopithecus habilis*.) Leakey's find proved to be nearly 2 million years old and revealed the existence of a creature who had a surprisingly small apelike body but a bigger brain, half again as large as the brain of any other hominids living during the same period. The face, too, is changed. It is significantly more delicate. From identifying the lower face bones, the palate, and four teeth, it is clear that the facial anatomy takes a distinctly human direction.

*Homo habilis* made the transition from a vegetarian diet to one that also included meat, a pivotally important step in the evolution of the face. Meat requires much less chewing than fibrous plants. Large canine teeth (helpful in shredding the harder covering of many edible plants), and bony crests were necessary to give attachment to the massive muscles that moved the lower jaw of the plant-eating primates. For the meat eater, however, large canine teeth, large jaws, and bony crests were unnecessary. Hence, the changes that occurred were in the direction of a more refined and humanlike head and face. By reducing the size of the teeth—and hence of the jaws necessary to hold the roots of these teeth—room was afforded for an expanding brain and the development of a more sophisticated vocal apparatus.

*Homo habilis* was succeded in the fossil record by *Homo erectus*, the man who stands erect. This ancient line lived in Asia, Europe, and Africa. The first fossil remains of *Homo erectus* were found in 1891 at Trinil in Java. Further finds provided an overview of *Homo erectus*'s million years on earth. Early *erectus* faces are more massively built than the later specimens. The teeth are fairly small and the cranial capacity grows from about 850 cc to over 1,000 cc (compared with a modern average of 1,300 cc). The increasingly larger brain is housed in a high, less rugged skull. At the end of their time on earth, casts of the brain cavity reveal a brain completely human in its proportions, if not yet in its organization.

By at least half a million years ago, fire was a great technological force that was reshaping the contours of the *erectus* face in a kind of chain-reaction process. Fire not only created warm zones for

To gaze on the faces of early man is an intriguing thought, but to the Russian artist and paleoanthropologist Mikhail Gerasimov, it was a passion and his life's work. For him the reconstruction of a fossil head was a three-dimensional jigsaw puzzle in which bone fragments were pieced together and layers of clay were added to simulate muscles, tissue, and skin until a portrait of an individual emerged. His techniques, based on modern human patterns of skin thickness and texture, opened up new avenues for forensic science and the reconstruction of the human face. His Cro-Magnon reconstruction is a familiar face. It is our face. Faces such as this one gave birth to art and music.

socializing, which led to a quantum advance in face-to-face communication, but it also changed eating habits. Fossil teeth, which as we have seen are sensitive indicators of evolution, suggest that cooking dates back to these times. Softer foods may have put less of a strain on the large jaws and powerful jaw muscles. These became small, along with the molar teeth. Changes such as these affected the overall design of the face and skull.

The demands of group living made new kinds of communication behavior mandatory. As a species, these prehuman *erectus* ancestors were challenged to get along, to cooperate and communicate with one another, and to operate as a group. Both cooperation and communication depend upon speech as well as expressive behavior. The process of developing speech manifests itself in structural changes of the lower jaw. The lower jaw becomes more refined. The points of attachment for the tongue muscles become enlarged. *Homo erectus* could not have been fully articulate, but this hominid was probably able to put thoughts into words, as we do today.

Though we do not know why, *Homo erectus* left Africa and embarked on journeys into Europe and Asia a million or more years ago. *Homo erectus* traces

Starting with a plaster cast of a damaged skull, Gerasimov reconstructed the missing parts and gave a face to this ancestral female. Though his reconstruction features the pronounced Neanderthal brow ridge, it has been suggested that the evolution from *erectus* to *sapiens* can be seen in this face.

Over the course of his career Gerasimov sculpted many Neanderthal faces from fossil evidence, including the famous adult male from the cave La Chapelle-aux-Saints in France. His many Neanderthal reconstructions show the range of variation of *Homo sapiens neanderthalensis*.

have been found in many places, which suggests that a bigger brain gave *Homo erectus* an enhanced ability to adapt to new environments. *Homo erectus*, in fact, built up an evolutionary momentum that was to propel it inexorably toward modern humankind.

We have two kinds of evidence that mark the transition from the *Homo erectus* face to the face of *Homo sapiens*. The first is a scattering of teeth and jaw fragments from a number of sites in France and Morocco and two skulls: one from Swanscombe, England, the other from Steinheim, Germany.

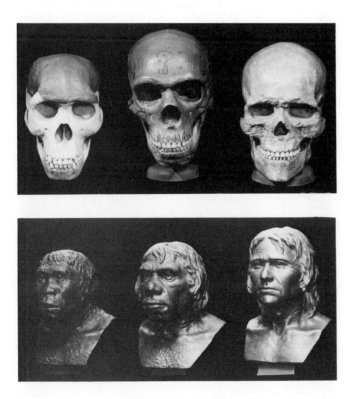

J. H. McGregor was another anthropologist-artist who tried to create posthumous portraits from fossil skulls. In the 1920s, he shaped these *Homo erectus*, *Neanderthal* (La Chapelle-aux-Saints male skull), and *Cro-Magnon* faces for the American Museum of Natural History.

Michael Anderson is a modern practitioner of the art and science of facial reconstruction. This series of photographs shows, from skull to nearly finished face and figure, another reconstruction of the famous La Chapelle-aux-Saints Neanderthal. To re-create this portrait, Anderson used ultrasound measurements that are based upon chimpanzee and human standards. He then adapted these standards to the individual being modeled. In addition, he used skin-depth data based on human cadavers. Compare Anderson's reconstruction of the La Chapelle-aux-Saints male skull with the ones done earlier by Gerasimov and McGregor. It is clear that advances in the art of facial reconstruction have given us a completely different image of the way our ancestors looked.

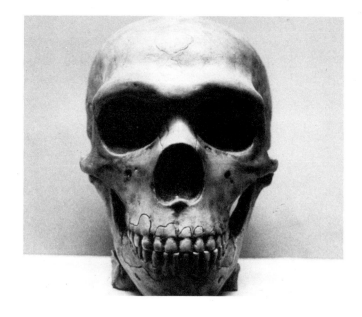

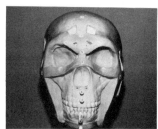
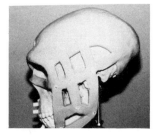

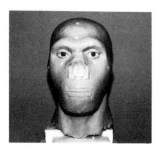
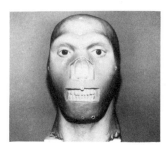
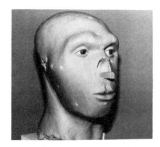

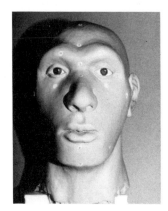
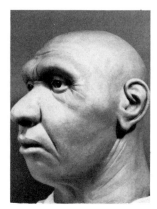

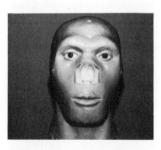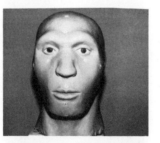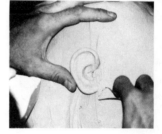

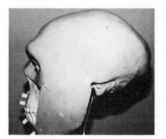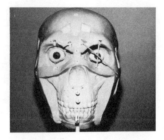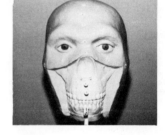

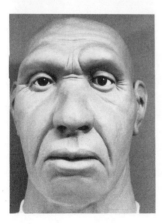

Commissioned by the Maxwell Museum of Anthropology at the University of New Mexico, Anderson is working on a series of realistic life-size reconstructions of our fossil ancestors. The La Chapelle-aux-Saints male stands on the right. Besides the La Chapelle Neanderthal man, Anderson is reconstructing a 3.5-million-year-old female *Australopithecus afarensis* and a *Homo habilis* male dating back 2 million years.

The Steinheim and Swanscombe women are between two hundred thousand and three hundred thousand years old. Both skulls possess pronounced brow ridges and heavy faces, but the back of the head is very similar to ours. The Steinheim woman's brain was 1,170 cc (exceeding any known *erectus* females who had come before) and the Swanscombe woman's brain was 1,270 cc. Both skulls are clearly intermediate types, as neither displays the sloping-sided skull shape of *erectus* seen from the back; both are rounded toward the crown, very much the way ours is.

It appears that the evolutionary processes leading to the emergence of more modern individuals from *Homo erectus* were working more swiftly on the back of the head than on the face. In terms of the face's appearance, the most dramatic change in its structure and appearance came in tandem with a decrease in the size of the chewing apparatus, including the

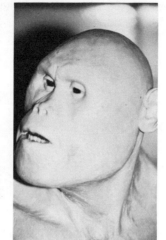
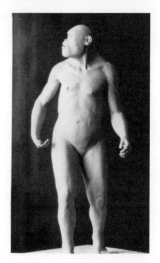

AUSTRALOPITHECUS
AFARENSIS FEMALE

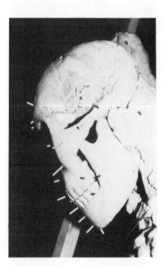

HOMO HABILIS MALE

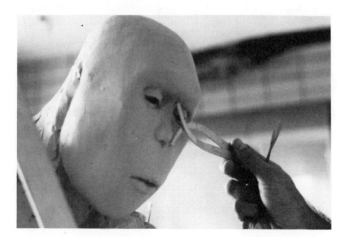

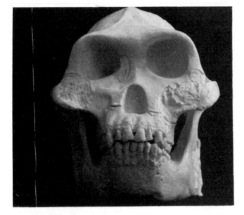

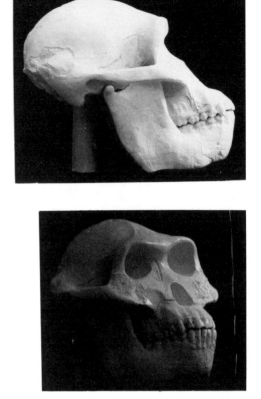

ridge of bone over the eyes, the cheekbones, and the bones that support the teeth. But perhaps the evolutionary change that was to have the greatest effect on how our faces look today was the enlargement of the brain—particularly the forepart. It is clear that the brain evolved by natural selection in circumstances where greater brainpower enhanced prospects for survival. In this scenario, skill fosters wisdom, wisdom fosters skill.

> *The head is more than a symbolic image of man; it is the seat of foresight and, in that respect, the spring which drives culture.*
>
> JACOB BRONOWSKI

It was after the hominids started to do cultural things that the brain grew in size and complexity— for the making of tools to deal with the result of

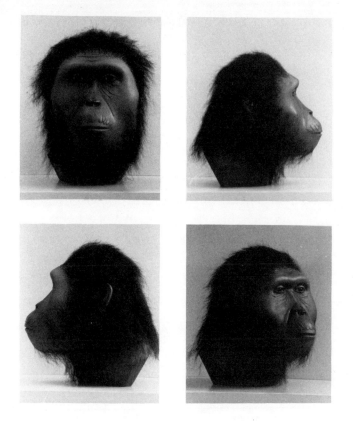

Compare Anderson's reconstruction (based on Dave Arter's skull reconstruction) of a male *Australopithecus afarensis* with the female he is working on for the Maxwell Museum. (See pages 16–17). In this case, Anderson used a completely different technique and the face's appearance is based on reconstructing the musculature (as Gerasimov did) rather than on skin-depth data. According to Anderson, this technique is more accurate as the musculature is clear from the skull's bone structure. "I do exactly what the skull tells me," Anderson says. "It all goes together like a puzzle." Interestingly, because the skull is such a strong indicator of the look of a face, these two individuals share an overall *afarensis* look in spite of the differences between the two methods.

cooperative hunting and the making of gathering implements and containers imply foresight and planning, as well as a complex system of cooperation and face-to-face communication. Obviously there was a selective advantage to cultural behavior and a premium on individuals who could learn a lot and learn quickly. Selection favored the smart. They bred smarter offspring. Skill and cunning, both products of the brain, enabled them to survive and flourish. In this way human beings created an environment of their own making, an environment in which individuals were dependent upon one another and upon their self-created culture for survival. Communication is crucial in this circumstance. Selection favors whatever mutations produce improved interpersonal communication; whether it is in the speech organs or in the musculature of the face, expressive behavior is subject to selection too.

Selection favors those with the prospensity for

getting along, and in a real sense this yielded faces that were more effective communicators. In other words, selection put into the wiring those qualities and propensities that made for a successful social and cultural face.

Around two hundred thousand years ago or so, a sentient responsive human face appeared. It was *Homo sapiens neanderthalensis,* and this species appeared with a brain even larger than that which is housed in our modern heads, but with a different face that was characterized by a huge bony visor about the eyes instead of eyebrow ridges and a forehead that sloped back. The Neanderthal nasal aperture was wide and the whole midface projected forward over an appropriately long jaw. But though Neanderthal's jaw is enormous, he has virtually no chin. A chin, it turns out, is a distinctly human feature of the face.

Neanderthals lived over a considerable period of time. Through the millennia they underwent important changes, especially in the shape and appearance of their faces. These changes apparently differed from place to place. In the Middle East, for example, Neanderthalers were becoming more like modern humans, while in Europe Neanderthalers were evolving toward the classic large-faced type with jutting brows and low, narrow skulls. The reasons for this are unknown, but it has been speculated that the European branch was isolated from the main genetic pool by glaciers and could not share in the important evolutionary improvements that appear to have been made in the Middle East.

Among the Neanderthals, we observe the arrival of several traits we associate with being human. Like us, *Homo sapiens neanderthalensis* buried their dead, painted their faces and bodies for ritualistic reasons, and committed murder. Indeed, Neanderthalers made many significant contributions to the development of human culture, including specialized weapons and distinct tools for scraping and chopping. They lived in caves, wore clothes, and united in organized packs. These circumstances set the stage for increased social activity and more formalized social organization. All this placed new demands on the face, as it became increasingly important to get along with others.

Though no one knows when we acquired the ability to speak, we know it had a feedback effect, for the ability to speak is in the shape and musculature of the mouth, tongue, soft palate, pharynx, and larynx as well as the brain.

Over time, as the muscles of the face became more specialized, they became more adept at maintaining social relationships. Small bundles of fibers developed and branched off from the broad bands of muscles like secondary roads until the muscles became capable of animating the face with precision and subtlety—ultimately empowering it to communicate information about the intentions of the expressor as well as to alert fellow creatures to certain aspects of the environment.

A great many Neanderthal remains have been discovered in Europe, North Africa, western Asia, and the Middle East. The human tide spread into every corner and every ecological niche, moving across deserts and over mountain ranges. People from each generation advanced in waves of no more than a dozen miles or so. Our Neanderthal predecessors may be regarded as a type representing a stage of human evolution all over the Old World. Anthropologists suspect that Neanderthals were virtually indistinguishable from modern humans in movement, in the use of the hands, in thought, and in language production. Neanderthals, as a species, displayed a wide range of variation in physical appearance, just as human beings around the world do today. The traditional view holds that modern humans are related to the Neanderthals, having descended from them. But recent genetic studies suggest something different: that, anatomically, modern humans may have emerged from Africa around two hundred thousand years ago and spread throughout the world. Other kinds of evidence, such as skull fragments discovered at St. Césaire, France, in 1981, show that *Homo sapiens neanderthalensis* and *Homo sapiens sapiens* were contemporaries.

Now that *Homo sapiens neanderthalensis* and *Homo sapiens sapiens* are regarded as two subspecies of the same genus *Homo*, the question is: What is the relationship between them? Anthropologists do not agree as to what it is. One theory is that a biological effect called neoteny may have been at work to produce quite quickly a more "youthful" version of the Neanderthal face. In his book *The Human Revolution*, Desmond Collins has recently posited a biological mechanism by which the Neanderthal population as a whole might have evolved into modern man: "Neoteny is the process whereby species become sexually mature and capable of reproduction at a less fully adult stage of development." A number of juvenile skulls of Neanderthals have been found and they all—including the ones with the classic features—more closely resemble adult *Homo sapiens sapiens* skulls than adult Neanderthal skulls do. For that matter, the skulls of baby chimpanzees do the same. It might be said that modern faces display numerous childhood or neotenous traits. Collins proposes that *Homo sapiens sapiens* may simply be the direct descendant of *Homo sapiens neanderthalensis* by means of the rapid operation of neoteny. The opportunity for neoteny to do its work upon the Neanderthals, who after all had already arrived at a modern sort of brain size, perhaps lay in the effects of human culture: cooking to render meat more digestible and less in need of chewing, and the improved tool kit that brought food to the mouth and did away with the need for big teeth in big, powerfully articulated jaws. The reduction of the jaw and its attachment areas on the cranium meant a reduced face and reduced skull ruggedness all around—the most noticeable areas of difference between Neanderthal and modern man. Under this view, neoteny has conferred real evolutionary benefits, physically manifested in a more childlike skull, behaviorally manifested in playfulness, inventiveness, and mental flexibility, which are surely among the most useful attributes in the survival game.

Whether or not neoteny was the mechanism of change, the appearance of fully modern faces in the shape of the Cro-Magnon reveal that powerful evolutionary forces were at work, driven by a complex interaction of physical and intellectual capabilities within a self-created framework of culture. These forces, in less than a million years, added nearly one pound of gray matter to the human brain, much of it in the forepart, where thinking, planning, and learning take place. As additional neurons crowded into the brain, the forehead bulged forward and outward and the cranium became rounded. These forces probably operated on many populations, driving them into the *sapiens* state simultaneously, so that by forty thousand to thirty-five thousand years ago a new face appeared on the scene. This new face was more refined, more intelligent, and capable of articulate speech. It had a capacity for compassion and learning, for foresight, for processing complex information. This is your face and mine. This is a face that spread into all the habitable regions of the globe, establishing homes in every kind of environment, including the Arctic. This is when the diverse cultures of man began to appear. We call these citizens of the world Cro-Magnon by convention, although, in strict archaeological terms, Cro-Magnon refers to the people who inhabited the caves and rock shelters in the limestone gorges of the Dordogne in southwestern France.

Our Cro-Magnon ancestors, perhaps no more than a million individuals, were isolated from one another early in human history by deserts, oceans, mountain ranges, and other barriers. In isolation, individuals within the groups mated. Traits were passed down through the laws of heredity, creating

**ENVIRONMENT SHAPES THE FACE**
It is clear that the total human population is divided along geographic lines, for there are many physical differences that distinguish us from one another as groups and that can be attributed to adaptations to the environment.

"gene pools" in which visible and nonvisible biological traits were preserved and perpetuated.

In time, population growth expanded the "gene pool," enlarging the body of genetic material. The result is that modern human faces come in many varieties. There are the well-padded faces of the Eskimos and the slender faces of the Manchurians. There are the light-skinned, long-nosed faces from northern Europe and the dark-skinned, flat-nosed faces of tropical New Guinea and the African Congo. What do these facial differences mean, if anything? This question has been the subject of an ongoing debate.

Some anthropologists believe that the physical differences that distinguish us from one another as groups were acquired as adaptations to the different climates into which our human ancestors moved. They theorize that the tightly curled hair of some tropical peoples emerged to protect the head from heat, while the Tibetan's sparse facial hair evolved because a beard would freeze against the face and prove dangerous. Desert life, on the other hand, forged a functional high-arched nose so that it would humidify the dry desert air before it reached the delicate lung tissue, and the Eskimo's flat, thickly padded face and eye fold (a fatty layer under the upper lid) may have evolved to provide protection against subzero temperatures.

The Darwinian revolution simplified our understanding of human geographic variation, but even Darwin recognized that adaptation to the environment did not account for all the visible differences between groups and did not begin to answer the question of why people from different places look different from one another.

Darwin's explanation in *The Descent of Man* in 1871 suggested that many physical characteristics about the face, such as skin color, eye color, and lip variability, could not be explained by natural selection because they did not confer any special advantage in the creature's battle for survival. But Darwin felt they could be explained by sexual selection because they played an obvious role in securing mates—either by attracting an individual of the opposite sex or by intimidating a rival of the same sex.

*Not one of the external differences between the races of man is of any direct or special service to him.*

CHARLES DARWIN

Many of the traits produced by sexual selection seem arbitrary, such as variations in skin color, or the thickening of the lips, or the extra fold in the eyelid. These features may have appeared naturally in early human populations living in isolated pockets around the world. In time, these distinct features became fixed—standards of beauty by which one selected a mate. In this way, sexual selection helped entrench different traits in different places.

UCLA physiologist and writer Jared Diamond has labeled this evolutionary mechanism "survival of the sexiest" because certain traits—such as skin color and eye color, as well as lip and eye shape—evolved in lockstep with the group's ideas about what is attractive.

"Survival of the sexiest" works like this: in a group where frizzy hair is preferred to straight hair, straight-haired individuals are going to find fewer and fewer mates. But the frizzy-haired individuals are going to leave plenty of offspring. Eventually, the genes for straight hair cease to exist in the population. Another scenario: frizzy-haired individuals mate only with other frizzy-haired individuals. Straight-haired individuals mate only with other straight-haired groups. The end result is that there are two distinct groups. Interestingly, new studies of how people actually select their mates show that people do tend to mate with individuals who resemble themselves in every way, including hair, eye, and skin color.

But as Darwin and many others since have pointed out, whether the hair is straight or whether it is frizzy has no adaptive value except in relation to some arbitrary standard of beauty, so it's likely that such traits and aesthetic preferences did evolve together and contribute to the limitless range of human diversity.

Darwin's ideas about sexual selection were generally rejected and ignored in his own time. Even today, many biologists hold that many visible differences, such as skin color, evolved through natural selection. The usual explanation is that people from sunny places have black skins because the abundance of melanin protects them against the sun's rays. Fair-skinned people, on the other hand, who live far to the north are pale so they can benefit from

light skin, which allows more vitamin D to be absorbed.

The problem with this hypothesis, according to Jared Diamond and others, is that it simply does not hold up to scientific scrutiny. The evidence makes it difficult to cite sunlight as the chief selective factor in molding skin color. Consider the following examples. Eskimos live in the north but are far from pale. Tasmanians live with relatively little sunlight, yet they are dark-skinned. Some of the people living in the sunniest parts of tropical Southeast Asia are far from black, and no original inhabitants of the Americas had black skin, regardless of how close they lived to the equator or how much sun they got.

The fact is, classifying groups on the basis of the face's physical appearance is fraught with danger, though some physical anthropologists continue to search for new and better ways of classifying human populations. Other physical anthropologists believe that it is impossible to classify all the world's different peoples because the range of human variation

THE LIPSCOMB FAMILY PORTRAIT
The passage of genes between members of the population occurs under many different circumstances. The result is not a uniform blend but incredible diversity even within a single family.

is too great even within groups. The advocates of this position point out that mixing is the rule, not the exception. The earth's people have migrated around the world since the earliest times and whenever people have scaled geographic barriers they have come in contact with other human groups, mated, and produced children who combined the different traits of their parents.

*No argument has ever been advanced by any reasonable man against the fact of differences among men. The whole argument is about what differences exist and how they are to be gauged.*

JACQUES BARZUN

Increasingly, scientists are turning their attention to the causes of human variation rather than the classification of groups. It is now clear that there are a number of genetic mechanisms operating to promote variation among and between human populations. Five are considered most important. The first is sex.

Sex delivers new gene combinations, guaranteeing an endless variation on the theme. Sex is the means by which the species is reproduced and maintained from generation to generation. Sex makes it possible for genes from two totally unrelated family lines to come together at fertilization and create a person (a new genetic combination that was previously absent) who possesses mutations that occurred in quite separate people of the past. (From the evolutionary standpoint, the fundamental materials of evolution are the hereditary particles, which are contained in the chromosomes of the sex cells of the male and female members of the population. These hereditary particles are called genes and they have the capacity to change.)

The second mechanism that ensures diversity is mutation. Any sudden change in a gene that is transmitted to future generations contributes to variation. The mutation comes for better or worse. There are a number of speculations as to what causes these mutations. Some suggest they are a result of cosmic rays penetrating the earth's atmosphere. Others point to the natural radioactivity from the soil. Still others suggest that among the properties of genes is an inherited capacity to undergo physical change. Whatever the cause, gene changes do happen and changed individuals are born. If their differences prove useful, they thrive better than others, live longer, and produce more children—some of whom will also possess this new and useful trait caused by genetic mutation.

Natural selection is the third mechanism that promotes variation, just as Darwin said it was.

The fourth important mechanism of human variation is isolation. In isolation, mating is selective. Most people choose mates who are attractive to them and who look the most like them. In this way, "gene pools" form. Isolation may result from geographic barriers, as it did in prehistoric times, when the people south of the Sahara Desert in Africa did not mate with the people north of the Sahara because they could not survive the trek across the desert; or it can be caused by social barriers, as it is today under the South African system of apartheid, which separates groups just as forcefully as do geographic barriers.

The fifth mechanism contributing to human variability is genetic drift. Genetic drift occurs when the breeding population changes. This happens mostly in small populations, where the departure of a few individuals or the arrival of a few outsiders may dramatically alter the genetic composition of the group.

By now you may wonder why are there so many safeguards to ensure human variability. The reason is that diversity endows our species with a high degree of adaptability, so that if there are any changes in the environment there are likely to be individuals (genotypes) who will be able to respond to the challenges of the changed environment.

From the evolutionary perspective then, the past has given rise to the present and in the process has produced a human species comprised of diverse populations, nations, and cultures. But just as evolution has guaranteed human diversity, it has also ensured singularity; that is, that each and every one of us will be different, so that in the course of our lives—from conception to death—each of us can develop virtually any identity that lies within the human possibilities.

# 2

# Identity

*Out of the great number of faces that have been form'd since the creation of the world, no two have been so exactly alike, but that the usual and common eye would discover a difference between them.*

WILLIAM HOGARTH

Each of us is a concrete biological unit. We are conceived and born at precise moments and we each exist in a well-defined dimension of time and space. Throughout this lifespan we bear an intangible dimension that is our identity. We experience identity as a diffuse feeling which is interwoven with all other feelings and which is hard, if not impossible, to isolate and describe—that is, until we look in the mirror. And then identity is suddenly personified. It is the face you see reflected. It is you. Rather like a calling card, your face establishes your identity and introduces you to others.

The matching looks of twins
inspire a certain voyeuristic
curiosity. They are the ultimate
in fascinating faces. But why
should they be so intriguing?
The answer is probably because two faces with the same
apparent identity is contrary to
our basic notion about self and
individuality. We expect individuals to be unique. Indeed,
twins probably have an altered
sense of self, as their faces are
not unique—they share an
identity with each other.

*Adventure most unto itself*
*The Soul condemned to be—*
*Attended by a single Hound*
*Its own identity.*

EMILY DICKINSON

Webster's describes identity as the sameness of
essential character, the sameness in all that constitutes the objective reality of a person. The dictionary
definition points to unity, oneness, persistence of

personality, and individuality, all of which suggest a lasting set of fundamental characteristics that can be known. For human beings, these characteristics are encoded on the face. They are a visible index to what is by nature invisible. In the mind's eye, face and identity are one and the same.

Your face's physical appearance was determined at the moment of conception in a kind of genetic roulette when twenty-three maternal and twenty-three paternal chromosomes united to form a set of instructions for the development of a new individual: you. This mixing of genes ensured two things; first, that you wouldn't look exactly like anyone else on earth and, second, that the way you do look would develop and take shape according to a set schedule, just as it does for all members of our species.

That schedule begins at conception and all human faces develop and change along predictable lines. The first visible development that seems to shape the face occurs in the first few weeks of life, as the whole head becomes dimensional to accommodate a rapidly growing forebrain. By five weeks the face has an eye bud growing. By the eighth week, when the fetus measures no more than an inch, it is recognizably human, with lips, nose, eyes, and eyelids. By eleven weeks growing bones and cartilage provide structure and give the face its form and shape. Skin, muscles, and soft tissue flesh out the support. The face is unmistakable, as a two-month fetal head is almost half the body length. Outside factors, such as German measles or malnutrition, can affect and sometimes disfigure the developing face, but for most, after about 266 days, a new and healthy face emerges to face life.

At birth the face is about one quarter of its adult size. The forehead is high, the nose is rather flat, and the face may appear chinless. During the first year the face will nearly double in size. Throughout childhood and adolescence the bones and cartilage grow, changing the proportions of the face. By the time one is around twenty-five years old, the face

Identity is the stamp of individuality. Everyone has his or her own identity. Each grows and develops in a unique fashion. Growth and change proceed from within. Identity is perceived from without. It has been said that infants are characterless, in that they show less individuality in the face than do adults. This suggests that some facial identifiers may emerge and find expression during development. Every face changes dramatically in the course of a lifetime. But in spite of all the changes, the essence of identity is clear and unmistakable throughout. Art historian E. H. Gombrich has written that "all growth and decay cannot destroy the essence of the individual's looks."

has reached physical maturity. The bones have fused and the muscles are in peak condition. The subsequent changes of adulthood are subtle and more gradual. By the age of thirty-five or forty, the natural course of events begins to take its toll and a unique set of permanent lines and creases become clear. Aging occurs as the skin, the soft tissue, and the muscles lose elasticity. By forty-five or fifty, the skin begins to sag around the neck. Wrinkles form between eyes, to the side of the eyes, in the upper and lower eyelids, and in the forehead. Between the ages of sixty and seventy years, the muscular lips lose their elasticity and slowly settle into a permanently wrinkled condition. The nose broadens and flattens. Sometime toward the end of the seventh decade, the eyes lose their luster because the white sclerotic membranes develop a yellow cast caused by changes in the blood vessels. The pupils can become clouded. Aging changes the skull and alters the face's appearance. The contour of the jaw slims down and becomes more rounded. Teeth loss causes modifications in the size and shape of the jawbones. In general, by the eighth decade the bones have grown brittle, the skin has lost most of its elasticity, and the face is a shadow of its former self. And yet,

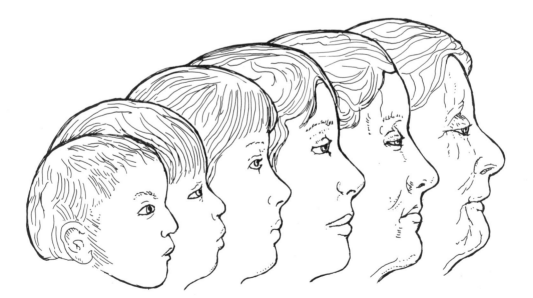

despite these changes, the essence of an individual's identity remains visible. Indeed, time seems to etch it more clearly than ever.

*Aging people should know that their lives are not mounting and unfolding but that an inexorable inner process forces the contraction of life.*

CARL GUSTAV JUNG

*With age we lose the face mask we've come to see as ourselves.*

JULIUS FAST

*Old age: the crown of life, our play's last act.*

CICERO

Though all human faces physically develop along predictable lines, the notions that one has about one's face and identity are shaped by a multitude of environmental and cultural factors. Identity has become one of those complicated aspects of self that we constantly strive to understand and objectify—a task made even more complicated by the fact that there are many ways to think about identity—all of which are personified by the face.

FACT   While the proportions of the human head have not changed for millennia, the body has grown enormously in comparison.

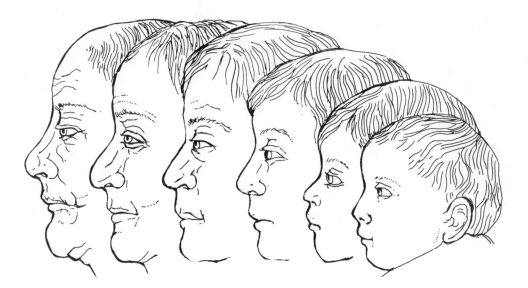

Rembrandt's self-portraits reveal the face to be an ever
changing world. And yet certain marks of identity with-
stand the ravages of time. Can
you identify them?

A CONUNDRUM What
does it mean that, when
we are young, we want
our faces to look older;
and when we are older,
we want our faces to
look younger?

Consider your gender identity, for example, or
your generational identity. Both kinds of information
about you are encoded on the face and are immediately apparent to anyone who glances at you. Indeed, both have a profound influence on how you
are perceived and identified.

Most species identify kin by smell. We humans

do so by face. This has important ramifications. Melvin Konner, a biological anthropologist from Harvard, has suggested that recognizing identity by face "may be the original adaptive basis of our keen interest in faces: the 'Are you related to so-and-so?' reaction." Recognizing identity might have helped males to detect cuckoldry in the faces of their alleged offspring, he suggests. This keen sense of identity recognition may also have served an adaptive function by playing some role in our sense of what constitutes facial attractiveness and negatively in our capacity for bigotry.

That faces reflect a family's identity is clear in the face of the famous Hapsburg clan, an old line of European royalty. The classic Hapsburg family face features a curious pouting lower lip and protruding jaw, which have appeared in scores of Hapsburgs since the fifteenth century. Although most

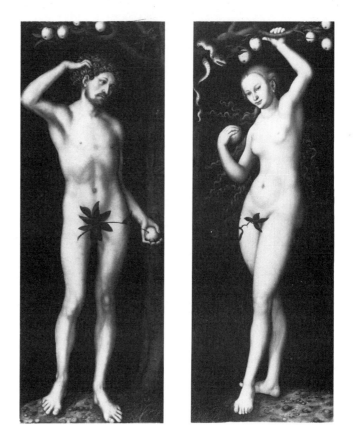

ADAM AND EVE
Adam and Eve, the names of
the original human couple in
the Hebrew Bible, have come
to personify our identity as
men and women.

family resemblances may not be as obvious as they
are in the Hapsburg faces, we all look to the face to
establish the family connection. Indeed, when a new
baby is born, the first question often asked is: Who
does he or she resemble? From then on, comparisons
are made with other members of the family. Family
resemblances are pointed out. The question is frequently asked: Are you related to so-and-so? The
answer profoundly influences how you feel about
yourself and your face.

It is commonly thought that people who live
together for a long time come to look alike and have
a shared identity. This might be because people who
live together develop similar facial habits and
expressions.

*Once he takes on self-image expressed through face
he will be expected to live up to it.*

ERVING GOFFMAN

The front teeth of the upper jaw normally bite over the lower jaw, but in some families the upper jaw and the upper teeth bite behind the lower front teeth. Sometimes, too, the lower lip protrudes. Such is the case with the Hapsburg family. The persistence of these dominant genes has been demonstrated in generation after generation of this famous ruling family. Note the trait on the faces of Emperor Maximilian I and some members of his family. The trait can also be seen below in the faces of Emperor Charles V, Philip II, and Maria Theresa, Archduchess of Austria.

There is no question that identity has many facets and many meanings. In the last forty years, social scientists have attempted to puzzle them out. One of these scientists, Erik Erikson, a leading figure in the field of psychoanalysis and human development, has spent a lifetime exploring the role and meaning of identity. It is he more than any other researcher who has charged the word "identity" with meaning

One of the world's great art mysteries has been the identity of the model for Leonardo da Vinci's *Mona Lisa*. This puzzle has been the subject of much speculation. Lillian Felman Schwartz claims to have solved the mystery. Employing computer-based image-processing techniques, she has produced striking evidence that the *Mona Lisa* is Leonardo's self-portrait. Her theory is based on historical data as well as on her now famous "Mona Leo" image, whereby the only existing Leonardo self-portrait (a red chalk drawing executed in 1518) was juxtaposed with Mona Lisa.

To create this image Leonardo's self-portrait was flipped, scaled, and aligned with the *Mona Lisa*. The result was a striking composite, revealing remarkable similarities in the two faces. Dr. Schwartz has called the congruences of the two images so striking as to preclude coincidence. "Artist and model were one and the same," Schwartz has written. "The *Mona Lisa* is Leonardo da Vinci's portrait of himself."

There is other suggestive evidence. While Leonardo kept precise notes about his other paintings, there is not a word about the *Mona Lisa*. In addition, Leonardo was fond of puzzles and paradoxes. His portraits of others carried clues as to the identity of the subject. Schwartz suggests there is such a clue in the *Mona Lisa*. Leonardo is known to have been

fascinated by knots. The neckline of Mona Lisa's dress is ornamented with an unusual type of knotted pattern, a sort of basket embroidery. The Italian word for the osier branches that are used in this kind of basketry is *vinco*. The verb *vincire* means "to lace or knot."

Recently, Dr. Schwartz has uncovered evidence of a "hidden" *Mona Lisa*. In her first finding she hinted at the possibility of a female model as the first subject of the *Mona Lisa*. Through some computer programs, a comparison between the X ray of the *Mona Lisa* and a cartoon Schwartz traced to the Hyde Collection in the Ad-

irondacks, she has now identified the first model as Isabella, Duchess of Aragon. She has suggested that when Leonardo left Milan he carried the unfinished work with him. The new technique he was developing, *sfumato*, provoked him to continue working on the now famous composition without the duchess as a model. With his own features always present, Leonardo turned to the mirror and used his own facial structure to complete the now celebrated painting.

"Mona Leo" by Lillian Felman Schwartz. (Program by Gerard Holzmann.) Copyright © 1987, Lilyan Productions, Inc.

and changed the way we perceive our individual identity as well as our social identity. In fact, because of Erikson, the word "identity" has entered the vocabulary of a wide circle and come into common usage.

Erikson's observations are clinical and his theories psychoanalytical. "Identity," according to Erikson, regardless of culture, provides an individual

CORPORATE IDENTITY
The faces of these individuals announce their identification with a particular group. This tendency to adjust our own identity to conform to a group's identity appears in all human populations and takes many forms and fashions.

*When we wish to establish a person's identity, we ask what his name is and what station he occupies in his community. Personal identity means more; it alludes to a subjective sense of continuous existence and a coherent memory. Psychosocial identity has even more elusive characteristics, at once subjective and objective, individual and social.*

ERIK ERIKSON

IBM CORPORATE TYPES

THE CLERGY

NEW ARMY RECRUITS

with the ability to experience herself or himself as something that has continuity and sameness and to act accordingly. Having studied identity formation in many different cultures and social settings, Erikson has concluded that a normal human being goes through eight stages of personality development. In each period, from infancy through maturity to old age, the individual faces a specific crisis. If all goes well, the individual emerges after each crisis with a more fully developed personality and a clearer sense of individual identity.

In less technical cultures, present and past, self-concept was probably much simpler and far less powerful in its effects than now. People's roles were standardized, so that each person knew more or less from the beginning of his or her life what was expected. There was comparatively little scope for variation of life-styles, occupations, or roles within relationships. In contrast, an urban industrial society offers the individual a great variety of roles and opportunities and makes self-concept a complex affair for most people.

The term "identity crisis," according to Erik Erikson, was minted during World War II to describe "shell-shocked" patients who had lost a sense of personal sameness and historical continuity. Erikson further popularized the expression "identity crisis" and vested it with a broader meaning, concluding that ". . . in some young people, in some classes, at some periods in history, the identity crisis will be noiseless; in other people, classes, and periods, the crisis will be clearly marked off as a crucial period with an unescapable turning point." Erikson concluded that identity formation was a necessary step in individual and collective development. Further, he recognized that identity had many faces. According to Erikson, humans have a built-in need for a psychosocial identity as well as a personal identity. This need was anchored in sociogenetic evolution and evolved gradually as humankind became more conscious of itself and assumed responsibility to and for itself. This, according to Erikson, is when mankind divided into "pseudospecies" and when one's sense of identity began to coincide with the group's identity. About collective identity and the notion of "pseudospecies," he wrote: ". . . sociogenetic evolution has split mankind into pseudospecies, into tribes, nations, and religions, castes and classes which bind their members into a pattern of individual and collective identity, but, alas, reinforce that pattern by a mortal fear of and a murderous hatred for other pseudospecies."

Even before Erikson, pioneering psychologist Sigmund Freud focused on identity and character. He saw the early years as being decisive in the formation of one's identity. Freud believed that life's instincts, such as hunger and sex, operate through a form of energy called the libido. This energy is charged and discharged through sensitive erogenous zones, such as the mouth, anus, and genitals. The infant's discovery and first uses of its libidinous impulses (energy) occur in three stages: the oral, anal, and phallic. Freud suggested that, if the child passes through each stage successfully and does not suffer gross frustration at one stage or another, then it will be more likely to have a fulfilled integrated sense of self. Looking in the mirror each morning under such circumstances proves positive and pleasant.

Psychologist Gordon Allport was another investigator of individuality and identity. He saw ordinary adults much as they see themselves, in terms of appearance and readily identifiable characteristics. He taught the trait theory of personality, compiling from Webster's a list of some 17,953 characteristics that, according to him, epitomized personalities. Personality, he believed, was composed chiefly of traits such as honesty, skepticism, and kindness. These characteristics motivated behavior and made an individual act consistently under many different circumstances.

Another investigator, Harry Stack Sullivan, espoused the "interpersonal" theory of personality,

which held that an individual was shaped chiefly by the nature of his relationships with others, beginning at birth and continuing throughout life and not including just the actual dealings with others but also relationships that are remembered from times past, imagined during waking hours, or fantasized about in dreams. If human interactions are rewarding, Sullivan maintained, personality and one's sense of identity develop favorably. Social disapproval, on the other hand, is a powerful and negative determinant in one's conception of self and notion of identity. Under these circumstances, looking in the mirror can have devastating ramifications.

*A strong sense of personal identity is the product of two things: a policy of independent thinking and the possession of an integrated set of values. Since it is his values that determine a man's emotions and goals and give direction and meaning to his life, a man experiences his values as an extension of himself, as an integral part of his identity, as crucial to that which makes him himself.*

NATHANIEL BRANDEN

Erikson has said that the more one writes about the subject of identity, the more the word becomes a term for something as unfathomable as it is all-pervasive. This may be correct, simply because knowing faces is a mental task dependent upon a visual construct in the mind. It is for this reason that the art of caricature gives some insight into the ambiguous nature of identity, for a good caricature captures the essence of identity with a minimum of visual information, suggesting that what information is conveyed is critical to identity recognition.

What is caricature but a visual shortcut, a potent distillation of the key ingredients that make up the distinctive features that identify a specific face? Caricatures exaggerate the features that constitute a face, but they do not simply distort the face's features. They make the distortion relative to a tacit understanding of what is unusual about the face and what is not.

A caricaturist knows that a face is perceived as a whole: an arrangement of three-dimensional relationships. A caricaturist captures the essence of a face by taking information from several points of view, compressing it, and distorting it in such a way that it becomes a kind of shorthand—an image that stands for something much more complicated. In the past, grotesqueness was part and parcel of caricature. Artists such as Honoré Daumier developed techniques of caricature as a pungent means of social and political comment. Today artist-scientists such as Susan E. Brennan of Stanford University are exploring the power of caricature to communicate identity for different reasons.

Brennan first became interested in the potential of caricature to encode identity when the Defense Advanced Research Projects Agency approached MIT's Media Laboratory to investigate teleconferencing with the express purpose of finding better ways to transmit good facial likenesses. At the time, Brennan was affiliated with the Media Laboratory. She and her colleagues initiated an investigation called "Transmission of Presence" and grappled with the problem of how to send an image that captured the essence of an individual's identity in order to make face-to-face teleconferencing possible. The group asked such questions as: What is the minimum facial information necessary to communicate identity? Brennan proposed caricature as a solution to the problem, for her work with caricatures had convinced her of their effectiveness in communicating identity quickly and effectively.

To demonstrate her theory, Brennan developed a computer program that created caricatures by distorting them according to what is unusual about the face. Her software compares the photograph of the target face with an average face stored in the memory of the computer. The features of the target face that differ most from the average face are scaled up in size and rendered in line drawing. Brennan exaggerates the differences between the line drawing and the average until an acceptable likeness is found. Then the caricature, which now clearly encodes identity, can be animated and transmitted with speech over telephone lines.

IDENTITY AND CARICATURE

These caricatures were generated by a computer program devised by Susan E. Brennan of Stanford University. To draw a caricature the program must be supplied with a digitized version of a real face and an average face. Both the average face and the target face are represented by 186 points,

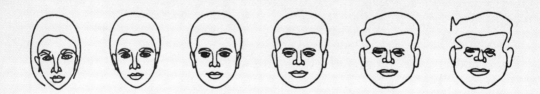

each of which has two coordinates. The resulting list of 372 numbers for each face is a point in face space and any two faces in face space can be connected by a straight line and averaged or "in-betweened." "In-betweening" is related to a trick that computer animators use. It works like this: the norms in the computer program are made up of sets of several dozen real faces in a data base of several hundred. Points are chosen that outline the feature of each face, and the points are labeled with respect to a set of matrix-based coordinate axes. The coordinates of corresponding points on each face are averaged to give the norm for that point. Brennan exaggerates the differences between the line drawing and the average until an acceptable likeness is produced.

Since any two faces in face space can be joined by a straight line, one can ask the program to generate a transitional sequence from one face to another. Brennan finds such sequences particularly intriguing when the two end-point faces are male and female. On facing page, her program transforms Elizabeth Taylor into John F. Kennedy.

Brennan points out that there is a natural limit to recognizable exaggeration. Eventually a caricature loses its human quality and degenerates into a chaotic state which Brennan calls "facelessness." Note the last image in the Ronald Reagan sequence.

Brennan and her colleagues learned from their inquiries that, when a caricature is exaggerated and recognized, it is recognized immediately—about twice as fast as realistic line drawings of the same face. This has led some investigators to conclude that, when we remember a face, we remember it as a caricature—a kind of shorthand symbol that encodes identity and epitomizes individuality.

In spite of the fact that an individual's identity is ambiguous and multifaceted, it is clear that it is built in: fixed in the body's maturational plan. Therefore the face is the best means of identifying an individual.

Since the face is the best means of identifying a person, an accurate facial description is a major factor in apprehending a criminal. Unfortunately, our ability to remember faces, compared with our ability to recognize faces, is poor. As a result, police departments use witness recall systems to facilitate the identification of criminals.

Most people are familiar with police composite pictures—those disembodied impressions of the faces of criminals issued to the media in the wake of a crime. They are best known by their trade names: Identikit and Photofit.

Identikit is an American product and Photofit was introduced in England. The original Identikit, invented by a California policeman, Hugh McDonald, appeared in 1959 and consisted of line drawings printed on acetate sheets. When appropriate sheets were superimposed on each other, they fused a composite "face." Identikit includes 130 hairlines, 102 chins, 40 lips, 37 noses, plus an assortment of eyebrows, scars, glasses, age lines, beards, and hats.

Photofit was created by Jacques Penry and was introduced in England with the support of the Home Office. Photofit depends on over 550 photographs of actual face features that are printed on thin cards. These cards can then be pieced together like a jigsaw puzzle to make faces fit. The French use still another system, called Portrait Robot, that depends on an

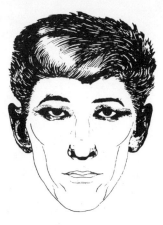

MAKING FACES FIT
This is the first police composite picture issued by Scotland Yard. It led to the identification of a murderer, Edwin Bush, in 1961.

artist drawing an impression based on a description. Though these techniques to facilitate witness recall are popular with police departments the world over, they have not proved very effective in apprehending criminals.

Why have faces proved difficult to describe and even more difficult to composite into a satisfactory and recognizable likeness? It is believed that compositing systcms are simply not effective in identifying criminals because they are neither flexible nor inventive. Unlike the human face, their possibilities are limited. Psychologist Kenneth Laughery compared faces made from Identikits with those sketched by artists and found that the latter more closely represented real faces. It seems an artist can produce an almost infinite number of faces; but the Identikit and even the new computer identification programs are limited in the number of possibilities they can create.

But there is another reason why these kits may not be so effective in identifying criminals. Identikits rely on descriptions of features. The idea is to isolate the features, describe them, and then make the faces fit. The problem is, identity is a quality of individuality that is globally apprehended and depends upon a great deal more than the specific qualities and characteristics of individual features. What you see and recognize in another person is ultimately determined by the unique pattern created by the whole picture the face presents. That is identity. It's

## FACES ON TRIAL:
## "IVAN THE TERRIBLE"

The question of identity and facial features highlighted the recent war-crimes trial of John Demjanjuk in Jerusalem. Demjanjuk was accused of being "Ivan the Terrible" of Treblinka concentration camp, where more than 850,000 persons were put to death by the Germans. "Ivan" operated the poison gas engines and was charged with sadistically torturing and beating prisoners to death. Several photos of Demjanjuk were entered into evidence. They included (among others) a blowup of the Trawniki ID card that was allegedly issued by the German SS in 1942, a driver's license issued in East Germany in 1947, and a 1951 U.S. immigration photograph. These photos were compared with the prisoner's face as it appeared at the trial. Specifically, twenty-four points and measurements were compared and evaluated, including the gap between the eyebrows, the base of the nose, the nostril rims, the corners of the mouth, the upper lip, and the position and configuration of the ears. A West German photo identification expert, Reinhard Altmann, using an electronic method of mixing and blending these photographs, created composites which he testified indicated that there was a very high likelihood the photographs were of Demjanjuk. The jury convicted Demjanjuk, believing that even after forty-six years Demjanjuk's face was unmistakable.

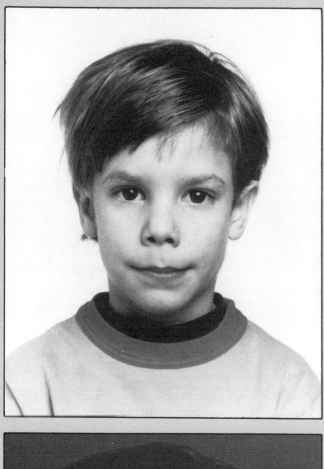

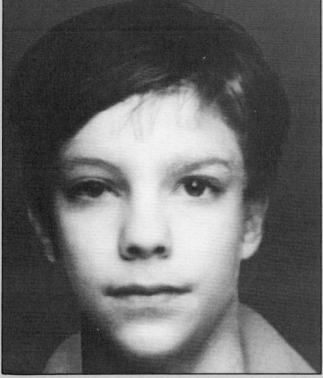

Nancy Burson's patented process is used by police departments in their search for missing children. Burson uses videographic techniques to "warp" the face of a missing child to show us what that face would look like over time. A case in point: several years ago, first-grader Etan Patz set out to school and has never been seen again. Law enforcement officials admit that one of the most difficult aspects of the ongoing search is that Patz would now be a teenager, making his childhood photographs hopelessly outdated. In a patented process, the photograph can be "stretched" to predict what the subject will look like in the future. Burson's technique uses a TV camera, which scans the subject's face, then feeds that visual information to a digitizer, which translates it into computer language. The computer then "warps" the face in a way that imitates the effects of aging. Although there has been no success in the Patz case, Burson's work has helped the police identify and find other children who had been missing for a long time.

Mistaken identity has long been the stuff of screwball comedies, but in real life it can be devastating reality. In many criminal incidents, eyewitness identification is the key to seeking and winning a conviction. Unfortunately, eyewitness identification is easily biased, subject to error, and an important source of injustice in the criminal justice system. Inaccurate identification involves two kinds of errors: identification of the wrong person and failure to identify the right person. These problems in witness identification were made clear in a Wilmington, Delaware, case in 1979 in which seven witnesses to six different holdups picked the same unlikely suspect out of a lineup: Bernard Pagano, then fifty-three, a Roman Catholic priest. In spite of the number of witnesses and the sworn testimony, the witnesses were wrong. Ronald Clouser, thirty-nine, later confessed to the series of crimes.

not the details of the features. It's not the spacing between features. Rather, it is the interrelationship among all of these things taken together that enables us to recognize the identity of a criminal or the face of a friend. You don't take faces apart analytically. Most of the time you can't even tell what you are looking at when you look at a face because verbal processes have little to do with visual recognition. Identity is encoded on the face and remembered as a whole. Though elusive and hard to define, it is experienced on many different levels, not the least of which is that identity enables us to carry out an important social skill: recognizing one another as individuals.

# 3

# Recognizing Faces

We humans are not solitary animals. We are genetically social. We need to be part of a group. Our ability to recognize others—to know friend from foe—is a valuable talent and has been central to the evolution of our complex social life. Social life, in fact, demands recognition accuracy for maintaining social contact, and position in one's community requires one to recognize and accord individuality to a number of people. The very success of our species depends on this skill.

The learned art historian E. H. Gombrich has suggested that face recognition is automatic and dependent on the two factors of resemblance and biological relevance: the greater the biological relevance an object has for us, the more we will be attuned to its recognition. Faces are extremely relevant from this point of view. Most scientists would agree with Gombrich, for it appears that there has been strong selectional pressure to improve the speed and efficiency of face recognition so that today all members of the human species demonstrate an amazing capacity to recognize and identify on sight an unlimited number of faces despite all the possible ways a face might look at any given time, including moment-to-moment expressions, the changes that accompany age, and all the paraphernalia of glasses, headgear, and makeup. We humans can often recognize a face at a glance after only a single exposure and after having encountered and stored a vast number of other faces. It is believed that we can do so because there is a special structure in the brain that develops automatically and takes shape according to the same genetic schedule that shapes the rest of the body. This perceptual apparatus, which is highly sensitive to faces, enables individuals to initiate and maintain relationships; of all life's undertakings, none is more important.

It has been known since the nineteenth century that injuries to a certain part of the brain can cause a total loss of the ability to recognize people. This condition, identified and named by French neurologists, is called prosopagnosia. It means, literally, "not knowing people." To prosopagnosics, faces may look like a cubist Picasso portrait, or may appear to have features in the wrong position, or the face may be so fuzzy it is beyond recognition. Tragically, in some cases, the impairment is so severe that prosopagnosics are unable to recognize their own faces in the mirror.

According to the late Dr. Norman Geschwind, an expert on this rare syndrome, what is most remarkable about this disorder is its specificity. Generally, it is accompanied by few other neurological symptoms. Most mental tasks, including those that require processing of visual information, are accomplished without much difficulty. A patient can usually read and correctly name seen objects. What he or she cannot do is look at a person or at a photograph of a face and name the person. It is not the identity of familiar people that has been lost to him, only the connection between the face and identity. Dr. Geschwind pointed out, "When a familiar person speaks, the patient knows the voice and can say the name immediately. The perception of the facial features also seems unimpaired, as the patient can often describe the face in detail and can usually match a photograph made from the front with a profile of the same person. The deficiency seems to be confined to forming associations between faces and identities."

For a long time it was commonly thought that the right hemisphere of the brain was specialized for face recognition. It was believed, therefore, that damage to the right side resulted in prosopagnosia. But PET scans of the brain's behavior have revealed something different: it always takes damage on both sides of the brain to result in prosopagnosia. Experts now believe that both sides of the brain are responsible for this crucial ability and that each side of the brain contributes something different to face recognition: the right half of the brain may contribute more to the overall recognition of the outline of the face, while the left side may be better at picking up small details. Whatever the division of responsibility, it is now clear that the two sides of the brain work together to make us experts at recognizing faces.

Biologically speaking, face recognition is a highly specialized form of pattern recognition. Our brains are neurologically organized to recognize patterns in general and faces in particular. In fact, the pattern that constitutes the face is what is sometimes called a "preferred pattern" because we are predisposed to make sense out of it. E. H. Gombrich has called the pattern that is the face a "privileged motif," one

*The most beautiful thing we can experience is the mysterious. It is the source of all true art and science.*

ALBERT EINSTEIN

*Nobody has ever expected me to be President. In my poor, lank face nobody has ever seen that any cabbages were sprouting out.*

ABRAHAM LINCOLN

*Something about my face must have struck Mr. Karno as being amusing, as he engaged me at once to play the comic villain as a foil to Mr. Harry Weldon.*

CHARLIE CHAPLIN

## FACE RECOGNITION
## IN THE BRAIN

Identifying and remembering faces is a mental process that takes place in the cerebral cortex—the newest part of the brain, where thinking takes place. Some scientists believe that the neural network on the underside of both occipital lobes, extending forward to the inner surface of the temporal lobes, is the region that is specialized for rapid and reliable recognition of human faces. According to them, it is here that one learns to discriminate thousands of different faces over the course of a lifetime.

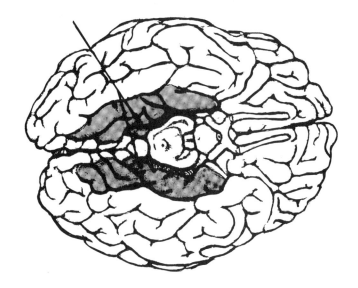

that we respond to easily. He suggested that, "whether by instinct or by very early training, we are certainly ever disposed to single out the expressive features of a face from the chaos of sensations that surrounds it. . . ."

This ability to single out faces with speed and

## WHEN DOES A
## PATTERN BECOME
## A FACE?

With very little visual information, you recognize this person. Why? What makes it possible for your brain to organize these shaded squares into a clear mental image? You can do it because you have an inborn talent for recognizing faces quickly and efficiently. Biomedical engineer Leon Harmon created this portrait to study the limits of face recognition.

FACT Although there are many, many pictures of Abraham Lincoln, he is never smiling.

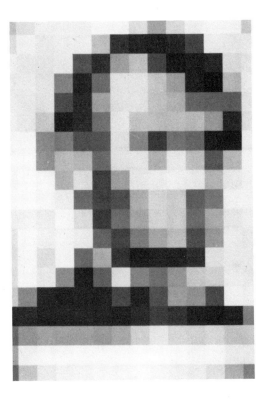

efficiency can be investigated experimentally by asking how much information is required for recognition and what information is most important. The late Leon Harmon, a world-renowned biomedical engineer, applied his considerable talents to answering these questions. He and his colleagues designed a series of experiments that were directed to understanding face recognition. One in particular asked how little information (in the sense of "bits" or picture elements) was required to represent pictorially a face so that it could be recognized. He explored what he called the "threshold" of recognition by creating "block portraits" out of picture elements based on shades of gray. This process, known as spatial quantization, consisted of breaking down the picture information into elementary building blocks. First the picture is divided into picture elements (abbreviated as "pixels"). Each pixel is a gray square that is the average of all the information in the same square of the original. Up close these portraits appear to be an assemblage of squares. Viewed remotely, a face is perceived and recognized.

THE THRESHOLD
OF RECOGNITION
Test your "threshold" of recognition. Here are eight block portraits of a famous subject, each at a different level of resolution. How much information do you need to recognize this face? Note that, once you see the individual and recognition has been achieved, it is difficult not to see it. Leon Harmon remarked, "It is as though the mind's eye superposes additional detail on the coarse optical image . . . as if some kind of perceptual hysteresis prevented the image from once again dissolving into an abstract pattern of squares."

## DOMINO-PIX™

Domino-Pix™ shows you another kind of pixelated portrait, one in which the pixels are the ends of cleverly arranged domino pieces. This is made possible by a computer algorithm that determines the placement of dominoes that best renders the image. It works like this. First a picture is taken of the subject. The picture is processed by computer into 440 pixels (individual picture elements). The computer program arranges these picture elements from brightest to darkest. Through a complex process, the computer then assigns the best domino to represent these pixels. Next, the computer creates the pattern, but it is your brain that turns the pattern into a portrait. For comparison, newspaper photographs are produced using a so-called halftone technique that essentially consists of breaking up the photograph into a set of black and white picture elements (dots). Typically a newspaper halftone uses eighty-five pixels per inch. These pictures, by comparison, use one pixel per inch. How many faces can you identify?

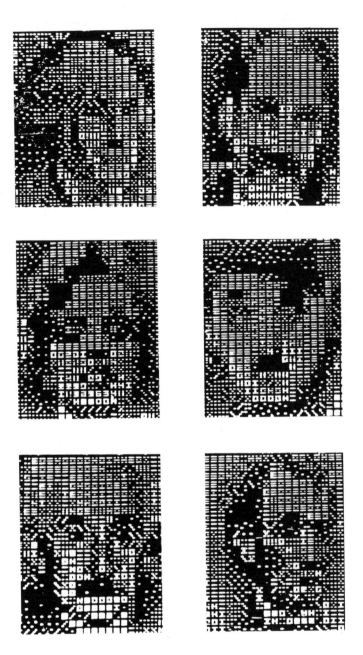

Because faces are a "preferred pattern" we tend to discover them everywhere—even where they don't exist. What a strange sort of perception it is that makes us imagine we see a face in the fire or on the moon. These faces, of course, do not exist in the real world no matter how uncanny the likeness; but they do exist in the mind's eye and show to what extent a group of shapes can be read as a face over all other possible readings.

## FAMOUS FACES

We seem to have a mental model for famous faces and that may be the reason we can easily recognize a famous face even when the picture has been distorted.

## JACQUES COUSTEAU

This four-by-three-foot work of aquatic art is displayed at San Francisco's Exploratorium. Up close, what you see is a collection of seashells and bits of coral. But when you stand back and look from afar, a detailed portrait emerges of the marine explorer Jacques Cousteau. The artist-scientist Ken Knowlton (widely known for his pioneering work in graphics and other computer research) began with a photograph of Cousteau that he digitized and reduced to pixels in shades of gray on a twenty-eight-by-thirty-eight-inch grid. He then worked to find the optimal correspondence between the cells of the grid and the shells. In this case, the seashells and bits of coral act like picture elements. Once again it is your brain that has turned a complex pattern of carefully arranged seashells and bits of coral into a familiar face.

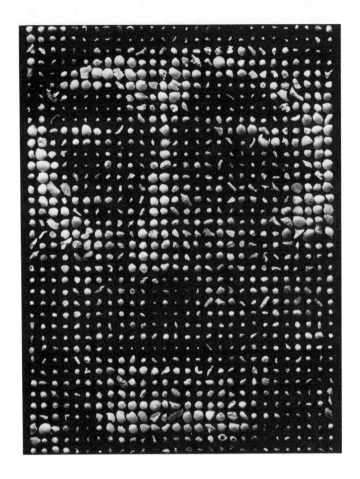

Though we are genetically equipped to recognize faces, it is an ability that we must cultivate and learn. This learning process is activated at birth and isn't complete until around eighteen years of age, when one can discriminate among an almost infinite number of faces.

A number of researchers, each with different areas of expertise, are trying to ascertain just how it is that we acquire this ability. Some work with infants, though this is understandably difficult. Others work with teenagers and college students. Still others work with people of different racial groups in an attempt to gain insight into this human ability. Those who work with infants point to research that indicates that newborns look at the outside edges of faces. As early as age three weeks, infants prefer the image of the human face to all other images. Between five and seven weeks, vision has improved and baby starts to return its mother's gaze when she talks to it. By the eighth week, babies can discriminate their mother's face from the faces of strangers. By three to four months, infants not only prefer a human face but usually smile in response to it. Next, infants come to prefer familiar faces—especially mother's. Indeed, the primal visual image —that which we first focus upon and recognize —is mother's face.

At about five months, babies can tell the difference between photographs of men and women, and some can recognize the face two weeks later even though they were only shown the picture for a minute. By seven months, babies can recognize people they see frequently. It must be remembered, however, that much of the research of behavioral scientists in this area of face recognition is the subject of debate. Since infants cannot tell us what they recognize, it is very hard to corroborate the data.

It has been demonstrated that pubescent teenagers for a short time actually lose their keen sense of face recognition. No one knows exactly why, but scientists speculate that large jolts of sex hormones may interfere with this ability temporarily. One researcher, MIT psychologist Susan Carey, suggests it may be both hormonal changes and a cognitive reshuffling that occurs during puberty that interfere with face recognition.

A study of long-term recall and recognition for persons, names, and faces was undertaken, using materials taken from high school yearbooks of people who had graduated from high school as many as fifty years prior to the study. Subjects were able to identify photographs taken from their own high school yearbooks with an accuracy of ninety percent after an average of thirty-four years since graduation. Of course the pictures had been viewed many times over the years but still this is a very high level of performance.

LIKABLE FACES AND
UNLIKABLE FACES
According to John Mueller, Martin Heesacker, and Michael Ross, psychologists at the University of Missouri, unlikable faces are more distinct and, therefore, recognized more steadily. They conducted two experiments. In the test 84 students were shown 160 black and white yearbook portraits. The portraits were of 80 men and 80 women. None had unusual features such as glasses or beards. The 32 most likable and the 32 least likable were shown to test subjects once, then again forty-eight hours later. The subjects found it more difficult to remember the likable faces.

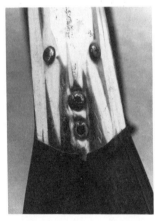

## DISCOVERED FACES

The image of the human face is a "preferred pattern" in that faces seem to take precedence over all other images when the visual scene is at all unclear. Here is a collection of discovered faces. How many do you see?

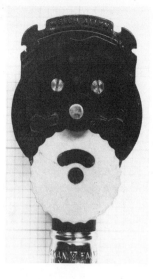

## FACES BY DESIGN

**EMBEDDED FACES** Salvador Dali often embedded faces in his paintings. In this one he embedded Houdon's famous sculptured bust of Voltaire. It was Dali's way of honoring the great philosopher for his courageous crusade against tyranny, bigotry, and cruelty. Dali admired Voltaire's critical capacity, his wit and satire. He felt him a kindred spirit and honored him in several works. This one is titled *The Slave Market with the Bust of Voltaire*.

**FACES THAT SMILE—FACES THAT FROWN** Dr. Roger Shepard, a Stanford University psychologist, believes that there are certain regularities about the world which we have deeply internalized. This is particularly true of faces. Because we consistently experience faces in a certain way, we tend to see them in our mind's eye in a particular way. Consider this illusion that Dr. Shepard has created to test this notion. Are the faces smiling? Or are they frowning? Rotate the images and you will discover that the faces do both. The illusion results because your built-in perceptual system draws conclusions even from conflicting clues. You can be told about visual illusions until you consciously understand them but it will not affect your experience of them. You can't undo them, according to Shepard, because your perception depends upon a highly efficient machinery over which you have no control.

It is also true that people differ in their ability to remember a particular face. One common finding is that many people have difficulty distinguishing individuals from different racial groups. Drs. June Chance and Alvin Goldstein of the University of Missouri have been studying cross-racial recognition for a number of years. According to them, all groups appear to be equally inept at recognizing individuals from other groups. There is great debate as to the meaning of these findings. Some suggest familiarity

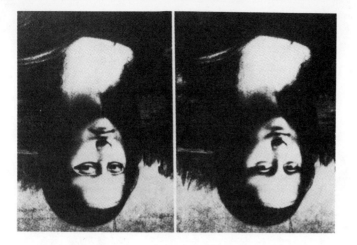

UPSIDE-DOWN *MONA LISAS*
Here are two upside-down *Mona Lisa*s. One of them, doctored by Bela Julesz, a psychophysicist at Bell Laboratories, shows how prior experience affects what we see. Turned right side up, the distortion appears far worse, in comparison to the familiar view of the face. Because we know this face, we expect it to look a certain way and our perceptual machinery insists on seeing it as we expect to see it.

and attitude are the main ingredients in recognizing individuals. Others, like behaviorial scientist Roy Malpass, at State University of New York at Plattsburgh, suggest it's not just familiarity but the quality of the interaction between individuals that is important; that is, recognition depends on the roles different people play in your life. Having studied face recognition for many years, he suspects that we constantly categorize faces. Faces are either significant, like family, friends, and business associates, or

FACES AND VASES Here the faces and vase compete for recognition in this tesselation. Why? Because the eye deceives the mind when an object and its background vie for recognition. In an illustration of this perceptual principle known as figure and ground, the profiles of Britain's Prince Philip and Queen Elizabeth greet each other from opposite sides of this porcelain vase created for the Queen's Silver Jubilee in 1977. The royal faces reveal themselves as figures, transforming the vase into a white background.

By the age of two, a child recognizes the face he sees in the mirror as being his own. With the development of a self-concept, children begin to see themselves as individuals and they begin to experiment with their identity. They do this by playing with their faces—by pushing and pulling, by making funny faces.

they are "other." Unless members of other races play a significant role in one's life, they'll be lumped into the outsider category and their faces will not be easily remembered. As young children we learn to use discriminating cues that help us classify the good guys and bad guys within our own group. "Outgroupers" are categorized as all alike. Who has not heard the expression, "They look all alike to me"? There may be a kernel of truth in this statement as the evidence is consistent that people of different groups do have trouble recognizing individuals of other groups, but the reason is certainly not because all blacks or Asians or whites look alike. On the contrary, Chance and Goldstein's massive anthropological study of

diverse groups around the world proved that all groups are equally variable in the face. They demonstrated that our ability to recognize faces of people from other groups could be improved with instruction, though it is still unclear whether this improvement would last over time.

A common question asked is: Can we improve upon our natural ability to recognize faces? In fact, there is very little information available on face recognition training but it appears that, while it may be possible to improve recognition for other-race faces (for which there may be an initial deficit), training for own-race faces produces no effect and possibly may even decrease recognition performance.

It is no accident that a mother's face is eight or nine inches away from the baby's eyes. This is the precise distance at which a newborn is able to focus. Focusing on mother activates the brain's face recognition program.

The reason this may be so, according to one theory, is that by the time one reaches adulthood one's ability to recognize faces will be at its most proficient because the social utility of accurate and efficient face recognition will have induced individuals to become as good at it as they can become.

Though the process of face recognition is extremely complicated and researchers remain uncertain how we actually accomplish it, they do know that face recognition occupies a very special place in human visual experience and that it is far more important to everyday life than the ability to recognize any other class of objects.

# 4

# Asymmetry: The Riddle of Sidedness

*Our notion of symmetry is
derived from the human face.*

PASCAL

At a glance the face appears to have perfect bi-
lateral symmetry; that is, the right side of the face
seems to be a mirror image of the left side. This
apparent anatomical symmetry, however, is an illusion. Most faces are surprisingly asymmetrical, with
clear and distinct differences between the two sides.
This two-sided pattern appears to be universal
among all human faces, in all cultures, in all parts
of the world, and possibly extending back into prehistory. It is only close scrutiny that reveals the apparent differences between the two sides. The classic
demonstration for sidedness—or laterality, as it is

**COMPOSITES**

The two sides of the face are asymmetrical, though long exposure to our own face or, say, the face of a friend may blind us to such differences. It is only through special procedures that we can focus on the differences. The classical demonstration is photographically to create composite faces, one from two left halves of the face, one from two right halves. This is done by reversing the halves and joining them at midline. In this way we can analyze the ways in which the two sides appear to differ. For most people, one composite is noticeably thinner than the other. Also, one composite may appear happier than the other if the mouth corner turns up on the side because that effect is doubled. The above images were made using video software developed by Ed Tannenbaum.

sometimes called—is photographically to create composite faces: one made from two right halves of the face and one made from two left halves of the face. These composites clearly reveal a face's asymmetrical nature.

Consider your own face. If you look at your direct image in a mirror you will discover many differences between the right and left sides of your face. You may notice for the first time that your face looks "tilted" or "crooked" or even that one eye seems slightly higher or larger than the other. You may discover that one cheek has an indentation or that it is thinner than the other one. You may find that one side of your mouth turns up or down slightly. If you are like the majority of people, your right ear is placed lower on your head than your left ear and there are small but detectable differences in the size and shape of the ears. But what do these differences between the two sides of the face really mean, if anything?

In order to put the face's asymmetry in perspective, it is necessary to look for a moment at the two-sided brain, which is ultimately responsible for the differences, both visible and behavioral, that we perceive between the two sides of the face.

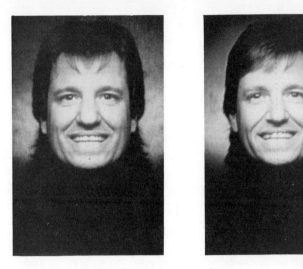 

That the brain is a divided structure and that each side has different talents and different specializations has been known for more than a hundred years. It was in 1861 that Paul Broca, a French surgeon and neuroanatomist, pointed out that damage to a particular part of the brain consistently resulted in aphasia, or speech disorder. Broca went on to make another important discovery about the two-sided brain: he showed that, while damage to an area on the left side of the brain (now called Broca's area) produced aphasia, similar damage to the corresponding area on the right side left the faculty of speech intact. From this he concluded that the two sides of the brain are specialized for different things when it comes to language and speech production. Since then, from brain-damaged patients as well as normal subjects, neuroscientists have learned a great deal about the brain and the different specialties of the two hemispheres.

In the 1950s Roger Sperry and his colleagues at the California Institute of Technology conducted research that demonstrated that the two sides of the brain have special though complementary powers. The left hemisphere deals in analytical and verbal skills; the right side is adept in space and pattern perception. The left hemisphere deals in the abstract symbols of language and numbers. It is logical, linear, and talented in the sequential in processing information. The right hemisphere, on the other hand, grasps things as a whole. It generates mental images of sight, sounds, touch, taste, and smell. It compares relationships and is termed holistic and simultaneous in its thinking.

In addition it was discovered that each side of the brain looks at the other half of space. In other words, if you look at a person's face and fix your gaze on the nose, the half of his or her face on your left projects to the right side of your brain, while that half of his or her face on your right projects to the left side of your brain. Rather than seeing two separate sides of the face, you see the whole face because a special four-inch-long, quarter-inch-thick highway connects the two. This highway of nerve fibers is called the corpus callosum and it is responsible for integrating information from the two hemispheres so that you construct a composite "picture" of a whole face in your mind.

In terms of motor and sensory behavior, the right side of the brain activates many of the muscles on the left side of the face while the left side of the brain controls many of the muscles on the right side of the face. Movements such as frowning, smiling, and wrinkling the forehead are normally produced by the simultaneous symmetrical contractions of the muscles on both sides of the face. But, you will notice, the expressions produced are asymmetrical. This is because the muscle actions on one side of the face are stronger than they are on the other side.

Over the last hundred years, attention has been focused on understanding how structural asymmetry could lead to a favoring of one side of the body or other. A recent theory claims, but it has not yet been proved, that a composite made from the two left halves not only looks different from one made from the two right halves but also indicates the subject's current emotional state more clearly and intensely.

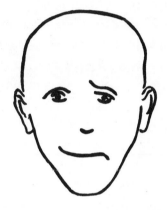

Julian Jaynes, a psychologist from Princeton University, believes that recognition of facial expression is primarily a right-hemisphere function. According to him, one important judgment for a human being is the recognition of facial expression. There is considerable survival value in being able to decide whether a person is friendly or unfriendly. Jaynes designed an experiment to test his theory. The two faces you see here are mirror images of each other. He asked more than a thousand people which face looks happier. He reports that, quite consistently, about eighty percent of right-handed people chose the bottom face with the smile going up on their left. They were judging, according to Jaynes, the face with their right hemispheres, assuming of course that they were glancing at the center of the face. He suggests that there is a tendency to judge facial expression by the left visual field. Fifty-five percent of the left-handers chose the upper face as happier, suggesting that it was the left hemisphere making the judgment.

The reason this is so, some speculate, is that the left side of the face reflects the work of the right hemisphere's concern with negative emotions such as sadness or anxiety, while the right side of the face reflects the left hemisphere's role in the expression of more positive moods such as happiness, joy, and laughter.

Investigators point out that in a face-to-face encounter your left side is the one more likely to be projected to the viewer's left, or verbal, side, which is not as skilled in face recognition or in the processing of emotional information as is the right side of the brain. According to this view, it is possible that the greater expressiveness of the left side of the face has evolved to compensate for the relative inferiority of our left hemisphere in such nonverbal behavior as the recognition of faces and emotions. Theories like this, however, are disputed by many scientists, who observe that there is no hard scientific evidence that either side of the face gives different information about character, personality, or emotions. The only evidence we have of information contained in the face's asymmetry is that an expression made deliberately is more asymmetric than if it occurs naturally and spontaneously.

What research does show is that there is a wide range of behaviors that are lateralized, at least to some extent, toward one or the other cerebral hemisphere. The late Norman Geschwind suggested that this has been advantageous in the development of the human animal simply because it increases intelligence, adding another string to the intellectual bow.

Geschwind along with many other investigators suggested that the roots of the divided brain lie deep in our prehistoric past, when early hominids found it necessary to use the arms independently of each other. This required an asymmetric arrangement between the two hemispheres, since each hemisphere was responsible for controlling the movement of only one side of the body. As one arm or hand began to be used more, the argument goes, the hemisphere controlling it specialized. This ultimately resulted in significant differences between the abilities of the two sides and may be why we humans have a hand preference—that is, that we are most comfortable using either the right or the left hand.

The decisive influence may well have been the evolution of upright walking or bipedalism. The evidence, according to University of Auckland psychologist Michael Corballis, who has examined laterality from comparative, developmental, evolutionary, and genetic perspectives, suggests that this occurred in the genus *Ramapithecus* (the common ancestor to *Homo habilis* and the Australopithecines) and was brought about by the transition from a woodland habitat to the open savanna of East Africa some 12 to 14 million years ago.

Anthropologists Richard Leakey and Roger

Lewin have made a strong case for this hypothesis, suggesting that three factors may have favored the evolution of an upright posture. One was an increased need for protection against predators. This was achieved by brandishing branches or by hurling projectiles. Another was surveillance, for having a commanding view of one's surroundings was a clear advantage. Finally, the ability to carry things was a great asset to those who had to gather food and take it back to a central point.

In addition, bipedalism would have freed the hands from any direct involvement with locomotion. The hands could then evolve new specializations, such as feeding, food gathering, manipulation, and the use of tools and weapons. This, in turn, would have freed the mouth from some of these activities and also allowed it to specialize somewhat for communication. These influences make up a complex system of mutual reinforcement and feedback that over the course of millions of years may have led to an increasingly lateralized brain and body. Other investigators, like Julian Jaynes, contend that human consciousness, which we understand as a product of cerebral lateralization, evolved much more recently, perhaps since the time of Homer around three thousand years ago. This theory is highly controversial and Corballis has suggested that it is extremely unlikely that cerebral lateralization could have evolved over so short a time span. He believes that, though the evidence for cerebral asymmetry among our prehistoric forebears is difficult to obtain, there are clues from which the experts can hypothesize. For example, anatomical asymmetries, comparable to those in modern human brains, can be detected in prehistoric human skulls, as the surface of the brain leaves an imprint on the inside of the skull. It was from just such fossil evidence that Raymond Dart concluded that the Taung baby was not a true ape but, rather, a member of a new, more humanlike species. Other investigators point to de-

tectable right and left differences in the skulls of Neanderthal man, particularly in the skull found at La Chapelle-aux-Saints in France.

Though the evidence is sketchy and incomplete, it does suggest that sidedness has evolved over millions rather than thousands of years and that the asymmetries that we recognize on the face probably result from the fact that the two sides of the brain are specialized for different kinds of information processing. It is also clear that cerebral lateralization is relative rather than absolute, that both hemispheres work together, and that both make important contributions to everyday activities such as recognizing faces and emotions.

In the normal course of events, and among the majority of people, environment and culture play only a minor role in modifying or reinforcing this biological disposition to sidedness. Time, however, accentuates the apparent differences between the face's two sides, making them more pronounced and therefore more noticeable. Since hereditary factors play a key role in the shape of the bony structure of the face as well as in the patterns of the fibers of the skin, they are probably the reasons why some faces grow to be more asymmetrical than others.

The fact that we are physically asymmetric may also account for the fact that we humans see the cosmos as well as ourselves as subject to two opposing influences. In other words, we have a tendency to dichotomize our reality and see it in terms of polar opposites such as right-left, up-down, Yin-Yang (which literally means the dark and sunny side of a hill).

*Nothing oppresses the heart so much as symmetry.*
VICTOR HUGO

Long a source of curiosity, this phenomenon of sidedness has led not only scientists and researchers

but philosophers and artists through the ages to puzzle over and theorize about the mechanisms that give rise to asymmetry. For centuries investigators have postulated various theories to account for the fact that our faces and bodies are functionally asymmetrical. In ancient Greece any deviation from symmetry was viewed as another example of man's ungodlike imperfection. Aristophanes declared that man had been created as a sphere, with his face toward heaven and his buttocks to the ground. There was no right or left side. But when mankind grew arrogant and angered Zeus, he split man into halves. Zeus tossed the two halves to Apollo, who turned the newly made face forward, creating a right and left side. Zeus further warned that if mankind continued in its impertinence, he would split them once more and they would then hop on one leg.

The Pythagorean Table of Opposites, recorded by Aristotle, linked the right side with maleness and the left side with femaleness. The right was associated with the straight, the light, the good, and the square; the left was associated with the cold, the dark, the bad, the crooked, and the evil. These ideas may have emerged from the half-forgotten mysticism of our paleolithic past.

Today there can be little doubt that different cultures attach different values to left and right sides of the face and body. The Chinese are apparently rare among human societies in that they bestow special honor to the left side while most other cultures

PLAYING WITH SIDES
Each of the nine faces is a composite picture of a noted celebrity couple, linked by marriage or career (or both). How many can you identify? If you have trouble identifying the individuals, cover the left or right side of the picture.

consider the left side to be sinister. Among the Nyoro of East Africa, properties associated with the right include man, brewing, health, fertility, life, the even, the hard, the moon, fidelity, and cattle. The opposite properties are associated with the left: women, cooking, sickness, poverty, barrenness, death, the soft, the sun, and chickens or sheep. The people of Morocco attach great importance to the twitching of an eyelid: twitching of the right eyelid signifies return of a member of the family or some other good news, whereas twitching of the left eyelid is a warning of impending death in the family. The Maoris of New Zealand are said to have believed that if a person experienced a tremor during sleep the body had been seized by a spirit. It was critically important to observe which side of the body was afflicted, for a tremor on the right side foretold good fortune and life, whereas a tremor on the left half meant ill fortune and even death. To the Maoris, the right was the side of the gods, as well as the side of strength and life, whereas the left was associated with demons, weakness, and death.

One aspect of the two sides of the face that has received attention through the ages is whether or not there is a better side for portraits and photographs. One study showed that portrait painters tend to show more of the left cheek than the right. The researchers considered a range of possible explanations but the question of why this is so remains unanswered, though intriguing.

*I am convinced that life, as it manifests itself to us, is a function of the dissymmetry of the universe or the consequences of this dissymmetry.*

LOUIS PASTEUR

Asymmetries, it turns out, are visible in the human embryo only fourteen days after conception. This suggests that asymmetry is a preprogrammed property of our species and of human development. In fact, human laterality appears to embody those very talents that set us apart from other species, namely, our sophisticated abilities to communicate and to manipulate. It is tempting to try and stretch its meaning and to conclude that laterality provides a key to understanding other uniquely human characteristics. However, there is no evidence to support such a notion. Rather, it seems that the asymmetry we recognize on the two sides of the face is a relatively surface manifestation of the evolution of language and other skills that have become lateralized in the human brain.

Andreas Vesalius was a gifted Renaissance physician who emphasized that the only true source of anatomical knowledge was the human body itself. In 1543 he published a landmark text, *De humani corporis fabrica libra septem (The Seven Books on the Structure of the Human Body)*. This beautifully illustrated work revolutionized neuroanatomy and revealed for the first time that the brain is responsible for the general shape and appearance of the human face and cranium. It is believed that these illustrations of the brain were done in the Venice studio of the great painter Titian. They are based, like other illustrations in this book, on the dissected brains of an executed criminal. In the illustration on the bottom, the membrane has been cut away, to reveal the corpus callosum, the highway that connects the two hemispheres.

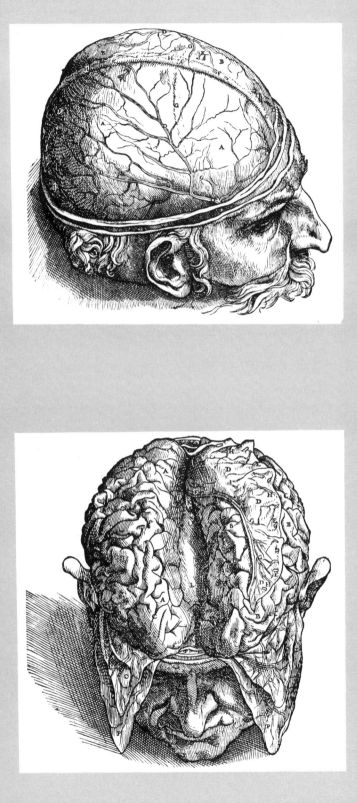

# 5

# More Than Meets the Eye

*Man is only man at the surface.*
*Remove his skin, dissect, and*
*immediately you come to the*
*machinery.*

PAUL VALÉRY

The faces of modern humans—and there are nearly 6 billion on earth—come in an infinite variety. We often sort them into categories based on size, shape, and proportions. We think of faces as long, broad, flat, beaky, hard, soft, swarthy, pallid, rosy, cheeky, plain, ugly, or beautiful. The list is almost endless and yet, different as we are on the outside, we have much in common on the inside.

Behind every face is an enlightened machine— the brain. Composed of a complex network of nerve cells and fibers, the brain requires a rich supply of blood and consumes approximately a quarter of the body's energy. Weighing less than three pounds, the brain stores more information than all the libraries in the world and is the essence of our humanity. This divided structure, orchestrates all behavior, including that which is expressed on and by the face. You might think about the face as the brain's theater, where what is happening on the inside is displayed on the outside for all the world to see—or not see, as the situation requires.

*In the human head there are forces within forces within forces, as in no other cubic half-foot of the universe that we know.*

ROGER SPERRY

The skull, sometimes called the dome of thought, is essentially a protective housing for the brain and the foundation for the face. The smooth vault of the cranium is built of eight bones and immovable joints called sutures, which in Latin means "seam." These jagged sutures not only hold the bones together but are designed to dissipate shocks and blows to the head. The exterior of the cranial bones is smooth and curved but the inside is convoluted, conforming to the contours of the brain. It is as if the skull is a mold for this organ of perception and thought and feeling.

Of the eight bones in the cranium, the most prominent is the frontal bone, the single bone making up the forehead and the forward part of the skull. There are two parietal bones that join at the midline of the top of the skull and serve as walls enclosing the brain. The occipital bone forms the undersurface of the rear of the skull. On either side of the skull, beneath the parietals, are located two temporal bones, which contain canals that lead to the middle and inner ear. Two less obvious bones are located below the cranium and behind the eyes. One is called the sphenoid bone, the other the ethmoid bone.

The face, though a smaller surface area than the

cranium, is composed of more bones, including seven pairs of bones and one unpaired bone. Two nasal bones form the bridge of the nose and meet at midplane. Behind the nasal bones are the vomer bones, which make up the bony portion of the tissues dividing the interior of the nose into two nostrils. The partition is the septum, which is not bony but cartilaginous, tough and elastic, which you can feel when you try to bend or twist it. Behind the nasal bones are the lacrimal bones. Most of the front of the face, from the eye to the upper jaw, is stiffened by the maxillary bones. These bones meet at midplane and make up the upper jaw and part of the upper border of the mouth. They run under the cheeks and reach up to the eye, forming part of the orbit. Behind the maxillaries in the roof of the mouth are the palatine bones, so called because they make up the palate (the roof of the mouth). The zygomatic bones make up the sides of the face and form the bony overhang above the upper jaw. These, sometimes called cheekbones, give each face its unique appearance and are highly prized by many different cultures. The zygomatics also stretch to the border of the eye and make up part of the orbit. Each orbit consists of portions of seven bones of the face and cranium.

All these bones of the face are immovably joined to one another and to the cranium. The face's only movable bone, and it is the largest one, is the lower jawbone called the mandible. Hinged to the upper bones, the mandible is a strong curved bar of bone that holds the lower teeth. When you open your mouth, this is the bone that drops down.

Sinuses are an important part of the skull's design. They are actually architectural air pockets that create hollow areas that have an opening linked to the nasal passage. (*Sinus* is a Latin term meaning "any hollow with but one opening.") These hollow areas serve a dual purpose: they lighten the skull and create spaces in which the voice can resonate. The sinuses are lined with tiny cilia that act to swirl

## THE BONY FRAMEWORK OF THE HEAD AND FACE

The skull is a protective framework for the brain and the major sense organs. It is comprised of twenty-three bones. After puberty, sex differences become apparent: male skulls grow significantly larger than female skulls and display a more pronounced brow ridge. Female skulls, on the other hand, are thinner and more delicate.

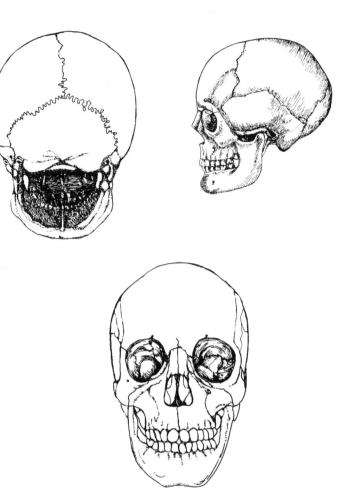

liquid through the narrow openings that connect them with the nasal passages. Sometimes a cold or allergy will cause the mucous membrane linings to swell and close the passage, making it difficult for them to drain. Without free movement of air, pressure builds up and causes what is commonly called a sinus headache.

Sinus problems, in general, are the result of our upright posture. It seems that in four-footed mammals the sinuses drain easily. But when our ancient ancestors became bipedal and walked upright, the sinuses tipped and assumed a somewhat horizontal position. With this evolutionary change, drainage became inefficient, particularly when the passage to the sinuses becomes blocked by a cold or an allergy.

Some people are more prone to sinus problems than others. This is probably due to the fact that in some individuals the opening leading to the nasal passage is particularly small.

Teeth are another key element in the face's design. Teeth vary greatly from one group to another, from individual to individual, in size, proportions, fissured patterns, and cusp numbers. Harder than bone and made of calcium phosphate, teeth are set in the upper and lower jaws, giving the human face much of its shape and contributing significantly to its appearance. Teeth originated among the primitive, sharklike fish. At first they were all the same size and shape and there were many of them. When they wore down they were simply replaced. The evolutionary trend, however, has been to reduce the number of teeth and the number of times they were replaced. Eventually teeth changed shape and specialized for different functions, making them more efficient. Today, human teeth are small, considering our size and weight. This is part of the reason why the human face has shrunk over a million years of evolution.

When you really think about the teeth and their supporting tissue you see how critical they are to their owners for oral health and functioning teeth are basic to an individual's biological welfare.

Teeth first appear in the developing fetus during the middle months of pregnancy. By the seventh

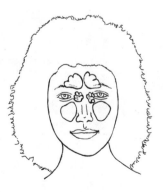

SINUS CAVITIES
There are four groups of sinuses or air pockets located in the frontal, ethmoid, sphenoid, and maxillary bones. The frontal sinuses are located above the eyebrows. The largest sinuses are located in the maxillary, or cheekbones. The ethmoid pocket is behind the bridge of the nasal cavity and the sphenoid sinuses lie in a bone that cradles the brain. Generally, we are only aware of our sinuses when they become irritated because of a cold or allergy.

## THE TEETH

Teeth vary in size and shape and in their location in the jaw. In the front, there are the incisors, which are wedge-shaped with a cutting edge. Behind the incisors are the canines, which are conical and specialized for tearing. Next come the bicuspids, sometimes called the premolars. They have the appearance of double canines. Farthest back in the mouth are the molars, which are specialized for grinding. The differences between the teeth enable them to work together to help you chew and digest food, to help you speak clearly, and to help your face keep its shape.

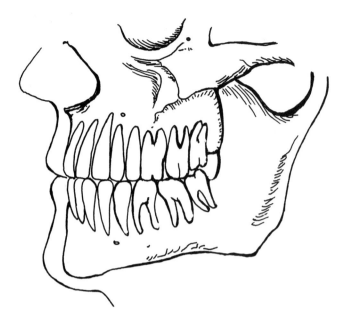

## CLOSE-UP OF
## MARLENE DIETRICH

In order to create the caved-in facial look that was uniquely hers, Marlene Dietrich had her upper rear molars removed early in her career.

*Every morning I look into the mirror and thank God for my high cheekbones.*

SUZY PARKER

month the lower front incisors have a shape close to their final form. By birth the upper incisors are almost completely formed. Both the top and the bottom incisors erupt when the child is about one year old. Humans grow two sets of teeth: a set for the young jaw and one for the mature jaw. Normally, all thirty-two teeth have appeared by age twenty-one.

The "wisdom" teeth are in a special category. The human jaw rarely grows large enough to accommodate them and often they must be surgically removed. In some people they may not even erupt. Scientists interpret this as a sign that the wisdom teeth may be on their way out, evolutionarily speaking. This would reduce the number of teeth in *Homo sapiens* to twenty-eight, which is probably enough to deal with the modern human diet.

A malocclusion (bad closing) interferes with the proper function and performance of the teeth and

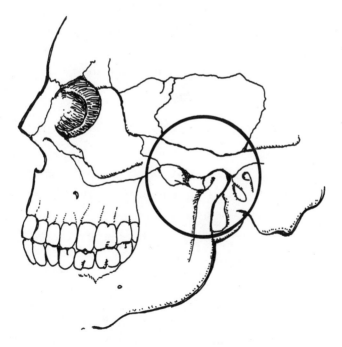

## TEMPOROMANDIBULAR DISORDERS

Do you suffer from a dull, aching pain around the ear, often radiating into the face and sometimes into the neck, back of the head, and shoulders? Are your jaw muscles tender? Do you hear clicking or popping noises when opening or closing your mouth? Do you sometimes have difficulty chewing or do you get certain kinds of headaches—sometimes of migraine proportions? Do you experience ringing in your ears, sinus pain, and dizziness? If you have answered yes to any of the above, you may suffer along with roughly twenty percent of all Americans from the often overlooked, misdiagnosed, and complex dental condition known collectively as temporomandibular disorders. The temporomandibular joints are the hinges located on either side of the face that connect the lower jaw to the skull. Each temporomandibular joint has two sections that permit the hinge and gliding actions needed to open the mouth widely. The joints work in concert with the facial bones and five pairs of muscles to open and close the mouth and to move it forward, backward, and from side to side. Any disturbance in this facial symphony can trigger the characteristics of TM (which is what this disorder is popularly called) because, when muscles and joints don't work together correctly, muscle spasms result and these produce pain, muscle tenderness, and tissue damage.

may create an unsightly appearance. Orthodontia, the branch of dentistry that deals with correcting irregularities of the teeth, can improve not only appearance but also the structural relationship between the teeth. Improving the structural relationship improves the functional efficiency of the teeth.

The human face is a compelling image because of its remarkable powers of expression. It is the facial musculature, in conjunction with the bone, cartilage, soft tissue, and skin, that makes expression possible. There are many muscles just below the surface of the skin. These muscles crisscross each other in many different directions and make possible a rich repertoire of complex, subtle, and beautiful movements. It is estimated that the twenty-two expressive muscles on each side of the face are capable of producing as many as ten thousand different facial actions or expressions, though the average person routinely uses fewer, perhaps no more than two thousand.

Most facial expressions are brought to life by the simultaneous action of many muscles. These muscles are anchored to the bones of the skull and attached to the soft tissue of the face. When a muscle contracts in response to a message from the brain, the unattached end is pulled closer to the attached end so that the skin and tissues lying on top of the muscle will be made to move, creating wrinkles or folds in the skin. In this way the corner of the mouth, for example, is pulled upward into a smiling position.

FACT It takes seventeen muscles to smile and forty-three muscles to frown.

*The movements of expression give vividness and energy to our spoken word. They reveal the thoughts and intentions to others more truly than do words, which may be falsified.*

CHARLES DARWIN

The facial nerve is a mixed nerve, meaning that it performs more than one job. Its sensory fibers

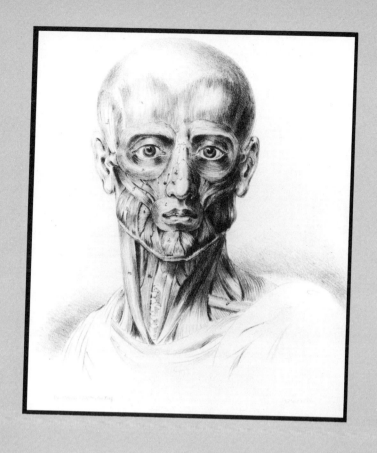

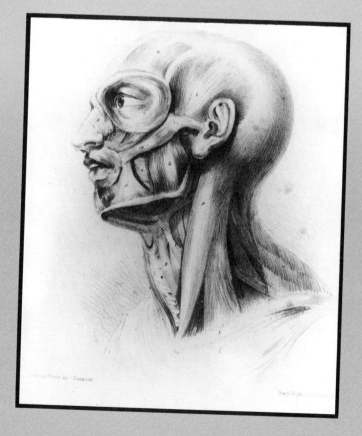

## THE FACE MUSCLES

Based on dissections, these illustrations done by George Simpson around 1825 reveal the inherent beauty of the face's musculature arrangement and highlight the major muscle groups: (a) frontalis; (b) temporal; (c) orbicularis oculi; (d) compressor naris; (e) levator labii superioris et alae nasi; (f) zygomaticus minor; (g) zygomaticus major; (h) masseter; (i) buccinator; (j) depressor anguli oris; (l) orbicularis oris.

arise from the forward two thirds of the tongue and it is through these that the sensation of taste reaches the brain. In addition, its motor fibers lead to the various muscles of the face and give rise to the face's expressive behavior.

*The patterns of facial nerves are about as different as the river systems on different continents.*

GORDON ALLPORT

Stripped of its covering, the structure we know as the human face is a marvelous, highly efficient biological machine composed of many specialized parts that work together to make our faces sentient and responsive. And though we seldom pass in front of a mirror without checking out our reflections, we rarely if ever consider that there is much more in a face than at first meets the eye.

# 6

# The Wrapping

Your skin is a remarkable organ exquisitely adapted to its many functions. It is an armor of keratin, the same protein that makes up hair and nails. It shields your vital organs from a multitude of irritants and microorganisms. It is a container that holds in lifeblood and acts to ward off the harsh ultraviolet rays of the sun. A supple and biologically rugged cellular renewal system, your skin is always at work protecting its precious cargo.

At the same time that the skin protects and preserves, it embodies the sense of touch, it is the principal organ of sexual attraction, it is a temperature-regulating system, and, as the skin absorbs ultraviolet rays from the sun, it converts chemicals into vitamin D, which your body needs for the proper utilization of calcium.

A strong and rugged wrapping, the skin is actually an array of different layers, each having its own properties. Much like plywood, the skin's strength is a function of these layers.

The outermost layer and the immediate buffer to the environment is the epidermis. Although this is the thinnest of the three layers, it is an effective barrier to the outside world. Next comes the dermis, which is a layer of connective tissue containing blood vessels, hair follicles, sweat glands, and sebaceous glands. It is the dermis that gives bulk to the skin. Finally, there is the subcutis, which is flexible, fatty, and fibrous.

A network of nerve endings in the skin makes it possible to feel sensations of touch, pain, heat, and

ZONES OF THE SKIN

The zones are shown in this cross section. The dermis is supported by the fat-rich subcutaneous stratum. Above the dermis is the epidermis: a zone of living cells capped by a horny layer of dead cells filled with the fibrous protein keratin. Melanocytes are the pigment cells responsible for producing varying skin colors. These lie at the base of the dermis.

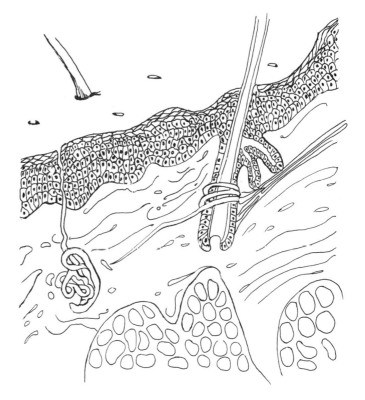

cold. It is the nerve network that facilitates a delicate communication between the outside world and the inside world in an ongoing effort to maintain the system's equilibrium.

Temperature regulation is possible because the skin is extremely well supplied with blood. If the environment is cold and the body needs to conserve heat, the blood vessels in the skin contract. When the environment is warm, blood vessels relax and expand, providing a free flow of blood. During muscular exertion, when great quantitites of heat must be dissipated, blood flow through the skin is maximal. This accounts for the red face you get when you exert yourself.

The skin's texture and characteristics vary from place to place on the body, and the face is no exception. In most people, the skin of the eyebrows is thick, coarse, and hairy. The skin on the eyelids is thin, smooth, and covered with almost invisible hairs. The surfaces of the forehead, the cheeks, and the nose are normally oily, while the chin and jaw are relatively greaseless. The skin of the forehead and cheekbones rarely has hair on it and the lips are hairless. In most men, the chin and jaws are hairy— so hairy, in fact, that bristles are visible within a few hours after shaving. In women, coarse facial hairs may sprout with age as a result of hormonal changes.

In some people the facial skin is taut; in others it stretches easily. In either type the skin is fundamentally elastic in order to accommodate the face's many subtle movements as well as to provide a flexible container for the ever changing mass. The skin's inherent elasticity is highly individual and largely determined by regional and genetic factors.

At any given moment, then, the way your skin looks depends on both genes and the life you experience. The genetic blueprint will determine the basic color and texture, thickness or thinness of your skin, the nature of the blood circulation, and the characteristics of the tissues beneath the skin. Age, on the other hand, and the climate in which you live will affect appearance and the skin's elasticity.

The development of skin begins very early in the human embryo and follows a characteristic life cycle, changing dramatically from birth to old age. In infants and children the skin is velvety, dry, soft, clear, and apparently hairless.

ENVIRONMENTAL
REALITIES
A harsh environment will take its toll, sooner rather than later. The most obvious indignities suffered by the face from a harsh environment include dry, wrinkled, and flaccid skin. That the skin survives these torments is a tribute to its toughness.

Troubled skin has long been the bane of adolescence. Medical experts point to fluctuations in sex hormones as the culprits. In fact, many of the most frustrating and seemingly untreatable complexion problems are the direct result of changes in levels of estrogen, progesterone, and testosterone during puberty, pregnancy, and menopause. Hormone-related skin problems are characterized by acne, uncontrollable oiliness, blackheads, whiteheads, dry patches, and eczema.

We actually know very little about the cause and treatment of acne, though we do know that the sebaceous glands are in some way responsible and that there is a hereditary disposition to acne that is connected to diet and hormonal activity.

Though sebaceous glands are little understood, we know that they produce sebum, an odd mixture of fatty acids, waxes, cholesterol, and cellular debris. This semiliquid mixture is toxic to living tissue and can cause a myriad of problems. Most sebaceous glands are attached to hair follicles. These glands are particularly prominent around the nose, the mouth, the insides of the cheeks, the border of the lips, on the forehead, over the cheekbones, and on the inside edge of the eyelids. In all these places, sebum coats the skin continuously. Even with normal production and regular washing, the oil-producing glands of the face create a condition favorable to acne. Some investigators believe that sebum helps the skin retain moisture and that it may kill certain forms of harmful bacteria. Others have dismissed sebum as a useless substance and sebaceous glands as archaic organs that do greater harm than good.

Acne results when bacteria is trapped in the sebaceous gland and the sebum turns to a fatty acid. The acid irritates the follicle and inflames the skin, causing a lesion. These lesions appear on the skin as pimples or cysts.

Virtually everyone experiences acne and as a result remedies have been numerous through the ages. A fourth-century Roman court physician recommended that the afflicted person wipe the skin with a cloth at the sight of a shooting star. By the eighteenth century, some physicians advised marriage as a cure, believing that masturbation caused acne. Recent research has produced a broad range of treatments including antibiotics, hormone therapy, and a derivative of vitamin A called 13-cis retinoic acid.

Acne scars can be obscured by dermabrasion, a technique of smoothing the skin with abrasives that was first practiced by the Egyptians. Although dermabrasion takes a long time to heal, it does result in a striking change in appearance.

Another secretion produced by the skin is sweat. The sweat that dampens the brow is produced by the eccrine glands. It is their job to cool the body, primarily by evaporation. Sweat glands are tightly coiled tubes buried deep in the inner layer of the dermis. Their ducts rise to the skin's surface through the pores. It is estimated that one square inch of skin contains about 645 sweat glands.

Up close you can see that the skin is pitted by sweat glands and hair follicles and is furrowed by intersecting lines. The lines indicate the general directions of elastic tension. Countless numbers of these lines, deep and shallow, together with the pores, give each face a characteristic topography.

HUMAN SKIN
SURFACE
This scanning electron micrograph reveals the dead epidermal cells that comprise the skin's surface. These dead skin cells flake off at the rate of about six hundred thousand per hour.

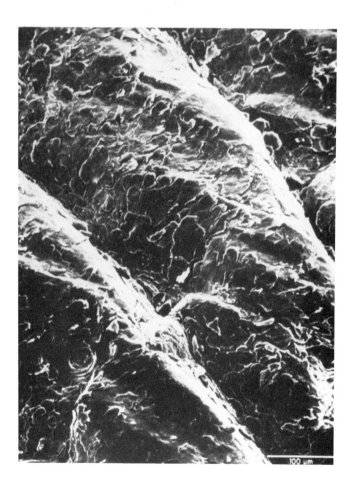

When children are very young, their cheeks are puffed out with "sucking pads." These fleshy areas on either side of the face elicit a powerful emotional response in adults, particularly in women. If you've ever wondered what makes a baby's face so endearing, it is the shapely cheeks.

These fine details are idiosyncratic to each individual, and time accentuates and emphasizes them.

The skin itself is separated from the muscles by a layer of fatty tissue which may be thick or thin, smooth or corrugated, according to age, sex, and genetic program. Important cushions of fat lie just below the skin of the face. These cushions profoundly affect what we see in the mirror. Notice the pad at the root of your nose. See the pad between the eyes. Notice other padded areas between the nose and upper lip and at the point of the chin that give your face its characteristic shape and contour. In the course of a lifetime, these fatty cushions will vary a great deal.

Birthmarks are abnormal distributions of blood vessels or pigment cells. There are several types. The port-wine stain, so called because of its red or purplish hue, is one type. It is composed primarily of enlarged blood vessels. This marking may be imperceptible in infancy but it can continue to grow over time and can sometimes cover as much as half of the face. "Mole" is a generic term for other markings on the skin. Like freckles, moles are concentrations of melanin. Although it is not known exactly how melanocytes form moles or why we get them, moles tend to be linked to heredity. Two major categories of moles have been identified: pigmented birthmarks, called congenital moles, and moles acquired after the first year of life. There is a visual distinction: a congenital mole is generally larger than five millimeters, flat and even in color, and frequently has coarse hairs growing out of it; an acquired mole, on the other hand, is usually smaller. It can be smooth or bumpy, one-colored or speckled, and it is hairless. Large congenital moles have a ten to fifteen times greater risk of developing skin cancer than acquired moles.

The skin is of enormous importance in the impression we make on others. Skin color, in fact, is our most visible difference and, though there is no basis for it, we often make judgments about others based solely on the color of their skin.

*When I was a boy the Sioux owned the world; the sun rose and set on their land; they sent ten thousand men to battle. Where are the warriors today? Who slew them? Where are our lands? Who owns them? . . . What law have I broken? Is it wrong for me to love my own? Is it wicked for me because my skin is red? Because I am Sioux; because I was born where my father lived; because I would die for my people and my country?*

SITTING BULL

*I have a dream that my four little children will one day live in a nation where they will not be judged by the color of their skin, but by the content of their character.*

MARTIN LUTHER KING, JR.

Remarkable individual variations in skin color occur even within members of the same group. Besides the network of blood vessels, the color of the skin is determined by melanin, a pigment manufactured by special cells called melanocytes. These melanocytes are evenly scattered deep in the epidermis. The prime function of the pigment is to absorb the sun's damaging ultraviolet rays and convert them into harmless infrared rays. The more pigment or melanin, the more efficient the absorption and the better the protection. Evolutionarily speaking, this protective quality has been an asset with high survival value to members of our species.

All human beings regardless of race have about the same number of melanocytes—the difference is, in dark-complexioned people, the melanocytes manufacture more pigment. When the face tans it is because the sunlight has activated these melanocytes, increasing their activity.

A freckle, or ephelis as it is technically called, is a small brownish, well-circumscribed spot on the skin that is a result of the pigment's gathering in clusters. This occurs in all skin colors but is most obvious in light skin. The tendency to develop freckles is apparently inherited and they generally begin to appear after the age of five. Apart from avoiding sunlight, there is no known way to prevent them.

The luster and transparency of the skin vary a great deal in different individuals. The skin is thinner, smoother, and more transparent in females than in males. There are differences, too, in the tissues supporting the skin: in young females there is usually more underlying fatty tissue, which is what gives the cheeks their characteristically smooth appearance.

The loss of this fatty support in both males and females during middle age may produce wrinkling because the skin and its underlayer may shrink at different rates. For everyone, gravity and activity ultimately take their toll as the skin loses its youthful elasticity and becomes wrinkled and furrowed with age.

Not all wrinkles are created equal. Some, like furrows on the forehead and the sag lines caused when gravity pulls your brows or jowls down, can't really be prevented. Those smile lines between the nose and mouth can't be prevented either, as this is the most used part of the face—always moving when we speak, eat, laugh, yawn, and smile. These lines represent an accentuation of preexisting congenital lines that become strongly emphasized with old age. But other wrinkles are not so inevitable. You may be able to forestall some major furrows by protecting your face from the sun's harmful rays.

Photoaging is the direct result of everyday damage caused by the sun's ultraviolet rays that penetrate the skin and injure the skin's cells. The effect of this damage over a period of years is what many people

PREGNANCY MASK
From the onset of puberty, and for many women throughout their menstruating years, the main dermatologic problem is oily skin. When the menstrual cycle stops, such as during pregnancy, the skin undergoes different changes and often benefits from the prolonged increase in estrogen levels and progesterone. However, twenty percent of all pregnant women are allergic to their own progesterone. For these women, elevated hormone levels cause a variety of skin problems, including a rise in the level of melanin, making them extremely sensitive to the sun. The result is what is sometimes called a pregnancy mask, a series of dark patches that commonly form around the eyes.

think of as aging skin. Photoaging occurs even when you're walking around doing your normal activities.

It is in response to increased ultraviolet radiation that the skin begins to develop a tan. Tanning, in fact, is a defense against additional damage. Overexposure to the sun results in a sunburn. The redness comes from increased blood flow to the area. This is the skin's way of speeding healing. Sun damage is cumulative and irreversible. There is no question but that steady tanning leads to premature wrinkles and discoloration of the skin and is responsible for the enormous increase in skin cancer.

The war against wrinkles is not new. It has been waged by women through the ages though the remedies have varied from region to region. In the Middle East, where beautiful skin is prized, women as far back as Bathsheba and Cleopatra used mud packs and oils extracted from plants and herbs to protect their skin against wrinkles and prevent the telltale signs of aging. Asian women historically have favored ginseng as a basis for antiwrinkle treatments. Common cold cream was invented by the Greeks, who used a mixture of olive oil, beeswax, water, and rose petals. It is the evaporation of water, which has a cooling effect, that gives cold cream its name. Though today's cold cream products are highly refined and have extra ingredients, the basic formula is the same. The early Vikings protected their faces when at sea with fish oils extracted from cod, salmon, and herring. Many modern Swedish skin products still feature these ingredients. In Mexico women attest to the high moisture-retention properties of the aloe vera cactus plant as a wrinkle remedy. Since ancient times Italian women have favored mud packs while Hungarian women use ingredients found in the stalk of the sunflower plant.

Today the war goes on. But though high-tech, antiaging wrinkle treatments today are plentiful, they are unproved. New work is being done in the United States to assess the effectiveness of a family of compounds found in plants, fruits, and sour milk called alpha hydroxy acids. The American Academy of Dermatology reported that these compounds may be a promising new antiaging treatment that causes a change in the structure of the skin, making it possible to reduce wrinkles, fade age spots, improve dry skin, and help reduce acne and scarring. The Academy continues to monitor current research in an attempt to determine just what concentrations of the acids produce the best results, how long the result will last, and whether alpha hydroxy acid treatments will work for everyone.

Tretinoin, marketed under the brand name Retin-A and available by prescription, is another antiaging cream that has been enthusiastically promoted by the media. The claim is made that it appears to reverse the signs of skin aging by reducing wrinkles, softening the skin, and lightening pigment spots. Researchers, however, are cautious and point out that not only is skin irritation a serious side effect but the long-term toxicity of Retin-A has yet to be determined. It is also not known whether or not the benefits last after treatment is stopped. Even more worrisome is the fact that tretinoin creates extreme sensitivity to the sun, and it is clear that sun damage contributes to the development of skin cancer.

The fact is, when it comes to wrinkles, the biological clock ticks inexorably and the most noticeable wrinkles on individual faces cannot be avoided, for they are the expression lines, such as frown lines between the brows, produced by continuous use of the same facial muscles. In any other part of the body, constant use of muscles would tone the area, but not so on the face. The expression lines deepen when you use facial muscles because the muscles of the face are attached to the skin, while in every other place in the body muscles are attached to the bone. Whenever you smile or frown you are actually pulling at the skin. It is this constant pulling that leads to furrows.

*Wrinkles merely indicate where smiles have been.*

MARK TWAIN

WRINKLE CONTROL
Sleep on your back. Pillows or
mattresses can cause tugging
on your face. Use moisturizer.
It won't remove wrinkles, but
because dry skin looks more
lined, a moisturizer can make
lines appear less noticeable.

Wear sunscreen daily to avoid
the wrinkles caused by photoaging.

Everyday facial tension is another factor in the creation of expression lines. Most of us don't realize how often we frown or raise our brows when the face is tensed. Nor do we realize that simple eyestrain, talking, being outside without sunglasses, or just concentrating on a task can cause the muscles of the face to bunch up into characteristic furrowed patterns.

Relaxation exercises can help ease the strain on your facial muscles and perhaps improve appearance. But facial exercise will not help. According to many dermatologists, facial exercises recreate the same pulls that you're trying to undo. Nothing short of plastic surgery will actually undo deep lines.

You are probably unaware of the many permanent organisms that live on your skin. Every square inch hosts an average of some 32 million bacteria. They are particularly abundant where there are plenty of nutrients, and that includes the face. You could wash your face with soap and water a hundred times a day and still never clear your skin of the countless bacteria that call it home. We acquire the bacteria at birth and thereafter the populations grow rapidly. Ironically, once some populations become established, they fill a niche in the skin's environment that harmful bacteria might otherwise occupy. These resident bacteria will fight off intruders in order to maintain their territory and in so doing protect us from more harmful intruders. The fact that our skin is constantly shedding also prevents many harmful kinds of microorganisims from gaining a foothold.

Though it is primarily harmful organisms that attract our attention, the overwhelming majority (both flora and fauna) are harmless and some may even be helpful. Consider the little-understood mite called *Demodex folliculorum*. This microscopic creature inhabits the hair follicles of the eyelashes, the chin, and the scalp of most adults. *Demodex folliculorum* is a narrow, wormlike creature that lays its eggs in the sebaceous glands and, after molting, travels in the night to find another follicle and a new home. Although this guest was identified in 1842, no one really knows what it eats or what role it plays in the skin's health.

There are other creatures that sometimes live on the skin but are not quite so benign. They include the red chigger and the scabies mite, for example, both of which are parasites. Some viruses also find the skin an attractive home. Herpes simplex, for example, resides in the head and is responsible for the common cold sore. Although advances have been made in treatment, no real cure exists for herpes simplex.

Of the resident fauna, *Pityrosporum ovale*, a common yeast, grows on the greasy surfaces of the nose, scalp, and ears. This plant can grow in number up to half a million per square centimeter. Though it possibly feeds on the fats in the skin it is believed to be harmless.

Hair is a specialized form of skin. It is largely ornamental and its purpose is still little understood. It is believed by some anthropologists that, as the human animal became differentiated from other primates through the slow stages of evolution, the body and face gradually lost its hair. In terms of the face, there is speculation that hairy faces may have interfered with expression and therefore with communication.

Some of the hair that remains on the face may serve a few useful purposes. Eyebrows, for example, keep dirt and sweat out of the eyes and may have evolved to facilitate social communication by accentuating the messages sent by facial expressions. Eyelashes serve as sensitive warning systems to close the eyes the instant an irritant gets near. Beards and

FACT: By the time an infant is born, it has as many hairs or rudiments of hairs on its face as it will ever have. The idea that face hair does not form until one matures is incorrect. Moreover, there is no substantial difference between men and women with respect to the number of hair follicles on the face.

mustaches, it has been suggested, are probably related to sexual dominance and may serve to intimidate rivals. At the time of male puberty, chin hair, mustaches, and the beard grow coarse and become symbolic of membership in the adult male ranks.

History tells us that men first cherished a beard for religious reasons. It was commonly believed that face hairs had to be guarded. Shaving was considered against nature. Continuously growing hair was regarded as an expression of vitality. This is why the cutting off of the beard was reserved for defeated enemies.

Other factors influenced the importance of face hairs. Because women generally couldn't grow beards, those who did were considered witches. A beard, then, was regarded as the special sign and privilege of manhood. In many cultures a long beard was used to distinguish members of the aristocracy. That is why in early Hebrew an elder was called "the bearded one." In the second millennium B.C., beards, more than crowns, were the sign of royalty and both Pharaohs and their queens wore false beards. At this time merchants, landowners, and members of the upper classes wore beards, but slaves and members of the lower classes were beardless. Ancient Persians considered the shaven face an absurdity, while the Hittites shaved everything— beard, mustache, and eyebrows. Alexander the Great ordered his soldiers to shave off their beards so they would not become convenient handles for their enemies. Early Romans wore beards until Sicilian barbers showed up and established a fashion of clean-shavenness. Emperor Nero meticulously preserved his beard in a golden pearl-encrusted box lest anyone get his hands on it for evil purposes. The English Queen Elizabeth I taxed anyone sprouting a beard more than a fortnight old and Charlemagne, who had a beard until he became Holy Roman Emperor, ordered his subjects to be clean-shaven. Beards flourished in the sixteenth century. They were waxed, dyed, powdered, and perfumed. Fran-

Today, in many parts of the world a beard is worn by the clergy as a sign of their wisdom and authority.

FACT The average man has somewhere between fifteen and thirty thousand whiskers on his face. He spends about ten minutes a day shaving and shaves off one pound of whiskers every ten years. Face hair grows at the rate of about a third of a millimeter per day. A common misconception is that shaving causes the hair to grow increasingly coarse. It is true that the stubble after shaving feels rough, but it is simply because the soft, tapered ends of the hair have been cut off.

cis I grew a beard to hide an ugly scar on the chin and all Frenchmen followed suit. A hundred years later the French considered it proper to be clean-shaven because Louis XIV was beardless. Eighteenth-century Spaniards did not wear beards simply because their king could not grow one. For nineteenth-century doctors, a beard was considered the trademark of an experienced physician; it has been said that without a beard a doctor found himself without patients.

Head hair is not essential to man but we are extremely proprietary about it and we go to great lengths to both care for it and groom it. On the average, we humans will sprout between 100,000 and 150,000 head hairs, depending upon hair color. Fair-haired people will grow more hair than dark-haired people. Redheads grow the fewest head hairs of all. Hairs vary in color, diameter, and contour. The dif-

Werewolf tales come from this affliction wherein the body produces a pathological abnormality characterized by an overabundance of facial hair and extreme sensitivity to light.

ferent colors result from variations in amounts, distribution, and types of melanin pigment in them, as well as from variations in surface structure, causing light to be reflected in different ways. Hairs may be coarse or so thin and colorless that they are nearly invisible. Straight hairs are round, while wavy ones are alternately oval and round. Very curly hairs are shaped and twisted like ribbons.

Each hair follicle on the scalp grows almost thirty feet of hair during an average lifetime or about five inches every year. Scalp hair is different from other hair on the body in that it will grow sometimes for years without falling out. Ordinarily, people lose between fifty and a hundred hairs a day.

Tales of the hair's becoming entirely gray overnight are myths. What actually causes hair to turn white is that the body's production of the natural hair-coloring agent, melanin, shuts down as one grows older. When and how much is genetically

Human hair comes in virtually
an infinite variety of types and
textures as well as a range of
color.

determined. Most people have a sprinkling of gray
by their mid-thirties and grow increasingly gray as
the years pass.

From an evolutionary point of view, according
to William Montagna, an expert on the structure
and function of the skin and hair, the most interesting aspect of man's hair is the baldness that de-

1.

2.

## HAIR APPARENT

One's hairstyle can be so distinctive that it becomes almost a trademark of the owner. Pictured here are twelve unusual heads of hair (including, in some instances, beards, mustaches, and eyebrows) of a dozen famous individuals past and present. Can you identify the individuals by the coiffures?

5.

6.

9.

10.

velops on top of the head. This baldness, he writes, is actually an extension of a natural process that occurs in all human beings and begins before birth. In the young fetus the entire head and forehead are covered with hairs. After the fifth month of gestation, the hair follicles on the forehead gradually become involuted and diminish in size. At birth the infant

3.

4.

7.

8.

ANSWERS
1. Princess Diana
2. Ronald Reagan
3. Bob Marley
4. George Washington
5. Albert Einstein
6. Captain Kangaroo
7. Farrah Fawcett
8. Elvis Presley
9. Bo Derek
10. William Shakespeare
11. Groucho Marx
12. Yul Brynner or Telly Savalas

11.

12.

may still have visible hairs on the forehead but in most cases they are gone by early childhood.

This same process of involution of follicles is responsible for balding of the scalp, which may begin in young men as early as the twenties. Curious as it is, considering that normally head hair will grow to an almost unlimited length, the explanation lies in

## THE SCALP

(a) This scanning electron micrograph, magnified 300 times, shows an oblique section through the scalp of a rhesus monkey. Some cut hairs (H) can be seen projecting from hair follicles. Both epidermis (E) and dermis (D) are seen. Note the large bundles of collagen fibers running throughout the dermis. Sections through the sebaceous glands (Se) are also evident.

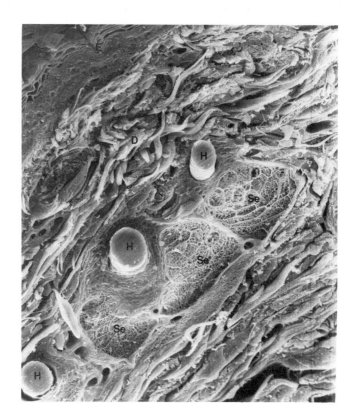

(b) On the scalp, as elsewhere on the body of most primates, hair grows from tiny oblong structures called follicles. Magnified × 1,500, this micrograph reveals that hair is made of highly keratinized dead skin cells arranged in overlapping scales. The visible section, called the shaft, grows about one half inch a month. It looks very much as though the hair is growing out of a cabbage because numerous desquamating cells, arranged concentrically around the base of the hair shaft where it emerges through the surface, are sloughing off. This is the scruff we think of as dandruff.

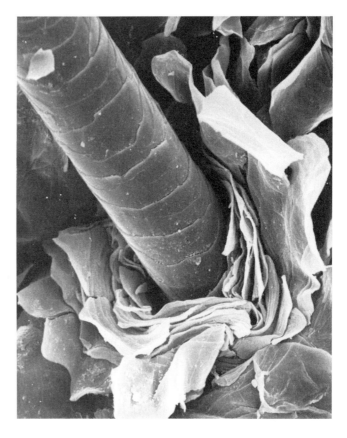

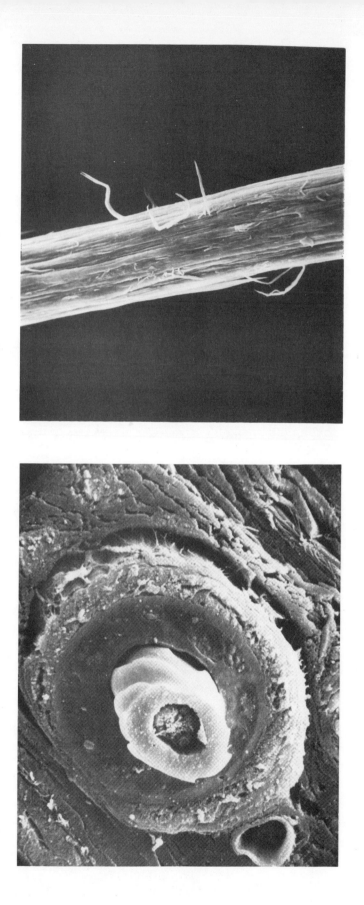

## BLEACHED HAIR

In the effort to enhance attractiveness, women and men subject their hair to systematic abuse, including pulling, stretching, heating, curling, dyeing, and bleaching. This human hair, magnified × 1,500, has been chemically bleached. Note that the entire outer cuticle (overlapping scales) has been destroyed by the bleaching process. Healthy hair usually survives such a treatment because it is fundamentally strong and resilient.

## CROSS SECTION OF HAIR

Hairs are manufactured by follicles. The size and shape of the follicles determine the shape and texture of the hair. Straight hair follicles grow straight hairs, curved follicles produce curly hair. The shape of a hair can be altered by both chemicals and heat. The number of follicles per square inch determines whether one has a thick head of hair or thin hair. Whether the hair is coarse or fine is determined by the diameter of the hair itself. All follicles grow at an angle to the surface. In the center of the follicle is the hair. Individual hair follicles are dormant for variable periods of time.

the action of androgenic or male hormones, which are paradoxically responsible for hair growth and for hair loss. As Montagna points out, "Once involution of the scalp follicles has taken place no agency will avail to grow a new crop of hair." The fact is that if a man's forebears were bald, chances are he will inherit the trait. Folk remedies, including massage, oils, creams, and vitamins, can do nothing to prevent or reverse the balding process.

Dandruff, which we think of as scruff that forms on the scalp, is an extremely common disturbance of the normal keratinization in which the rate of cell turnover of the epidermis on the scalp is uneven and may be as high as two or three times normal in certain places on the scalp. Most adults suffer the embarrassment of dandruff at one time or another.

All in all, we humans are extraordinarily dependent on the many properties of our skin. Though seemingly delicate, the skin is a remarkably complex, tough, and adaptable organ that serves not only as a protective armor but also speaks reams about us to other members of our species.

# 7

# Reading Faces

*There's no art to find the mind's construction in the face.*

SHAKESPEARE

The judgments we make about a person's character, rightly or wrongly, fairly or unfairly, are based upon our sensitivity to the total configuration of the face. And yet most people would disagree. They would tell you that they try to deduce character from reading an individual's anatomical features: a large nose, a purposeful chin, or narrow, shifty eyes. Reading the face's features in order to understand and ascertain character and personality is called physiognomy and it has a long tradition. In fact, it seems that there is something of the physiognomist in each of us.

About two thousand years ago Cicero, Rome's

could form an opinion about how much ability a man possessed. "The countenance," he remarked, "is the portrait of the mind, the eyes its informers." Beliefs like this made perfect sense at the time, for the majority of philosophers, poets, historians, and physicians agreed that knowledge about people could be attained by the systematic study of the face's features.

As early as 500 B.C. the philosopher-mathematician Pythagoras was looking into the faces of his prospective students in order to "see" if they were truly gifted. He allowed no one into his prestigious academy to study mathematics unless the facial appearance showed that the individual could profit from his teachings.

*A troubled countenance oft discloses much.*

SENECA

Aristotle wrote the earliest known treatise on physiognomy. The chief basis of his work was analogical; that is to say, people with facial features resembling a particular animal were thought to have analogous temperaments. Someone with a bulldog jaw, for example, was tenacious, just like a bulldog. In addition, in his *Historia animalium*, Aristotle said that the face revealed many characteristics including humor, talkativeness, meanness, steadfastness, fickleness, stupidity, courage, intelligence, impudence, and indecision. It was his opinion that men with small foreheads were fickle and those with rounded or bulging ones were quick-tempered. Straight eyebrows spoke of a soft disposition, while staring eyes were clearly impudent. Large-headed people, according to Aristotle, were mean, those who had a small face were steadfast, a broad face reflected stupidity, while a round face was an unmistakable sign of courage.

*There are often voice and words in a silent look.*

OVID

*The face is the mirror of the mind—and eyes without speaking confess the secrets of the heart.*

ST. JEROME

Hippocrates, the father of modern medicine, wrote about faces in his voluminous writings. He used the face as a source of diagnosis. On it he found indicators of health and disease. It was Hippocrates who gave a name, *facies Hippocratica*, to the face of one about to die. He described it this way: nose sharp, eyes hollow, temples shrunken, ears cold and contracted, with their lobes turned outward, the skin about the face hard and tense, the color of the face being yellow or dark.

But Hippocrates was not the only doctor of antiquity to depend upon physiognomy for medical judgments. Galen in the second century and the Greeks Adamantius and Meletius of the fourth century also found physiognomy useful in the practice of medicine. Face reading, in fact, was an honored profession and the relationship between face and character was celebrated in marble portrait busts that stood in public squares as well as in the family courtyards.

In Roman times a cult of collecting wax death masks and displaying them at home developed. These *imagines* were intended to be constant reminders of the dead person's character. In his *Natural History*, Pliny the Elder described how the *imagines* of death masks were taken from the corpse, incorporated into terra-cotta busts, and carried by family members in funeral processions in order to attest publicly to the character of the departed.

> *The face of man is the index to joy and mirth, to suffering and sadness.*
>
> PLINY THE ELDER

In Europe during the Middle Ages the art of face reading was employed by astrologers who mapped the face along with the stars. Even minor physical characteristics such as the lines of the forehead had significance and could be interpreted. For instance, on the forehead, straight lines denoted good fortune, winding lines denoted struggle, distorted lines denoted variety, mischief, and deceit. Many lines signified a changeable personality while simple and straight lines spoke of an honest nature and long life. Broken lines revealed the influence of Saturn and Mars and indicated a hot temper. Beliefs like this flourished and, for centuries thereafter, physiognomy would be inextricably tied to astrology and dependent upon the occult and magic for its explanation.

The Renaissance delivered a new advocate of physiognomy. His name was Giovanni Battista Della Porta. Influenced by the physician Hippocrates, Della Porta challenged the traditional approach to reading faces, which relied on astrology, and ushered in a new era in which observation and physiology were considered primary. Della Porta believed that both character and facial features resulted from a man's temperament, not from the stars. Judging character, he said, depended upon discerning the varieties of temperaments and the relationship of these temperaments to the features of the face. There were four basic and distinct temperaments. One was either sanguine, phlegmatic, choleric, or melancholic. These classifications, which originated with the Greeks, corresponded to the four basic elements from which the whole earth was composed: air, water, fire, and earth.

In addition, Della Porta resurrected an old approach that depended upon comparing human faces with those of animals in order to understand character. Under this system, a man who looked like a goat was considered to be goatlike or stupid. On the other hand, a man who looked like a lion was thought to be brave, strong and fearless.

Popular interest in physiognomy persisted and was given a new impetus in the second half of the eighteenth century by a Swiss pastor and teacher named Johann Caspar Lavater, who started a vogue for reading character from portrait silhouettes. Lavater declared that, from the shape and proportion

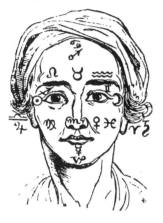

ASTROLOGY
AND THE FACE
As recently as the eighteenth century it was widely believed that the planets and stars influenced the face and personality. Though still popular today in some circles, astrology has absolutely no scientific basis.

A COMPARISON
This comparison by G. B. Della Porta comes from his book, *De humana physiognomia*, published in 1586. He claimed that important insights about character were to be obtained by making comparisons between humans and animals.

*If it were possible to shave the head of a queen bee, her profile would still be queenly and superior to the profile of other bees, and recognized as such by them. If it were possible to make a comparison between the heads of men and bees, one might well discover a fundamental index in the great alphabet of physiognomy.*

LAVATER

of the parts, he could describe the subject's disposition in depth and reveal the secrets of the mind. In the course of several years Lavater assembled a massive body of data on the subject of faces and, in 1775–78, he authored a landmark work, *Essays on Physiognomy*, which became a best-seller and was ultimately translated into many languages. This work was tremendously influential in cultivating popular interest in and awareness of physiognomy.

From the physiognomist's point of view, the whole of a man is written in the face and one's thoughts always appear in the features. The eyes and the mouth are the face's two major centers of expression: the eyes usually express the nature and level of a person's intelligence, the mouth shows strength or weakness of will.

Since ancient times, eyes have been the symbol of the sun and of divine omniscience. As a symbol, they stood for knowledge, judgment, and authority. Eye color was read for insight into nature and disposition. Reading character from eye color was especially popular during Elizabethan times, when a gray eye was considered sly, a brown one roguish. It was at this time that a blue eye was first called true, unless it had a dark ring around it, and then it revealed a debauched nature. Dark eyes, on the

other hand, were mysterious, while green eyes marked a jealous face. The power of the evil eye pervaded Elizabethan superstition, as it still does in many cultures around the world.

In America the Puritan minister Cotton Mather wanted to formalize the link between the eye and soul and created a diagnostic system entitled, "Moral Diseases of the Eye." Under his system, an "unchaste eye" becomes inflamed and squinting eyes reveal an animal low and base.

Today, we still unconsciously read intention in the eyes. We say that they can threaten or beam kindness. We say they can be wary or roving, quick- or dull-witted. Ralph Waldo Emerson once remarked that "The eyes of man converse as much as their tongues, with the advantage, that the ocular dialect needs no dictionary, but is understood the world over." Most people would agree, for it seems we all look to the eyes first when we encounter another

Speaking about this engraving, Lavater said that even a child would be able to "read" the mouth, eye, and forehead of this woman, whose features had once been so gentle and soft.

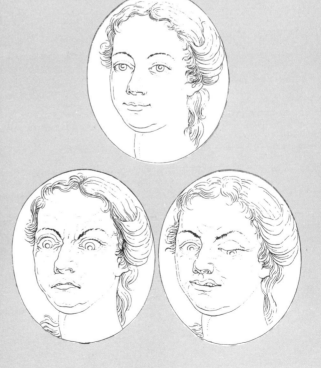

human being and we make instant judgments based on what we see in them.

To the physiognomist, the forehead and brow also deserve special treatment because, taken as a whole, they carry the stamp of an individual's moral and personal characteristics. When considered in detail, these features give a reliable idea of a person's strength and weakness as well as innermost thoughts and feelings. Eyebrows that touch are a sign of virility in the young and authority in the aged; they engender either admiration or fear. To the physiognomist, a person's aptitudes and the extent of one's abilities can be assessed from the shape of the bone structure of the forehead, its depth and curves, its proportions and irregularities. In order to determine whether a person is weak or energetic, sensitive or strong-willed, a physiognomist reads the nose: a large "Roman" nose is considered an indication of a powerful and aggressive person; an "aquiline"

*Shakespear.*

Lavater classified features in order to deduce character. He subjected famous faces to analysis and saw in Shakespeare's face the traits of a clear, capacious, and rapid mind.

*Contours des Yeux.*

According to Lavater, the eyes, whether vacant or terrified, courageous or dull, stupid or wise, ignorant or astonished, are the most faithful mirror of the soul.

*If you are fortunate enough to find a mouth which, though closed, is perfectly relaxed and natural, with well-proportioned lips, a characteristic forehead, sloping slightly backwards, gracefully and delicately shaped, with gentle mobile skin, free from coarse or deep lines—this is a head you will want to remember!*

LAVATER

Shakespeare found the "mind's construction in the face" and language in the eye, the cheek, the lips. To him, low foreheads were "villanous" and dull eyes "lack-lustre." Eyes could be powerful, too, "like Mars, to threaten and command." He wrote about "Pity-pleading eyes" and "a still-soliciting eye." He pointed out that a woman's eyes "sparkle still the right Promethean fire."

nose, shaped like an eagle's beak, is suggestive of strength of character. The size of the nose has been associated with sexual power or the lack thereof. When we say someone is "stuck up" we suggest that he or she has the nose in the air, a gesture associated with a contemptuous, superior attitude. When we call someone nosy we mean that he or she is intruding into someone else's business.

According to the physiognomist, the mouth is the spokesman of the mind and heart. A mouth may show strength or weakness of will. It can be generous or tight-lipped. The chin, too, can be read to assess an individual's strength and weaknesses. We still label a jaw "stubborn" and "set." We find cheeks full of meaning: they can be hollowed by grief or lined with wisdom. When we say someone is "cheeky" we consider him or her to be arrogant, insolent, or nervy.

*O! What a deal of scorn looks beautiful*
*In the contempt and anger of his lip!*
SHAKESPEARE

One of the most serious and persistent errors made by physiognomists, both past and present, was to make metaphorical generalizations that linked straightness of features to straightness of character. This kind of association we know to be without the slightest scientific foundation. Nevertheless, such pseudoscientific notions do not die easily and despite criticism physiognomics flourished for many centuries. By the beginning of the nineteenth century there arose another, equally absurd, system for reading character. It was called phrenology.

The brainchild of Franz Joseph Gall, a Viennese physician, phrenology was the systematic study of the shape of the face and skull. In its simplest form, this new technique postulated that, since the brain was the organ of the mind, it shaped the skull and

face and, therefore, there was an observable concomitance between a human being's mind—including one's talents, dispositions, and character—and the shape of the head and forehead. To understand more about a person's mind, disposition, and personality, therefore, one just had to examine the shape of the face and head.

Phrenology was introduced in the United States in the 1830s by Johann Gaspar Spurzheim, a disciple of Gall's. He traveled the Northeast, lecturing and winning converts. One such convert was Orson Fowler. Fowler was a student at Amherst College when he first heard a lecture on phrenology and was so taken with the idea that he devoted the rest of his life to proselytizing its virtues. He educated his fam-

THE NOSE
AS SYMBOL
Noses are frequently used as symbols in art to communicate character.

Phrenology defines and identifies the location of various mental faculties and qualities on face and head. In the middle of the nineteenth century thousands of ceramic heads were manufactured with the important areas mapped out. These were sold to the public to help them read faces.

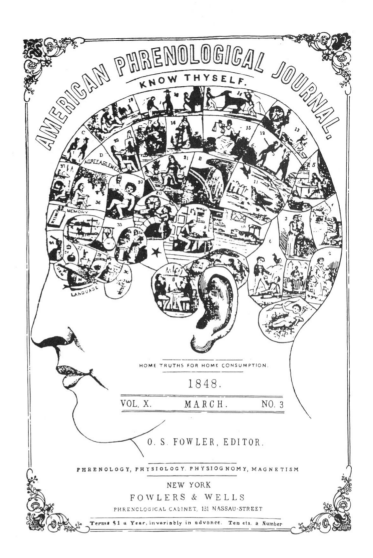

ily in the benefits of phrenology and together they traveled around the country, feeling heads, measuring faces, dispensing advice. They were in the vanguard of the phrenologizing fervor that swept America.

Mark Twain wrote about Orson Fowler in his *Autobiography:* "In America, forty or fifty years ago, Fowler . . . stood at the head of the phrenological industry. . . . One of the most frequent arrivals in our village of Hannibal was the peripatetic phrenologist and he was popular and always welcome. He gathered the people together and gave them a

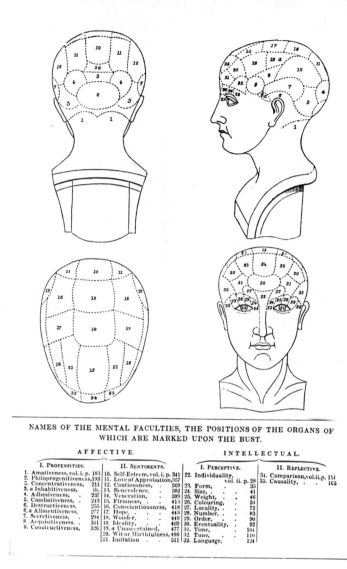

NAMES OF THE MENTAL FACULTIES, THE POSITIONS OF THE ORGANS OF WHICH ARE MARKED UPON THE BUST.

| AFFECTIVE. | | INTELLECTUAL. | |
|---|---|---|---|
| I. PROPENSITIES. | II. SENTIMENTS. | I. PERCEPTIVE. | II. REFLECTIVE. |
| 1. Amativeness, vol. i. p. 183 | 10. Self-Esteem, vol. i. p. 341 | 22. Individuality, vol. ii. p. 28 | 34. Comparison, vol. ii. p. 151 |
| 2. Philoprogenitiveness, 193 | 11. Love of Approbation, 357 | 23. Form, . . 35 | 35. Causality, . . 163 |
| 3. Concentrativeness, 211 | 12. Cautiousness, . 369 | 24. Size, . . 41 | |
| 3. a Inhabitiveness, ib. | 13. Benevolence, . 382 | 25. Weight, . . 46 | |
| 4. Adhesiveness, . 237 | 14. Veneration, . 399 | 26. Colouring, . 53 | |
| 5. Combativeness, . 243 | 15. Firmness, . 413 | 27. Locality, . 72 | |
| 6. Destructiveness, 255 | 16. Conscientiousness, 418 | 28. Number, . 83 | |
| 6. a Alimentiveness, 277 | 17. Hope, . . 443 | 29. Order, . . 90 | |
| 7. Secretiveness, 294 | 18. Wonder, . . 449 | 30. Eventuality, . 92 | |
| 8. Acquisitiveness, . 311 | 19. Ideality, . . 469 | 31. Time, . . 104 | |
| 9. Constructiveness, 326 | 19. a Unascertained, 477 | 32. Tune, . . 110 | |
| | 20. Wit or Mirthfulness, 490 | 33. Language, . 124 | |
| | 21. Imitation . . 511 | | |

gratis lecture on the marvels of phrenology, then felt their bumps and made an estimate of the result, at twenty-five cents per head. I think the people were always satisfied with these translations of their characters—if one may properly use that word in this connection; and indeed the word is right enough, for the estimates really were translations, since they conveyed seeming facts out of apparent simplicities into unsimple technical forms of expression, although as a rule their meanings got left behind on the journey. Phrenology found many a bump on a man's head and it labeled each bump with a formidable and outlandish name of its own. The phrenologist took delight in mouthing these great names; they gurgled from his lips in an easy and unembarrassed stream, and this exhibition of cultivated facility compelled the envy and admiration of everybody. By and by the people became familiar with these strange names and addicted to the use of them and they batted them back and forth in conversation with deep satisfaction—a satisfaction which could hardly have been more contenting if they had known for certain what the words meant."

Although the Fowlers' "science of the mind" was denigrated as "bumpology" by skeptics and later discredited by psychologists and neurologists, its vocabulary and ideology left an indelible mark on American culture. Who hasn't admonished someone to have his or her "head examined"?

## TWAIN HAS HIS HEAD EXAMINED

Remembering the itinerant phrenologists of his Hannibal days, Mark Twain was intrigued by the Fowler name advertised while he was in London. He made what he called "a small test of phrenology for my better information." This test consisted of Twain making two visits to Lorenzo Fowler. These visits were spaced three months apart. The first was made under an assumed name. For the second visit he used his famous nom de plume. Twain claims to have received conflicting analyses from the professor. The charts made out for him have not survived but Twain left a record of his encounters: "I went to him under a fictitious name. . . . I found Fowler on duty, in the midst of the impressive symbols of his trade. On brackets, on tables, on shelves, all about the room, stood marble-white busts, hairless, every inch of the skull occupied by a shallow bump, every bump labeled with its imposing name, in black letters.

"Fowler received me with indifference, fingered my head in an uninterested way and named and estimated my qualities in a bored and monotonous voice. He said I possessed amazing courage, an abnormal spirit of daring, a pluck, a stern will, a fearlessness that were without limit. I was astonished at this, and gratified, too; I had not suspected it before; but then he foraged over on the other side of my skull and found a hump there which he called 'caution.' This hump was so tall, so mountainous, that it reduced my courage-bump to a mere hillock by comparison, although the courage-bump had been so prominent up to that time—according to his description of it—that it ought to have been a capable thing to hang my hat on; but it amounted to nothing, now, in the presence of that Matterhorn which he called my Caution. He explained that if that Matterhorn had been left out of the scheme of my character I would have been one of the bravest men that ever lived—possibly the bravest—but that my cautiousness was so prodigiously superior to it that it abolished my courage and made me almost spectacularly timid. He continued his discoveries, with the result that I came out safe and

Daguerreotype portrait of Samuel Clemens (Mark Twain), circa 1850.

sound, at the end, with a hundred great and shining qualities; but which lost their value and amounted to nothing because each of the hundred was coupled up with an opposing defect which took the effectiveness all out of it.

"However, he found a *cavity*, in one place; a cavity where a bump would have been in anybody else's skull. That cavity, he said, was all alone, all by itself, occupying a solitude, and had no opposing bump, however slight in elevation, to modify and ameliorate its perfect completeness and isolation. He startled me by saying that that cavity represented the total absence of the sense of humor! He now became almost interested. Some of his indifference disappeared. He almost grew eloquent over this America which he had discovered. He said he often found bumps of humor which were so small that they were hardly noticeable, but that in his long experience this was the first time he had ever come across a *cavity* where that bump ought to be.

"I was hurt, humiliated, resentful, but I kept these feelings to myself; at bottom I believed his diagnosis was wrong, but I was not certain. In order to make sure, I thought I would wait until he had forgotten my face and the peculiarities of my skull, and then come back and try again and see if he had really known what he was talking about, or had only been guessing. After three months I went to him again, but under my own name this time. Once more he made a striking discovery—the cavity was gone, and in its place was a Mount Everest—figuratively speaking—31,000 feet high, the loftiest bump of humor he had ever encountered in his life-long experience! I went from his presence prejudiced against phrenology, but it may be . . . that I ought to have conferred the prejudice upon Fowler and not upon the art which he was exploiting."

Regardless of the label, the practice of reading faces for the express purpose of ascertaining psychological characteristics is a universal behavior practiced by all members of our species, though different cultural groups express this behavior according to their own rules and interpretations. In China, for example, face reading is an ancient and respected tradition reaching back into prehistory. The practice was first recorded in the time of Confucius. The object of reading the face was to discover something about a person's aptitude, personality, and potential. Face reading in China is still popular and practiced by professionals.

*Look into a person's pupils.*
*He cannot hide himself.*
CONFUCIUS

One principle of Chinese face reading is the idea that, "as above, so below." This means that the earth reflects the state of the cosmos. The order of the Celestial Sphere, or the cosmos, is reflected in the order of the Chinese imperial court, and the order of the court is reflected on the faces of everyone. Planetary influences are read to assess a person's vitality and fortune. Personality traits are linked with certain shapes and natural elements.

The universe, according to the Chinese, is comprised of two energies—Yang and Yin. The left side of the face is Yang and the right side is Yin. The left side represents the masculine and paternal influences, the right side maternal and feminine influences. Prominent bones are Yang and fortunate, so if you have a prominent forehead you will benefit. The sides of the face should be balanced; this ensures a balance of cosmic energy. On the other hand, if one side is dominant, that indicates an imbalance in your nature and personality. A Yang-dominant individual will have prominent features, little flesh, and will evidence a need to control others and drive hard

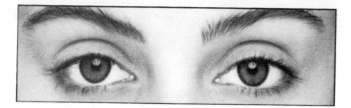

Everyone's eyes have a subtle, intangible quality that speaks volumes to a trained physician about one's physical well-being. In addition, a physician can often look into the eyes with special instruments in order to see the progress of some types of diseases, such as hardening of the arteries or kidney disease.

for power and success. If Yin is dominant, the features will be small and fleshy; the person may be submissive, underachieving, and overemotional.

The five major features are read with an eye toward evaluating potential for achievement and determining abilities and limitations. These features include the ears, the eyebrows, the eyes, the nose, and the mouth. There are also minor features, such as the forehead, cheekbones, jawbones, chin, and philtrum (the vertical groove of the upper lip). The ears are assessed for life potential. The eyebrows hold information about fame and fortune. The eyes mirror energy and intelligence. The nose is a symbol

*Who would believe that so small a space could contain the images of all the universe?*
LEONARDO DA VINCI

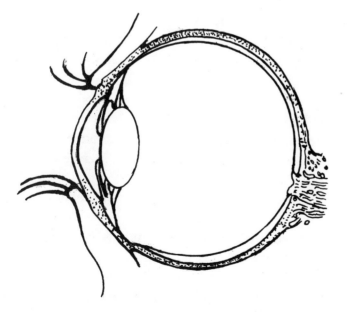

THE STRUCTURE OF
THE EYE IN
CROSS SECTION

The eyes are optical devices that gather, guide, and filter light, ultimately turning it into images in the mind. The eyeball is composed of three main layers. The sclerotic layer on the outside is white, semirigid, and it gives the eye its shape. The middle layer is called the choroid layer and it contains blood vessels. The inner layer, known as the retina, contains light-sensitive rods and cones. One point on the retina, the fovea, is the point of most acute vision. Another point, just over the optic nerve, is a blind spot. The cornea covers the iris, which is pierced by the pupil. Behind the pupil is the lens, which focuses light.

of wealth and achievement. The mouth epitomizes personality. If the mouth is slack and turned down, this is often the result of discontent and failure to realize potential. Through "inner rightness" the mouth can become firm and confident.

Unlike physiognomy and phrenology, which are both deterministic, under the Chinese face-reading system, you are not doomed by any feature. Rather, the Chinese believe that knowing your limitations means you can compensate for them; knowing your strengths means you can rely upon them.

*The face is the visiting card of the individual's general constitution.*

ERNST KRETSCHMER

Today's scientists read the face's features for another reason. They see its landmarks—the eyes, the ears, the nose, the mouth—as being the major gateways of perception, responsible for life itself. These features are crucial sensory systems that link the outside world to our consciousness. Through them, a constant flow of information reaches the brain and physical things become sensations to which we respond.

The eyes are recognized as the dominant sense organs of the human body. They provide eighty percent of the raw sensory data that reach the brain. Because we are vision-oriented animals, our eyes are stationed prominently top, front, and center. This insures a binocular view of the world which, as Cicero appreciated more than two thousand years ago, means our eyes "have the highest station to give them the widest outlook for the performance of their functions."

The eye is a remarkable structure about an inch in diameter with a light-sensitive retina at the back. The retina contains 137 million cells. Light becomes electric when it passes through the pupils and falls on the retina. Here the cells convert the light to electronic impulses that the brain receives and interprets. A hundred and thirty million of these rod-shaped cells are sensitive to black and white and 7 million cone-shaped cells are sensitive to color. The eyes are cradled into hollow bowls of bone. Seven of the skull's bones (the frontal, lacrimal, ethmoid, zygomatic, maxilla, sphenoid, and palatine) play a part in armoring and shaping each socket. A cushion of fat lines the socket. Muscles secure the eyeballs and rotate them to direct gaze with coordinated precision. At the center of the eye is the pupil, which controls the amount of light that falls on the retina. Around the pupil is the muscular, colored iris. This contracting disk is responsible for changes in pupil size. Contraction and dilation are involuntary and therefore they are reliable guides to our emotional responses to visual images. Our pupils, in other words, don't lie.

*Dim windows of the soul, eyes tell much about the human spirit.*

WILLIAM BLAKE

The eyelids guard the eyes from injury and keep them lubricated. The inner surfaces of the upper and lower lids, as well as the eyes themselves, are covered by a transparent membrane called the conjunctiva. This membrane helps keep the surface of the eye moist so that the eye can move freely. On the average, we blink twenty-four times a minute. In this way, the eyelids act as windshield wipers and prevent the eyes from drying out. Because you blink regularly, you spend five percent of your waking moments with your eyes closed.

The film of tears in the eye is composed of three layers: an outer oily layer that is secreted by glands in the eyelid; lacrimal fluid secreted by the lacrimal glands; and a mucous layer that forms between the cornea and the tear film. Though it is not known why, human beings are the only land animals with eyes that weep. It is interesting to note that emotional and irritant tears are different chemically.

*Tears, idle tears, I know not what they mean,*
*Tears from the depth of some divine despair*
*Rise in the heart, and gather to the eyes,*
*In looking on the happy autumn-fields,*
*And thinking of the days that are no more.*

ALFRED, LORD TENNYSON

*Four ducks on a pond,*
*A grass bank beyond,*
*A blue sky of spring,*
*White clouds on the wing;*
*What a little thing*
*To remember for years—*
*To remember with tears!*

WILLIAM ALLINGHAM

The nose, besides smelling, acts as a vital air-conditioning unit, warming, cleaning, and moistening the air we breathe before it reaches the delicate lungs. It also serves as an outlet for exhaled air. Every day the nose treats approximately 500 cubic feet of air. In a lifetime, the nose will snatch 13 million cubic feet of air in order to provide your body with life-giving oxygen.

An extremely complex structure, the nose is composed of many different parts. Two tiny but very important patches of tissue, one on the upper half and one on the roof of each nostril, are what enable us to smell the odor molecules in the air. This specialized tissue makes it possible for the average nose to distinguish 4,000 different smells. The sense of smell, or olfactory recognition, is the work of the nose and brain in concert. The nose is curiously linked with brain power and has been since the beginning of our primate past. In fact, the only brain cells that reach the outside of the body are the neurons that end up in the nose. This direct connection between brain and nose may account for the powerful feelings and vivid memories that a smell can elicit in the mind and body.

Ears are important, for they collect and deliver sound to the eardrums. Hearing depends on transforming a sound's mechanical vibrations to electrical signals that the auditory nerve sends to the brain for interpretation. This nerve contains about 30,000 circuits. The ear also regulates and maintains the body's equilibrium. The mechanisms of hearing and equilibrium are both housed within the hollow space in the skull's temporal bone.

Systematic studies have confirmed that the external ear is, in shape, pattern, and relief, an utterly individual feature, much like fingerprints.

Some people can wiggle their ears using muscles which once could tip the ear toward the source of the sound and sharpen hearing. Those who can wiggle their ears are able to use these special muscles attached to the outer ears. Though everyone has these muscles, not everyone can use them on command. Another interesting feature of the ear is that one out of four people has a small bump on the rim of the ear. According to Charles Darwin, this is one of the last surviving indicators that our ears were once long and pointed.

The mouth is one of the busiest parts of the face. Extremely mobile, we use it to eat, swallow, cough, yawn, snarl, and scream but we also use it for talking, whistling, smiling, laughing, and kissing.

Modern science recognizes other important landmarks on the face. The chin is an exclusively human feature that is crucial in the production of language and also may have evolved as a threat device. When we are angry, the chin juts forward. When we are submissive, we pull it back in. Males have heavier jaws and more protuberant chins than females; this gives them a more aggressive look. The cheeks are a palette where emotions are conspicuously displayed. The great ethologist Konrad Lorenz has emphasized the importance of these rounded contours in the signal of childlikeness, to which we humans are attracted. The behavioral scientist Irenäus Eibl-Eibesfeldt has proposed that the bulging cheeks of

**DIMPLES**
are caused by muscles in the face. When some people smile, certain muscles make dimples. Dimples occur more commonly among babies than adults and more commonly among girls than boys. Dimples are rated attractive by most people, perhaps because they create the illusion of a baby face.

children have evolved specifically as social organs, acting as signaling devices.

In Western cultures, cheeks have historically been the focal point of beauty and innocence. We associate pink cheeks with youth and vigor and attractiveness. Current research has demonstrated that cheeks are powerful structures that stimulate the release of strong feelings of parental love. According to Leslie Zebrowitz McArthur, a psychologist at Southern Methodist University, the key characteristics of a baby face are rounded cheeks, a high forehead, a small and rounded chin, and large eyes. The advantages of having a baby face, according to McArthur and her colleagues, may exist in diverse cultures. In general, adults with baby faces are seen as warmer, more naive, and honest. But they are also seen as weaker and more submissive than adults with mature faces. These perceptions seem to explain the tendency of people to view baby-faced people as less likely to commit premeditated crimes, such as robbery.

That the face serves as an erogenous zone has been made clear by investigators mapping nerve density and the skin's sensitivity. The nose, the earlobes, the eyelids as well as the mouth are extremely touch-sensitive. Under the right circumstances, this sensitivity can be amplified and can cause sexual arousal.

Therapists and physicians are trained to read faces in order to discover something about personality and general well-being. Freudians, in particular, believe an individual's personality has three sides and that these personalities are visible on the face. The superego, represented by the smile, strives for moral perfection. The id reflects anger and is the mainspring of human passions and drives. The id demands pleasure at any cost. The ego, on the other hand, is caught between these two extremes and tries to balance them. One's personality, in this view, is a constant tug of war among these three forces, each one striving to become dominant.

In summary, it has become increasingly clear that there is much to be read on the human face. And whether or not one is a formally trained professional, we all put our instincts to work when we read faces to get a better sense of who the other person is and where we stand in relationship to him or her. It is also clear that the instant judgments we make based on what we read in the face, affect the nature of our daily social encounters. Who has not thought, "There is just something about him I don't trust" or "She has an honest enough face"? These responses are powerful and have important ramifications, for whether our conclusions are right or wrong, our behavior reflects the judgments we've made about the person's inner self based on the individual's external features. In this sense, we are all physiognomists reading faces to distinguish virtue from vice, loyalty from treachery, candor from hypocrisy.

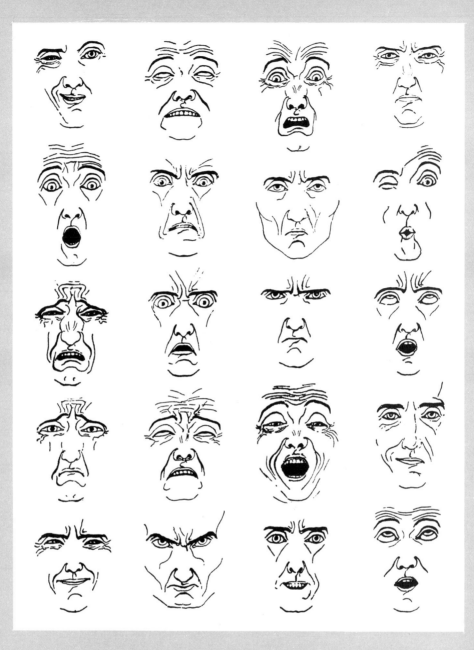

THE LANGUAGE
OF THE FACE
Facial expressions are a powerful, nonverbal communication system that broadcasts information about feelings.

# 8

# The Face of Feeling

Getting along with others is the key to the success of our species. Getting along is possible because we are equipped to communicate in very special ways. The face is central to that communication. It is the supreme center for sending and receiving social signals—signals that are crucial to the development of the individual and to the cohesiveness of family and society. Consider where we would be without our facial expressions, without a smile or a raised eyebrow, without a wrinkled nose or flared nostrils. Without this avenue of emotional expression, how could we live in groups and maintain relationships with other people? How would we know what is profoundly felt?

Though it is the brain that knows and feels, it is the face's job (often in conjunction with language) to communicate these feelings to others and let them know something about our intentions. The face communicates emotional information by registering rapid changes—on the forehead, the brows, the eyelids, the cheeks, the nose, the lips, and the chin. These changes are produced by the action of groups of muscles that are highly specialized for the purpose of conveying emotional information. In the course of a day, each of us uses hundreds of such expressions as we pass through the social events that engulf us. It is now clear that each expression that we produce has a personal history, sometimes a cultural history, and sometimes a more deeply biological history.

Charles Darwin was the first to subject the face to scientific analysis. He argued in his 1872 book, *The Expression of the Emotions in Man and Animals*, that expressions of the face are in large measure universal and innate and that they are adaptive responses necessary for survival. In Darwin's view, emotions are organized in the brain but communicated by the face. To come to this conclusion, he canvassed the anthropologists and ethnologists of his day for descriptions of patterns of emotional expression in human beings living in remote societies. Based on the information he collected and his own experience, he categorized some expressions as being universal and he questioned the part played by experience in shaping expressions. He compared expressive movements in infants and adults. He speculated on the adaptive significance of many movements and he proposed a neurophysiology of emotional expression. Yet his ideas had little influence on the thinking about such things during the late nineteenth century. At that time the public wholeheartedly accepted physiognomy as a legitimate science and defined character and personality

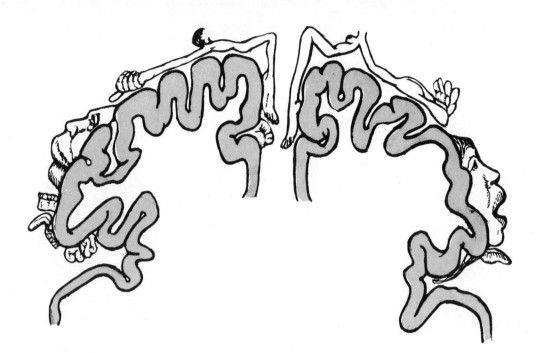

by reading the features of the face.

Today, many of Darwin's insights have been confirmed by a number of investigators, notably Irenäus Eibl-Eibesfeldt, Paul Ekman, Melvin Konner, and Carroll E. Izard. These researchers, each working independently and following a different approach, have demonstrated conclusively that all members of the human species share the same expressions for signaling the basic human emotions.

The German ethologist Irenäus Eibl-Eibesfeldt demonstrated that the face's behavior, which he labels social behavior, is preprogrammed to a decisive extent and that a whole series of motor patterns expressed on the face are inherited and innate. Doing field research on all five continents, he collected data on many different kinds of behavior, including greeting behavior, threat staring, pouting, gaze aversion, and kissing behavior. Using special cameras, he filmed his subjects without their knowledge and, at the same time, meticulously kept field notes and recorded the social context of the face's behavior, including what the person did before and after producing a given expression. Then he analyzed the film, breaking down the expression into

BRAIN WORK
Canadian neurosurgeon Wilder Penfield electrically stimulated the cortices of patients undergoing neurosurgical operations so that he could map the brain areas responsible for movement of specific parts of the body. He found the brain to be organized along functional lines. To illustrate his findings he designed a motor homunculus, a cartoon of the body surface drawn to scale and representing body parts aligned not according to their actual size but rather to the extent to which they are involved in skilled movements. Notice how much of the brain's work is devoted to the face's behavior.

ESSENTIAL
EXPRESSIONS

These simple stylized faces reveal the minimum information needed to communicate expressions of surprise, sadness, anger, happiness, angry pout, fear. Can you tell which is which?

the same emotional messages. Eibl-Eibesfeldt concluded from his data that many of our innate motor patterns, visible on the face, are the results of an ancient evolutionary inheritance. Witness the fact that we share with anthropoid apes some universal expressions, such as the threatening behavior of the mouth when it moves to expose the upper canines and announce rage. Although the usefulness of this action to human beings went out of fashion in Australopithecine times, both as a predation tool and as an actual social weapon, we still occasionally flash our canines and the effect is still intimidating. In that sense, our canine teeth are still a weapon.

Paul Ekman, a psychologist at the University of California at San Francisco, and his coworker Wallace Friesen have demonstrated that there exist biological universals in the expression of emotion and that they are at least partly genetically determined. Their investigations revealed relative uniformity in the use of facial expressions to denote fear, loathing, anger, surprise, and happiness. In one experiment they photographed Americans acting out these emotions and New Guinea highland tribesmen as they told stories in which similar feelings were emphasized. When individuals were then shown portraits from the other culture, they interpreted the mean-

ings of the facial expressions with an accuracy greater than eighty percent. Ekman later reported that after analyzing videotapes and photographs of the subjects that they "found that they moved the same facial muscles as do people in other cultures when feeling or trying to simulate these emotions." From this and other evidence, Ekman concluded "that these facial signs for emotion—the particular muscles likely to be recruited for each of a number of emotions—have evolved and are therefore universal."

In the early 1960s another researcher, Carroll E. Izard of the University of Delaware, turned his attention to the face and set out to identify and find objective evidence for the existence of specific emotions. He reasoned, like Darwin, that if a particular facial expression could really be interpreted as representing a specific emotion by people in all cultures, then that emotion could be said to be universal. To that end he set out to gather the evidence and ultimately made a case for the existence of ten genetically determined facial expressions. The expressions Izard identified include (1) interest-excitement, which he noted appeared to be the most frequently experienced positive emotion. This emotion is expressed on the face by wide eyes and a slightly open

### THE EYEBROW
### FLASH GREETING
To raise the eyebrow in greeting is a gesture distinct from other facial signals, according to Irenäus Eibl-Eibesfeldt. These artful illustrations, created by him from motion picture footage, illustrate the greeting action: at the moment of visual contact a smile is coupled with an abrupt arching of the eyebrows. The whole process is very rapid and, in almost all cases, the eyebrows are raised for only .16 second. Eibl-Eibesfeldt believes that the global distribution of this behavior suggests it is both inborn and universal to all members of the human species.

mouth and, according to Izard, it provides much of
the motivation for learning. This is the emotion that
fires the creative endeavor.

(2) Joy is identified as a highly desirable emotion.
Together with interest, it guarantees that human
beings will be social creatures. The smile of one
person elicits the smile of another. A beaming face
expresses an active state of joy and is characterized

by a sense of confidence. (3) Surprise is a reaction that is novel, unexpected, and sudden and is accompanied by raising the upper eyelid and dropping the jaw. It serves the useful function of clearing the nervous system so that the individual can respond appropriately to the sudden change he or she has experienced. (4) Distress or sadness indicates that one is discouraged and downhearted. Sadness serves

## INTEREST

According to emotion researcher Carroll Izard, interest with its attendant state of excitement is the most positive human emotion. Interest is the emotion responsible for providing the motivation to learn and develop skills and competencies.

the highly useful function of communicating to others, as well as the self, that all is not well.

(5) Anger is intended to disturb and frighten. Often it results from physical or psychological restraint or from interference with goal-oriented activity. Izard points out that anger may motivate destructive behavior, but it may also prove adaptive as a source of strength and courage when it is necessary to defend personal integrity or one's loved ones. (6) Disgust is elicited by anything spoiled and may have originally been a signal to the group of

According to Carroll Izard, the act of birth is the first occasion for distress or sadness. Throughout life, separation continues to be a common cause of distress and sadness. Another important and common cause of sadness is the real or imagined failure to live up to the standards set by oneself or others.

this fact. Disgust can literally make one feel nauseated. In addition, it can combine with anger and provide the motivation for maintaining personal standards, such as good body hygiene. (7) Contempt Izard refers to as the "cold" emotion. He suggests that contempt depersonalizes the individual or group held in contempt. (8) Fear is an emotion that affects every individual. It motivates the avoidance of danger situations and is characterized by raising the upper eyelids and tightening the lower lids and by a horizontal stretching of the lip. Izard points out that this expression and its attendant emotion can produce great toxicity as it is actually possible to be "frightened to death." An expression of fear suggests an impending disaster. (9) Shame, according to Izard, "may have emerged as a result of man's social nature and the human need for social community. If the child deviates from the norms established by family and community, he may be shamed." Shame can produce feelings of ineptness and isolation. On the other hand, shame avoidance can foster self-improvement. (10) Guilt has a close relationship to shame. It occurs in situations in which one feels personally responsible. Izard posits that guilt may be the basis for personal-social responsibility and the motive of avoiding guilt may heighten one's sense of personal responsibility.

From these studies and others, it has become increasingly clear that there are universal facial expressions (though the question of how many is in dispute); that they provide immediate and specific information regarding emotions; and that all social bonds are based on them. The close link between expression and emotion has developed over a very long time and has produced a powerful repertoire of expressions. Consider the all-powerful smile.

Studies of smiling conducted independently by psychologists and anthropologists reveal the smile to be a universal signal of friendliness and approval, and secondarily a signal indicating a sense of pleasure. For all members of the species, smiling behavior appears early in infancy. It is the result of brain development rather than of learning. Physician-anthropologist Melvin Konner reported that the infants of the !Kung San of the Kalahari Desert in Africa (the ! represents a click sound in their language) are nurtured under very different conditions than, say, American or European infants. Yet the !Kung San smile is identical in form to that of a European or American infant and the behavior serves the same social function.

Some scientists speculate that smiling evolved from laughter, and that the social smile, which is unique to humans, evolved as a special adaptation designed to strengthen bonds among people. It might have gone something like this: the first "social" bond established was with the mother. But there were outside forces demanding the mother's attention. Often she would have to leave her child to be cared for by another while she went off to

THE UNIVERSAL SMILE
*In an evolutionary sense, the most important things can easily hinge on a smile.*
MELVIN KONNER

gather and prepare food. These departures tended to weaken the bond between mother and child but demanded that bonds be established with the caretaker.

The smile, then, may have evolved in part as a signal for communication—to help make up for the handicap of the infant's immobility—to help the child establish social bonds with someone other than the mother. The forces of natural selection came into play. Infants capable of making a ready connection between such pleasant responses and their mothers learned to smile more often and received more care and attention than other infants.

Whatever the evolutionary mechanism or mechanisms, today the smile is essential. It is a powerful social response that serves a number of important functions and promotes the capacity to get along

with others. The smile gets us through the day. It says, "I am not aggressive." It says, "I beg your pardon." The smile is a gesture of friendship. It is also a kind of glue that bonds infant and parent. The smile fires romance and it is the stuff of childhood play. Melvin Konner summed it up when he wrote that the smile "has a subtlety, a multiplicity of meaning—an ambiguity—that is quintessentially human."

*When you call me that, smile!*
OWEN WISTER

*A cheerful face is nearly as good for an individual as wealth.*
BENJAMIN FRANKLIN

The first smile appears so early that it is usually never seen. Modern technology, in the form of the sonogram, shows us that smiles are not so unusual in utero. But it will only be after birth that the infant learns to attach this important reflex to appropriate circumstances.

On average, the first public smile is generated between the fourth and sixth weeks. This smile is so delicious that most parents can't help but smile back. In doing so, they initiate an exchange that will provide the foundation for all human social life. Because the smile elicits such a strong reaction, the baby soon realizes that his or her smile can cause happiness. This connection marks the beginning of the sense that one can have a pleasurable impact on the world.

It doesn't take much to encourage an infant to smile. Research has demonstrated that a very young infant will smile at a visual symbol of its mother— an oval shape with two dark dots placed where the eyes would be. The central stimulus is the sight of a facelike pattern. It turns out that the most compelling aspect of the face (pattern) is the eyes. Investigators suspect that the eyes are, in fact, the minimum amount of facial information necessary to arouse a smile in a young infant. To test this idea, investigators masked all the face's other features. Still the infant smiled but it took both eyes: smiling would stop when one eye was masked or when a profile was presented so that the infant could see only a single eye. It was also discovered that two glass balls or any other pair of shiny objects would produce smiling as long as they were roughly the same size, shape, and spacing as the eyes of a real person. Human eyes are both powerful and compelling, partially because they stand out against the more uniform background of the forehead and cheeks and partially because they are vital: they display color and light and movement.

The smile continues to develop, and after two months or so an image consisting of two bright spots no longer causes an infant to smile. Something more is required now for a response—first the outline of a nose becomes important and a little later the mouth, lips, and hair become part of the perceived picture. As the weeks go by and the perceptual system develops, the infant's impression or picture of the face is filled out in finer and finer detail until it becomes complete and is identified with a specific person, generally the mother.

By four months the universal baby flashes the "social smile" at a familiar face. This is a clear expression of pleasure. Soon the smile erupts into laughter. This reveals a more intense and complex emotional experience. As time passes, the child learns from experience all the things that can be accomplished with smiles and begins to employ them deliberately.

Experiments have shown that infants who receive no social stimulation after smiling will begin to smile less and less often. This, of course, suggests that feedback is absolutely essential to healthy emotional development. It is as if there were some hardwiring in the brain designed to set the infant on course but only experience will make it blossom.

Of all the ways of reaching out and communicating with others, the smile is clearly one of the most effective but it is not the only fixed, preset action performed by the face. Expressions of anger, disgust, fear, sadness, and surprise also work to communicate basic emotional states, are phylogenetically programmed, and show up early in human development. By means of ultrasound monitors, fetuses

FIND SADNESS

How much information do you need to recognize sadness? The first images are shown in low resolution ($12 = 3 \times 4$ pixels, or picture elements, per image). The faces are shown in successively higher resolutions. Each face displays a different emotion. Finally, a large number of pixels gives a lot of detailed information about the expression so it corresponds to a closer look at the face and you can unequivocally name the emotion expressed on the face. This is the face of the noted psychologist Paul Eckman, who has played a central role in the identification of these universal expressions. Notice that certain emotions, such as surprise, are relatively easy to identify at low resolution whereas others, such as anger and fear, need higher resolution to be discriminated.

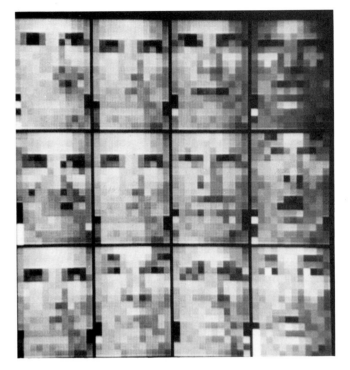

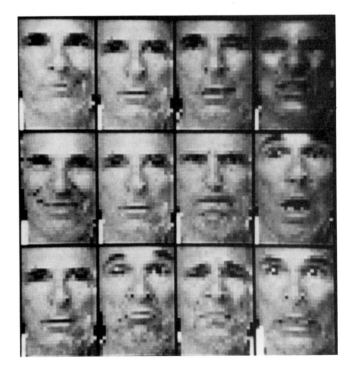

have been observed with looks of disgust as well as smiles on their faces. And congenitally blind infants, who have no means of imitating faces of those around them, exhibit the same expressions as sighted children.

Scientists who scrutinize babies' faces for clues to their feelings have found that newborns possess a rich repertory of inborn emotions and their faces speak volumes about how they feel. As early as the age of thirty-six hours, newborn infants can discriminate and imitate such key emotions as sadness and surprise. Within the first few weeks of life they seem able to register and communicate to their parents feelings of interest, disinterest, and disgust.

By three months an infant appears able to differentiate among several of the mother's emotional expressions. This suggests that the regulation and shaping of emotional responses begins in the very early weeks of life as the face mediates the relationship that develops between infant and mother.

Under normal circumstances, sadness will appear at around eight or nine weeks, after the baby

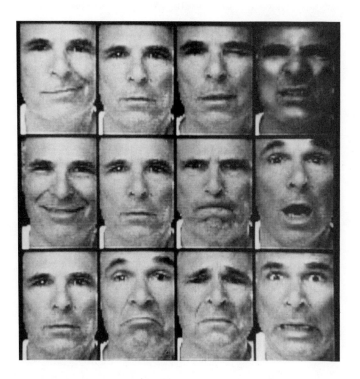

has formed a strong enough bond with the mother to feel sad when she leaves. This blossoming relationship with the mother also promotes fear, usually in response to someone the baby doesn't know. Experts mapping the stages of emotional development have found that most babies will express unmistakable anger for the first time at around four months, just when the infant has a clear idea of what he or she wants and also realizes that he or she cannot have it. The caretaker teaches the child how to manage the face's behavior so that it doesn't always cry out innermost feelings. This learning is crucial to social development, for if one does not learn to control the public expression of negative emotions one will find it hard to get along with other people.

A number of studies have shown that by six months most infants can tell the difference between posed versions of several facial expressions and the real feeling. It is clear that they prefer the real thing. They also prefer faces that are happy rather than sad, angry, or even neutral. In one experiment, in response to a mother's sad expressions, infants engaged in "mouthing" behavior that included lip and tongue sucking and pushing the lips in and out. This appears to be a self-soothing response to sad expressions.

Both pride and shame grow out of what other people think of us, and these emotions start to show their face sometime during the second year of life. A fifteen-month-old child is interested in the parent's response. Parental approval makes a baby feel proud. Disapproval makes him or her feel ashamed.

By the first birthday infants can determine whether a situation is dangerous or safe by reading the emotional message displayed on the mother's face. This was demonstrated by psychologists Joseph Campos and Mary Klinnert. Klinnert also used videotape to document how a mother's facial expressions influenced her baby's action. Her experiments showed that a mother's smile encouraged a child to explore and be happy. But when a mother grimaced

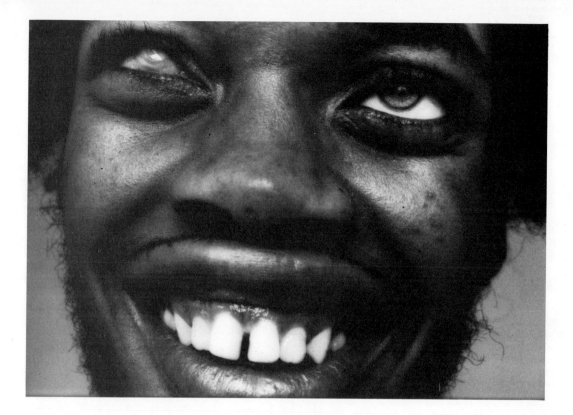

or showed fear most children backed off; some even cried. Angry expressions made babies uncomfortable and increased their physical movement. A mother's look of concern was enough to warn a child of danger. These data suggest how powerful the human face is as an organ of emotional expression and how talented it is as a medium of communication.

In producing emotional messages, certain features of the face play a key role in formulating the message. The eyes, for example, are important indicators of emotion. They collaborate with the other features of the face to show surprise, fear, anger, disgust, happiness, and sadness. These emotional states that we sometimes refer to as feelings are conveyed not only by the actual facial expression but also by the duration and fixation of the gaze.

For most primates, in an eye-to-eye situation, the duration of the gaze is indicative of the hierarchical position of the animal. In many species the submissive animal turns away grinning from the dominant individual. But in humans, perhaps because of a

**BASIC TRAINING**
Have you ever experienced a superior's authority when he or she stares straight at you? It is a disquieting feeling and creates a kind of internal stress and tension. Here, a sergeant exercises his power and authority over a recruit. By convention, the recruit may not look into the sergeant's eyes.

much longer juvenile period, eye-to-eye contact has evolved into a very complex social interaction that is of great importance to the species.

Human eyes are unique in that they have whites in order to signal gaze direction to their fellow humans. This is vital to follow the shifting attention of our social companions. In a normal two-person conversation eye behavior is predictable. As speakers, we begin a conversation by establishing mutual gaze with the listener. Then we break away. Then we look again to check for the listener's feedback. As we engage in conversation, we use our eyes to monitor our partner's interest, understanding, and acceptance of our words. We all tacitly understand that the length of the gaze is an indicator of attentiveness.

The anthropologist Irven DeVore has said that if two people look into each other's eyes for more than about six seconds they are either going to kill each other or make love together. We call the latter "making eyes" and this is the classic way to establish a more intimate relationship. Engaged couples "make eyes" a lot. Scientists call the syndrome "increased mutual gaze behavior" and it is clear that it is fundamental to our reproductive success.

Like the eyes, the eyebrows play a major role in communicating emotional information. Their changing positions signal mood changes very clearly as they contrast sharply with their surroundings. Paul Ekman writes that there are seven visibly distinctive eyebrow actions but only five are involved in emotional expression. The emotional expressions most dependent on the changing position of the brows include surprise, sadness, fear, and anger. We all recognize anger when we see it: lowered brows that are drawn together combined with tightened, lowered eyelids and pressed lips. Surprise is conveyed by widening the eyes and raising the eyebrows. In a sad expression the inner corners of the brows are raised and may be drawn together to signal unhappiness.

The mouth also plays a key role in signaling emotional information. Aside from talking, kissing, and eating, the mouth also works to convey and communicate information about changing moods and attitudes. The changes are signaled by different combinations of lip positions and the myriad combinations produce a broad range of emotional information. (It has been said that as we grow older the lips increasingly reflect the emotional state that has dominated our lives. This, however, is hard to document and does not take into account our genetic predisposition to a particular shape.)

Anger and fear both depend on the position of the mouth to transmit the message. The subtle difference between the two emotions is in the degree to which the corners of the mouth are drawn back. Desmond Morris, who has spent a good deal of his life studying human behavior, points out that in anger the mouth corners are pushed forward as if advancing on the enemy. In fear, they are retracted as if in retreat from attack. He also points out that human lips, unlike those of all other primate species, are strongly everted. That is, they are rolled outward to expose parts of the mucous membrane. This part

*The eyes of men converse as much as their tongues.*
RALPH WALDO EMERSON

*He speaketh not;*
*and yet there lies*
*A conversation in his eyes.*
HENRY WADSWORTH
LONGFELLOW

*A lover's eyes will gaze an eagle blind.*
SHAKESPEARE

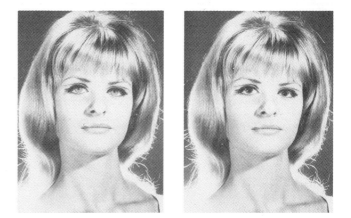

Compare these two photos. To which face are you attracted? In the early 1970s, at the University of Chicago, psychologist Dr. Eckhard Hess found that when a person is excited or interested or stimulated the pupils of the eyes enlarge. By instinct or by association, enlarged pupils make a person more attractive to the opposite sex—not because enlarged pupils are more aesthetically pleasing but because the reaction displays interest and stimulation. That is why you may have found the woman on the right to be more attractive than the woman on the left. (In both these photos the pupils have been retouched.) Dr. Hess reports, "The pupil is a very sensitive indicator of how people respond to a situation. When you are interested in something your pupils dilate." Hess calls pupil action "kinesic," meaning that it is an involuntary, nonverbal behavior pattern. This automatic behavior is why maintaining a poker face is so hard when you are holding all aces. Like it or not, your pupils dilate.

is both smoother and darker than surrounding facial skin. It is this dramatic contrast that helps accentuate the expressive changes of the mouth.

The lips work in another crucial way to communicate feelings. When one is aroused sexually, the lips become swollen and darker in color, which makes them both more sensitive to physical contact and also more conspicuous. This change in the lips is important to our mating behavior as we tend to mate face-to-face.

According to Eibl-Eibesfeldt, opening the mouth is a universal sign of curiosity. You'll notice that when you are listening to someone or when he or she is listening to you, quite automatically the mouth opens slightly. Eibl-Eibesfeldt has suggested that this behavior is probably an instance in which an expression of genuine curiosity has degenerated into a conventional mark of courtesy, denoting interest on the part of the listener. He came to this conclusion after analyzing his film studies of people around the world.

The cheeks are another of the face's features that work to communicate changing emotional states. It has been said that the cheeks are the part of the face most likely to expose one's true feelings because emotional changes are prominently displayed there. On the cheeks we notice the blush of shame or sexual embarrassment. This is where the heat of anger is likely to "boil up" and be expressed. In a truly aggressive person the cheeks become pale as the blood drains away from the skin in preparation for immediate physical action. Similarly, if one is scared, the cheeks will blanch, as the body prepares to meet the challenge.

The nose also plays a role in sending emotional messages, though it is less expressive than the other features of the face. It is, however, central in signaling disgust, when it wrinkles, or in anger and fear, when it will flare noticeably.

That feeling faces have the power to move us to expression and to certain subjective experiences is undeniable. A person who deliberately smiles is soon likely to feel happier. A person who feigns an angry face is soon likely to feel anger. Empathy is the capacity to participate in another's feelings; it is an important social mechanism whereby the feelings of one individual are transmitted and partially experienced by another. It is not entirely clear how such transmission takes place but the fact that it does is undeniable. A smile triggers other smiles. A sad or unhappy face tends to make others sad and unhappy. This empathetic communication between members of the species has had an inherently adaptive function. Indeed, it has bonded us to one another irrevocably.

The fact that we all share a language of emotion means that through our faces we can communicate basic feelings independent of culture and that emotional information can be deciphered without knowledge of language. But there may be more to feeling faces than just the communication of emotional information. Some investigators, like psychologist Robert B. Zajonc of the University of Michigan at Ann Arbor, are looking at facial expression as the first link in a chain of biological reactions that alter the brain's blood flow, temperature, and chemical environment. According to Zajonc, when we smile or frown we may not just be expressing our mood to the outside world, we may be adjusting our cerebral blood to match the situation we are in. In other

FLIRTING
Behavioral scientist Eibl-Eibesfeldt studied flirting around the world and has suggested that the basic movements of flirting are common to women the world over. These movements, which he calls a fixed-action pattern, consist of a smile of provocation and invitation which is then followed by a bashful lowering of the eyes and a momentary turning away. Visual contact is then resumed, and the motor sequence may be repeated. Eibl-Eibesfeldt found this behavior sequence as common to a Turkana tribeswoman in Africa as it is to a young girl on the French Riviera.

MASKED FACE SYNDROME
Parkinson's disease affects the basal ganglia in the brain and is often referred to as "masked face syndrome" because among the symptoms are a lack of expression, a kind of emotional deadness. Parkinson's robs the face of feeling.

DRINKING BLURS
THE MESSAGE
British researchers have demonstrated that drunks frequently get into fights because they misread the emotional message of the face. After a couple of drinks a subject was shown a series of photographs of a face and asked to identify the expression being displayed. The drunk consistently had trouble judging anger, disgust, and contempt. This inability to read faces accurately is what gets drunks into trouble.

words, facial expressions may be a means of controlling blood flow into and out of the brain, as well as a means of communication.

This idea was first proposed about eighty years ago by a French physician, Israel Waynbaum, in a book called *Physionomie humaine: son mécanisme et son rôle social*. In contrast to Darwin, Waynbaum refused to view muscular movements as the terminal stage of the emotional process. He attributed them to an internal regulatory role and argued that all emotional reactions in the face produce circulatory changes. These changes either mobilize energy or remove energy demands. It works this way: when facial muscles contract and push against the face's bony structure they can act as tourniquets on arteries and veins and thus can regulate facial and cerebral blood flow. Waynbaum suggested that the muscles that contract during laughter increase blood flow to the brain and create as well as convey a feeling of elation. He further offered the opinion that laughing had beneficial circulatory effects and, therefore, must be healthy. Haven't you laughed until you were red in the face and experienced a brief moment of euphoria? According to Waynbaum, the laughing person approaches a state of congestion. A hard laugh makes the face quite red. The contracted skin muscles that press on the jugular veins impede circulation. The result is that more blood remains in the brain. Test this idea. Pull the corners of your mouth apart by contracting the major zygomatic muscles, as if in an exaggerated smile. After several seconds, the frontal vein will be gorged with blood. Cerebral blood is momentarily restrained, causing temporary cerebral hyperemia, which leads to a surge of subjectively felt positive affect. Thus, claims Waynbaum, the zygomatic muscle acts as a ligature blocking the blood. From Waynbaum's point of view, laughing is like taking an oxygen bath. The cells and tissues receive an increased supply of oxygen, causing a feel-

Norman Rockwell

ing of exuberance. In contrast, sadness produces disoxygenation of tissues and attentuates vital processes. It is claimed that happiness leaves the face young because it involves only one major set of muscles—the zygomatic. In sadness, many muscles are contracted: the elevators, orbicularis oculi, orbicularis oris, corrugator, frontalis, pyramidal, and others.

Waynbaum questioned the popular term "emotional expression" to describe facial expressions as

*THE GOSSIPERS*
The human mouth is an effective signaling system, the most expressive in the animal kingdom. You don't need to hear the conversation to understand the language spoken in this 1948 painting by Norman Rockwell entitled *The Gossipers*. It turns out that the gossipers are slandering none other than Rockwell himself. Note the last two images.

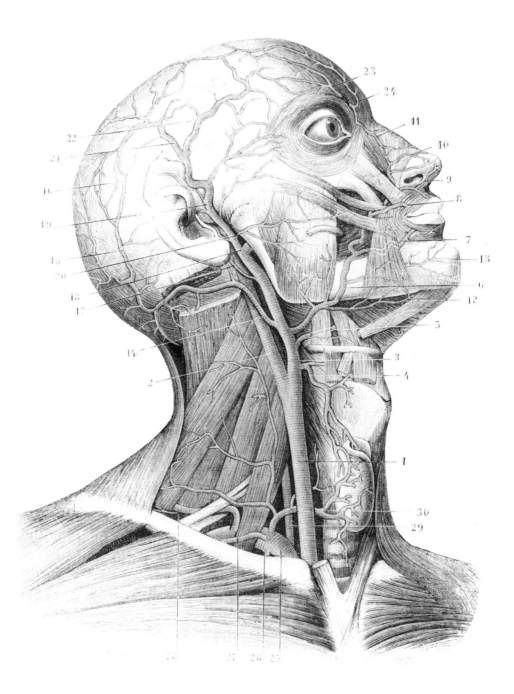

## CIRCULATORY SYSTEM OF THE HEAD

Israel Waynbaum argued in the late nineteenth century that facial expressions may create feelings as well as convey them by altering the flow of blood to and from the brain.

he feared that the very words, standard since Aristotle and reinforced by Darwin, implicitly fixed the role of facial expressions in the emotional process. The term "facial expression" implies the existence of an antecedent internal state which the expression externalizes and displays. It also suggests that the internal state needs to find expression on the face.

But it is by no means established that all facial behavior that is classified as expressive is caused by internal subjective states, according to Zajonc.

Zajonc does not dispute the fact that there are convincing data to support Darwin's contention that there are facial expressions with universal meanings. Rather, he points out, ". . . this does not explain anything about the dynamics or biological substrates of emotions." It doesn't explain, for example, why certain muscles behave the way they do.

According to Zajonc, Waynbaum's theory may answer the question of why the inner ends of the eyebrows are raised and the corners of the mouth depressed by a person suffering from grief or anxiety. This muscle action has the effect of creating temporary brain anemia, or ischemia, and is associated with negative affect, depressive moods, and unsound physical condition. In sad expressions, some of the face's muscles allow more blood to move out of the brain through the facial artery and increase the circulation of blood back to the brain. As a result the brain temperature and heart rate temporarily rise.

In the case of the fear expression, the eyes and mouth are widely opened and the eyebrows raised. Since opening the eyes and mouth allows freer blood flow into the facial artery, it slows cerebral blood flow and promotes a more vigorous draining from the brain in temporary readiness. As a consequence the organism may experience momentary dysphoria—the experience of feeling unwell or unhappy.

Waynbaum, his critics say, went too far when he asserted that the subjective experience of elation follows the smile, rather than the other way around. But there still may be something to the idea that facial expressions may create feelings as well as communicate them, says Zajonc. Why, for example, do we furrow our foreheads when we concentrate? The action forces the frontalis to contract and the forehead to furrow. The eyeball gets swollen and the

THE SNEEZE
The face is also the center for the display of behavior that is basically nonexpressive, though it can and often does send a signal to the onlooker. A sneeze is such a behavioral gesture. Its primary function may be mechanical in that it serves the breathing mechanism. At the same time it may also signal information about the presence of an allergy or a cold.

pupils dilate. The eyes often close, and the orbicularis oris as well as the masseter are contracted to make the jawbone project forward. By putting a tourniquet on the external carotid and on the facial veins, all these actions affect facial circulation, sending more blood to the brain. More cerebral blood means better brainwork.

This has been borne out by modern research. We furrow our brow when we concentrate to divert more blood to the brain by reducing the flow of blood to the face. For the same reason, when we are stuck on a problem, we may rub our chin or our forehead, push our face around the eyes, frown or pull an earlobe—squeezing blood wherever we can. Crying will do the opposite. Blood flow to the brain is diverted, causing a degree of anesthesia. According to Zajonc, a host of other mannerisms are universal in all cultures and are recognized as revealing internal mental states, such as thinking, problem solving, trying to remember, or making decisions. These are: rubbing one's chin, scratching one's head, frowning, biting fingernails or pens, pulling one's earlobes or eyebrows. If facial musculature can to some extent control cerebral blood flow we would have an explanation for phenomena that seem otherwise bizarre and for which no adequate explanation has been offered.

Migraine headaches are caused by vascular dysfunction, so migraine sufferers may unconsciously be adjusting cerebral blood flow when they make a variety of unusual mouth movements, such as licking their lips or biting the inside of their cheeks. These vascular actions may play some role in reducing external vasodilation.

Waynbaum rightly emphasized the connection between the vascular system and emotions, says Zajonc. Take blushing, for example. Waynbaum pointed out that blushing occurs after an intense emotion sends a sudden surge of blood to the brain. Though one might be embarrassed or ashamed, there is little that can be done to hide the heat of

*Anger raiseth invention, but it overheateth the area.*

LORD HALIFAX

this emotion. As in suppressed rage, mobilized energy and increased cerebral blood flow have to be relieved, so the facial muscles allow the surplus blood to drain into the face. Darwin, on the other hand, concluded that blushing occurred because the attention of others was focused on part of one's body. He wrote that blushing is primarily a social phenomenon and noted that "women blush much more than men." And blushing is not the only overt emotional response tied to vascular processes, according to Zajonc; sobbing, weeping, and frowning can be included, to name a few.

Waynbaum's most significant contribution, according to Zajonc, was to examine the role of facial movements apart from their expressive consequences. Facial movements, he points out, that are associated with emotion are not different from sneezing, coughing, and yawning. The universality of expressive behavior is therefore no more surprising than the universality of yawning and sneezing. All have a clear biological basis and can be ascribed to corresponding neuroanatomical structures and neurophysiological processes. What distinguishes them from emotions is that they are regarded as having no psychological instigating causes. But, being constant and universal, they can readily acquire communicative and symbolic significance.

But does a smile precede the feeling of happiness? Was Waynbaum right? There are no hard and fast answers yet. But it is true that the brain, like a computer, generates heat and is cooled by arterial blood. It is also true that brain temperature is important because any changes are likely to affect the activity of the neurotransmitters—those chemicals that are released at nerve endings and stimulate or inhibit the firing of a muscle or other nerve cells—and enzymes basic to its function. The whole truth, however, is much more complicated as our subjective state—the way we feel at any given moment—is dependent upon an intricate collaboration between a number of highly specialized systems that

*To redden with shame.*
CHINESE EXPRESSION

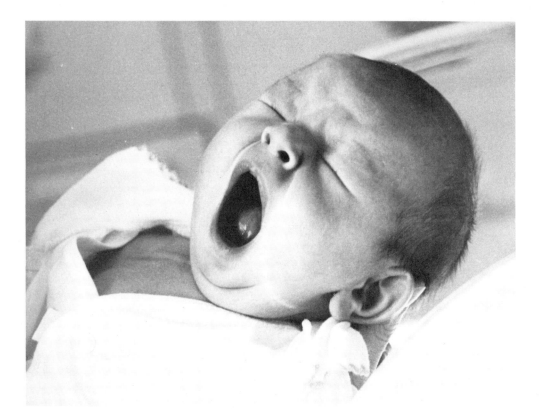

Have you ever noticed the power of a yawn and wondered about its biological significance? Yawning is contagious. Its power lies in its ability to transmit information and to move the group to joint action, in this case, to sleep. Yawning transmits a sense of fatigue and helps keep the group's circadian rhythms in sync.

together give rise to expression and serve to regulate and control the internal system as well as the external message, so it is not just figurative to say that the face of feeling provides much of the color, richness, and complexity of our lives. The Technicolor drama displayed there is part and parcel of an exquisite repertoire of human behavior. It appears to serve a variety of functions and may be of crucial importance not only in mirroring our internal states but perhaps in regulating them as well.

# 9

# Face Work

While it is clear that our biological inheritance equips us to express and display our feelings on our faces, cultural learning determines in large measure which emotions are permissible to display, to what degree they may be expressed, and to whom. In other words, right from the beginning, though we are primed for action, we are taught to manage our faces' behavior and to control the emotional messages displayed there. Put another way, our genes provide us with a reaction range but it is our culture that determines where in the range our behavior will fall, for it is culture that determines opportunities to observe, to decode, and to imitate.

The instinct to imitate is a very important spur to human development. It is the reason that we learn to behave in particular ways. Parents encourage or discourage certain actions in an ongoing give-and-take exchange. Children use their parents as aids to practice. They clamber around them, engage in face-to-face play, elicit certain reactions. All the while they are exposed to virtually thousands of facial expressions. These are internalized and adopted as their own. In the process, they learn to behave properly. So while emotions and their attendant facial expressions may arise on a built-in schedule, they wither or flourish depending on the basic give-and-take exchange between family members. (It is interesting to note that every human society is convinced of the rightness of its own approach to teaching correct face behavior.)

To what extent basic facial expressions are influenced by upbringing and tradition has fascinated a number of investigators, including Eibl-Eibesfeldt, whose film studies supplied numerous clues about how different cultures influence expressive behavior. He filmed such groups as the Samoans, the Turkana and Karamojo of East Africa, and the Shom Pen, who live on Great Nicobar Island in the Bay of Bengal, and discovered that individuals in these groups all appear uninhibited when it comes to sending emotional messages via facial expression. They seem self-assured and do not hesitate to expose their private selves to the gaze of others.

At the opposite end of the expressive scale, Eibl-Eibesfeldt found some human groups to be extremely inhibited in expressing emotion and speculated that they had developed a sort of control mechanism that held direct expression of emotional information in check. This was illustrated with particular clarity by the films he made in Benares, India, where faces tend to be masklike and immobile and where children are systematically discouraged from showing their feelings on their faces.

In southern Europe, Eibl-Eibesfeldt found, there were different rules for the display of emotional information. Here his films revealed that facial expressions tended to be pronounced but also artificial. Sympathy was often feigned for reasons of politeness. One man smiled at another even when ill disposed toward him. Eibl-Eibesfeldt speculated that culture had succeeded in intensifying innate facial signals and, indeed, the culture may simulate feelings that have not been present as a mark of breeding or in order to avoid dissension. His films also revealed that in conversation, the face of the listener often echoed what the other person was saying. If the speaker said something serious, the listener grew serious. If someone showed surprise, the listener performed a facial movement conveying the same feeling. This behavior, Eibl-Eibesfeldt speculated, was a product of tact, courtesy, and good manners and reinforced important cultural values. These faces, it seemed, worked by convention rather than as an expression of genuine fellow feeling.

One of the hallmarks of our humanity is that we have a vast capacity for learning and, when it comes to the face, children in all cultures learn to be perceptive in a certain way; they learn to have feelings attached to self and face. They learn to control their faces' behavior and mask their true feelings. These controls are based on the imitation of adult behavior and on culture-specific display rules. In this way, within the context of good manners, there arise a large number of facial movements that work in the service of a particular culture and cannot be understood easily by people from other cultures.

The display rules most Americans learn are clear. They learn not to display their emotions easily, in contrast to southern Europeans, Latin Americans, or even Middle Easterners. In the United States, showing one's anger publicly is unacceptable. The same holds true for the British upper class, who are taught to exercise great control over emotional expression and to avoid, at all cost, unbecoming behavior.

> *Never to master one's anger is a mark of intemperance and lack of training but always to do so is difficult and for some impossible.*
>
> PLUTARCH

> *A man should study to keep cool. He makes his inferiors his superiors by heat.*
>
> EMERSON

In Japan, all extremes of emotional expression are rejected: not only grief and sorrow but anger, frustration, contempt, jealousy, joy, and love. The Japanese are taught not to let their true emotions be seen. They abhor face-to-face confrontation and avoid it when at all possible. Children are taught to show happy faces to neighbors and friends lest they bring them pain or sorrow. In fact, in the Japanese culture, to lose control of one's emotions produces deep shame and humiliation, not just for the individual but also for the whole family.

These cultural rules are not arbitrary. They evolved along with history and society, though they may have lost their original function. Consider, for a moment, the Japanese practice of emotional restraint, which dates back many centuries, when all aspects of one's behavior, including facial expression, were carefully regulated. In the presence of one's superiors all emotions—anger, pain, grief, even happiness—were suppressed. Social rules of the time required that a person submit to any order issued by a superior with a pleasant smile and a properly deferential attitude and tone of voice. This was the time of the samurai knights, and a samurai could legally execute anyone he thought was not respectful enough. One can see how following the rules could have considerable survival value in such an environment.

Even today in Japan an individual who feels anger is likely to show it by excessive politeness and a neutral expression. A Japanese who shows anger the Western way is admitting publicly that he has lost control. The result is a considerable loss of face, which puts an individual at a disadvantage in any negotiation or face-to-face encounter.

In other cultures, different rules apply. In some Middle Eastern cultures showing anger, for example, may simply mark the beginning of an exchange in order to show that the negotiation is serious. In this case, a man may lose face if he does not show anger when it is considered appropriate and "manly" for him to do so.

Anger is a particularly interesting emotion to examine in the light of cultural learning—for what are good manners but society's organized system for anger management? Anger is the rush of adrenaline that prepares the body to respond to danger by fighting or fleeing. We recognize anger when we see it: the brows are sharply lowered and drawn together, the eyes are narrowed or squinted, and the mouth is open in an angular, squarish shape. It has been said that this facial expression is preeminently serviceable for the display of power. Its message is unmistakable: "Watch me. I don't like what you are doing. You are in my way. Danger!" Anger is the human hiss—programmed phylogenetically (during the course of evolution) and ontogenetically (during the course of the lifetime of the individual). Everywhere people get angry but they get angry in the service of their culture's rules. Sometimes those rules are explicit; more often they are implicit. Regardless, the rules usually serve to dissipate anger and resentment and maintain respect between disagreeing parties.

In a highly cooperative society like the !Kung San of Africa, the provocations of anger that we take

FORTUNE COOKIE:
*Short temper is a loss of face.*

for granted are strictly controlled by convention. Right from the beginning the children learn to manage negative emotions and are taught to cooperate at all costs. Quarrels often end with opponents staring at each other until one gives up, lowering the head and pouting. For a small group like the !Kung San, trying to survive in a harsh and unforgiving desert environment, getting along with one another makes society possible.

Whenever a group of people must cooperate in order to survive—whether it is on the frozen tundra of the Northwest Territories or in the arid bush of Africa—strict rules have evolved to settle disputes. The smaller the community, it seems, the more rigid the rules, though the spectrum of solutions might range from ridicule and gossip to punishment and isolation. Whatever the group's solution, the rules work to regulate both the feelings of anger and the expression of anger.

Among the Semai of western Malaysia *slniil*, or shame, is the typical response to anger, and this applies equally whether one feels the anger personally or is the recipient of someone else's anger. A man who feels *slniil* will avert his eyes from the target of his wrath and refuse to talk or listen to him, effectively retreating from the conflict instead of confronting or escalating it. In the end both parties to a Semai conflict feel shame.

When it comes to anger, the Arapesh of New Guinea criticize the provocateur. According to Margaret Mead, if two Arapesh are seriously angry with each other, one will hang a bunch of croton leaves as a reminder on his front door, which signifies that he will never again eat with the other man. The breach can only be healed if the one who put up the sign slaughters a pig. If you get angry in front of an Utkuhikhalingmiut Eskimo you will be ostracized for your childishness. Other Eskimo groups settle for a round of wrestling. Still others living in the Arctic Circle cuff one another's ears, while those who live in Greenland, on the Aleutian Islands, and

*And though hard be the task,*
*"Keep a stiff upper lip."*
PHOEBE CARY

the eastern coast of Alaska engage in singing duels. Singing duels are an interesting, culture-specific technique to dissipate anger. Each opponent in a singing duel sings. The style of the songs performed follows a traditional pattern, but the texts are individually composed for each occasion. In the end, the audience judges who was right and who was wrong by applauding the better singer, even if he is actually in the wrong.

The Mbuti of the African forest dispel anger with a good laugh. Other groups, including our own, use cursing as a mechanism to make sure that anger doesn't become excessive and threaten the delicate internal mechanism of the group. In the old days, the Jews of Eastern Europe had a litany of colorful curses that they would yell at an adversary: "May your teeth get mad and eat your head off." Or, "May all your teeth fall out but one, and that one has a cavity." Still today, cursing is common in many Western cultures where everyday life seems to be designed to provoke anger among and between people. Consider what happens in a traffic jam when someone cuts in front of you. There is no way for you to directly confront the perpetrator of so annoying a deed. Instead, you curse from afar and soon your anger is dispelled. In another situation, someone insults you. Your anger boils up. Your face gets hot. If you are permitted to reply in the same vein, your face may relax and cool. If not, you burn. If the person apologizes, your dignity is restored, your anger subsides, and you cool down.

We often think of anger as maladaptive but it is obvious that under certain conditions it was, and still is, an asset to be able to face a particular threat. On the other hand, as we evolved in a social context, anger management was of supreme importance in maintaining social relationships and attachments.

Anger, of course, is not the only facial expression that is subject to cultural rules and regulations. All universal expressions, even smiling, develop in a cultural context. Ray L. Birdwhistell, an expert in the

*There is a smile of Love,*
*And there is a smile of Deceit,*
*And there is a smile of smiles*
*In which these two smiles*
  *meet.*
WILLIAM BLAKE

study of body movement and nonverbal communication, studied the frequency of smiles in different parts of the United States. He concluded that, of all Americans, those who live in the southeastern part of the United States, smile by far the most while those who live in the Great Lakes states smile the least. In New England, cultural upbringing teaches that restrained smiles show polite reserve, while in the South children are taught that a smile denotes hospitality and good manners.

> *A face with gladness overspread!*
> *Soft smiles, by human kindness bred.*
> WORDSWORTH

It seems that humankind's tendency is to vary culturally whatever can be modified. Eye behavior, which plays a critical role in the face's effort to communicate, lends itself to cross-cultural comparison as there is a great deal of variation in eye behavior around the world and it is governed by strict though often unstated rules.

Eye contact is commonly used to describe a mutual locking of eyes. This is called "mutual gaze" behavior by the experts, who make a distinction between looking and seeing. When we look, we do so with the intent to discover, to decode, to get information. When someone is looking at you, you know it. You can feel the power of the eye to look.

The Spanish philosopher José Ortega y Gasset, in his book, *Man and People*, wrote of "the look" as something that comes directly from within "with the straight-line accuracy of a bullet." In citing the power of the eye to look, he distinguished "the look that lasts but an instant and the insistent look; the look that slips over the surface of the thing looked at and the look that grips it like a hook; the direct look and the oblique look whose extreme form has its own name, 'looking out of the corner of one's

eye.' " Every look, Ortega said, tells us what goes on inside the person who gives it.

In the American context, eye behavior and looking is predictable and has been recorded and documented by many researchers. It is clear from their work that there are strict and unstated rules. Catching someone's eye, for example, and locking into a mutual gaze indicates a willingness to communicate. On the other hand, avoiding the eyes of a stranger or breaking mutual eye contact after a brief good-will smile shows no desire for communication.

As urban Americans we practice what is called

"civil inattention" on people in the street. The display rules of "civil inattention" require that at about eight feet away a stranger will signal with eyes which direction he or she will take to pass. One does this by using the eyes, quick glances, and a slight inclination of the head in the chosen direction. Then the eyes are turned downward. The anthropologist Erving Goffman, author of *Behavior in Public Places*, calls this a "kind of dimming of lights while passing" and says that the quick look and the lowering of eyes are a message for "I trust you. I am not afraid of you." To strengthen the signal, one looks directly at the other's face before looking away. This particular pattern of communication works so well and so unconsciously that athletes use it all the time to "fake out the opposition" as they move up or down the field or court. Faking out the opposition simply means that a player sends a signal of intent to move in one direction and then abruptly moves in another.

Sometimes the rules are hard to follow, particularly if one of the two people is wearing dark glasses, for it then becomes impossible to discover intention. Is the person looking at you at all? The one wearing the dark glasses feels protected and assumes that he or she can stare without being noticed.

Elevator behavior is another kind of face work that is predictable and highly ritualized. We step into an elevator. Glance around. Face the door. Stare at the ceiling, at the floor, but not into someone else's face. If by chance we connect, we smile a brief, polite smile and turn away. The smile must not be too long or too obvious. It must say, "I am sorry we have looked, but we both know it was an accident." We say with our look, "I see you. I do not know you, but you are a human and I will not stare at you." The unspoken rule in an elevator or on a crowded bus is, Never stare into the face of a fellow passenger. That would clearly be an invasion of privacy.

In other circumstances, we may wish to catch

someone's eye, perhaps a friend in a crowd or a clerk in a store. In this case, we put our eye power to work and invite mutual contact. A good salesperson uses this kind of eye power to lure a customer to the counter. The anthropologist Edward T. Hall has described such tactics, which are used by solicitors and religious fanatics as they work airports and shopping malls in order to solicit contributions or signatures on petitions. First they try to establish mutual gaze at about twenty feet. The tactic is to lock eyes and pull you toward them with their gaze. But they don't make the move until you are quite near. Banking on your good manners and unwillingness to offend, they have you face to face before you know it. At this point, it is very difficult to extricate yourself. On the other hand, you may see them coming and signal early, "Leave me alone. Don't bother me. Step aside."

In the United States any gaze longer than ten seconds is considered staring and rude and is likely to induce irritation if not real discomfort. What is it about staring that seems mildly threatening? Generally our first encounter with this experience was when we played the childhood game of "stare you down." The rules were simple: two people face to face, eye to eye. Whoever blinked first or looked away, lost. You steeled yourself to play. "Stare you down" was a contest of power. When you played you were participating in an ancient ritual that today we understand as a social confrontation.

In the United States, in a normal two-person conversation, eye behavior is predictable. We do not look at others while we talk or listen to someone, nor do we look away for long periods of time. As speakers, we begin a conversation by establishing mutual gaze with our listeners, then we break away. At the end of a comment, we look to check for feedback and perhaps give the other person a turn at talking. As listeners, we look at a speaker finishing a comment to indicate that we desire to speak. When we avert our gaze we indicate that we do not wish to speak. When gazing becomes more and more infrequent, it signals an end to the conversation.

Throughout a conversation we use our eyes to monitor our partner's interest, understanding, and acceptance of our words. Both the extent of the gaze and the facial expressions combine to provide important feedback to the two parties. According to research reported in the *Journal of Personality and Social Psychology*, if we consider the person with whom we are communicating to be of moderately high status, our gaze and mutual gazing are moderate. But for low-status people we employ minimal gaze. If we are dependent in any way upon our conversation partner, our gaze tends to be longer and more frequent. We also seem to gaze more at people we like.

Outside the United States, rules for looking at each other are very different. The Tuareg of North Africa seem to stare at each other relentlessly while talking. Gaze behavior dominates their nonverbal language. It has been suggested that this is so because they cover the rest of their bodies completely, so that other forms of body language are masked. Edward Hall points out that many Arabs are particularly intent on "watching the pupils to judge response to different topics." This sensitivity to eye behavior may also account for the fact that Arabs often wear dark glasses even when indoors.

Since most English-speaking people regard a direct look into the face as threatening, it is customary for a speaker who does not wish to appear aggressive to avert his or her gaze. In Greece, however, to stare directly into the face is perfectly normal. When confronted with English speakers, Greeks often feel that they are being ignored, while the English speakers feel as if they are being stared at.

A gaze behavior comparison was made between the English and the Swedish. The results showed that the Swedes looked at their conversation partners less often than did the English, but when they did look, they held eye contact for a longer time. Anthropologists report that Luo men from Kenya may speak to, but not look at, their mothers-in-law.

The Mende of Sierra Leone always look a conversation partner in the eyes and are suspicious of anyone who averts his eyes: they believe that the dead reappear in human form and can be recognized because they cannot look a living person in the face.

Gender also affects the way the face behaves and displays information. Different cultures have different display rules. In the United States, crying is an unmistakable emotional signal. Tears signify sorrow, pain, or unhappiness, but men may not cry on pain of being considered "crybabies." Women, on the other hand, are expected to cry. Elsewhere, the pattern is reversed. Arab men may weep in public; women may not. In Iran, men are expected to be emotional and to weep easily. Women, on the other hand, are expected to maintain control and show an impassive, unemotional face. Tears are a signal of welcome for the Andaman Islanders, who weep profusely when welcoming long-absent friends and on many other social occasions.

Greeting behavior is another kind of face work that varies highly from culture to culture and group to group and is an important ingredient in social life. One puts the whole face to work in a greeting. It sends a clear message: "I want to initiate friendly contact."

The peacemaking significance of a greeting in our daily life is evident. Not greeting someone raises aggression even within a family circle. A friendly greeting can relax a tense situation. The reply to a greeting is an equally important confirmation of one's willingness for contact and to a certain extent it implies a pledge of benign intent.

In the United States, people who live in small towns are more likely to greet friends and strangers alike with smiles than those people who live in big cities. We are obliged to offer greetings when we enter a shop or strange house. In addition, we will greet a perfect stranger if we meet him or her alone

*Alas, how hard it is not to betray a guilty conscience in the face!*

OVID

somewhere out in the open. In this circumstance, if a greeting isn't exchanged one experiences an unpleasant feeling of tension.

The greeting rites of the central Eskimo tribes are idiosyncratic. A stranger approaches with arms folded and his head inclined to the right. He receives a powerful slap from the local man on his proffered cheek. The latter offers his cheek and receives a slap. This slapping duel can continue until one of the participants falls to the ground. Generally such greeting duels end peacefully and they serve their central function, which is to appease aggressive feelings and to underscore that which unites members of a particular group.

A nodding gesture is often a part of one's greeting behavior. Eibl-Eibesfeldt and his cameraman, Hans Hass, filmed greeting behavior in which nodding was central in many parts of the world and among a variety of ethnic groups. They found that the Waika Indians of the Upper Orinoco nod and so do the Turkana, Karamojo, and Bantus of Africa and the Balinese, Samoans, and Japanese. So far, he reports, he has not discovered any culture in which people do not nod when greeting.

The teachings of the Egyptian sage Ptahhotep contain the following precept: "Bend your back before your chief, your superior, and the administration of the king." This custom, known as *senta*, which literally means "breathing the ground." To do homage individuals would fall to the ground and kiss the earth. As a particular favor the subject was permitted to kiss the king's feet instead of the earth.

Kowtowing was one of the earliest forms of obeisance. The word derives from the Chinese *K'o-t'eu*, a term meaning "to knock the head on the ground." Kowtowing, a method of saluting a superior, was a widespread custom throughout China and Africa. Among the Sandwich Islanders, falling on the face is a mark of respect. Many forms of obeisance, still in use today, probably had their origins as acts to show absolute submission, which meant hiding the face—depriving it of its power.

Embracing and touching the face—when we pat it, caress it, and kiss it—attest to the many ways in which we can signal a friendly greeting. Of all these behaviors, kissing is very widely distributed.

*Respect kisses the hands, friendship the open brow,*
*Pleasure the cheek and blissful love the mouth.*
FRANZ GRILLPARZER

Greetings exchanged between ancient Persians differed according to rank. Equals kissed each other on the mouth. If one ranked lower than the other, each would kiss the other on the cheeks. In the case of a great difference in rank, the subordinate flung himself to the ground before the other.

When we blow a kiss we first kiss our own hand. The Bedouin smack their kisses in the air while shaking hands with a guest. Many people greet with the nose in a way similar to kissing. This is a friendly sniffing action in which the nose is pressed on the cheek or nose of the partner and lightly rubbed. In Burma this form of greeting is called *namtschui.* Sometimes the person greeting simply takes the other person's hand and rubs his own nose with it as Captain Cook reported of the New Zealanders and Charles Wilkes of the Samoans. We find greeting by rubbing noses among the Lapps, Eskimos, Waikas, and Malayans; on Madagascar, on New Guinea, and in the Polynesia area.

The "spittle greeting" of the Eskimos is unique. One foreign visitor described the greeting he received in the Bering Strait as follows: "Here a dirty skin was spread out on the boards on which I had to sit down and then one after another of them came up to me, embraced me, rubbed his nose hard against mine and ended his caresses by spitting in his hands and wiping them several times over my face."

The movement of embracing and caressing occurs in the greeting behavior of many people. In fact, all cultures have rules governing this behavior. And human greeting behavior seems to display a great number of peculiarities and great variation. In the Philippine Islands the custom used to be to greet newcomers by rubbing the guest's hand or foot over the host's face. An old Nigerian form of greeting is to kneel and rub foreheads together. Sticking the tongue out is a traditional gesture of greeting of the Maori tribespeople of New Zealand.

Greeting formulas in principle express the same as greeting gestures, namely, peaceful intentions, sympathy, submission, and desire to establish a bond. For all the multiplicity of forms, really what greeting behavior amounts to is a message: "I have peaceful, friendly intentions and I want to establish a bond."

Using the head and face to nod and shake to signal "yes" and "no" is a very common kind of face work in all cultures. The most widespread movement of "no" is the head shaking, a standard signal in cultures as separately evolved as the Papuan highlanders, the Yanomamo of Venezuela, the Himba of southern Africa, and the Kalahari Bushmen. Many Mediterranean and Mideastern peoples signal a "no" by jerking the head back while closing the eyes, sometimes turning the head sideways and lifting one or both hands in a gesture of refusal. The Ayoreo Indians of Paraguay wrinkle their noses as if they were reacting to an unpleasant odor. They close their eyes and often push their lips forward in a pout. The Eipo of New Guinea indicate a factual "no" with a headshake, and a refusal in a social encounter with a pout. Eibl-Eibesfeldt thinks that virtually all of these signals can be interpreted as ritualizations of the more direct, motor rejection to unpleasant physical stimuli—shaking off of objects on the head or the closure of the eyes, nostrils, and mouth.

Speakers of English punctuate their sentences with head movements. Arabs, on the other hand, use both hand and head gestures liberally. When

Arabs shake their heads from side to side the message being sent is "yes," not "no." To communicate "no" nonverbally they tilt their heads upward and lightly click their tongues.

The Ceylonese affirm by means of a rhythmical to-and-fro movement of the head. Some Italians signify negation by raising their heads and inclining them backward slightly.

We know that emotions can be expressed with deliberate intent, as with acting, or spontaneously. Because there are two different sets of nerves going from the brain to the face that control these dual means of expression, all humans can play their faces at will. The voluntary nerve pathways lead from the cerebral cortex; the spontaneous pathway comes from a more primitive part of the brain called the limbic system, located just below the cortex. At birth the spontaneous pathway is in charge. As we get older, we learn to control the muscles in our faces—to play them on command.

*I must prepare a face to meet the faces that I meet.*

T. S. ELIOT

*His face rarely moved, even in the face of extinction.*

IAN FLEMING'S 007

Voluntary expression may vary from something like making faces to a situation in which an individual feels a little of an emotion but wants to show much more of it. In still other instances an individual may want to feel an emotion and may use the facial expression in order to facilitate the experience of it.

*No man, for any considerable period, can wear one face to himself, and another to the multitude, without finally getting bewildered as to which may be the true.*

NATHANIEL HAWTHORNE

The psychologist Paul Ekman studied actors trained in the Stanislavsky method of acting. This method makes actors skilled at remembering and experiencing emotions and teaches them to become physically the character they play. When asked to create certain facial expressions, actors who practiced this method reported feeling the emotion that accompanies the expression. Instead, their heart rate and skin temperature also evidenced a physical change in being. Carroll Izard obtained a similar result when he traveled to the Soviet Union, where he tested actors trained in the Stanislavsky method and found that feigning these expressions can actually trigger corresponding internal sensations and physiological changes. The connection between producing the expression and instigating the feeling is

MAKING THE
FACE BEHAVE
Sometimes it is extremely difficult to make the face produce
a genuine expression of emotion. This series of photos
taken by the world-renowned
photographer Norman Seeff of
the actress Marsha Mason reveal just how hard it is, even
for the trained professional, to
make the face behave upon
command.

only close in anger, depression, fear, and sadness,
according to Ekman. Physiological changes do not
result from a feigned smile.

All in all, how the face works to display and send
information is the outcome of complex interaction
among biological, environmental, and social factors,
all of which conspire to make the face work in particular ways and according to specific cultural "display rules."

One's cultural display rules are extremely important, for there is a great deal at stake when people
encounter one another face to face. Erving Goffman
has written that all encounters require face work,
because all acts involving others are modified, pre-
scriptively or proscriptively, by considerations of
face.

Besides sending emotional
messages, the face communicates in other ways too. Face
researchers Ekman and Friesen
call one kind of information
displayed by the face "emblems." Emblems are behaviors that are substituted for
specific words or phrases. An
emblem is learned consciously.
The message is sent intentionally and deliberately. American
children, for example, use an
emblem when they stick out
their tongues or thumb their
noses at someone. A wink is
also an emblem. Its purpose is
to tell you something, though
that something varies from culture to culture. "Illustrators"
are another category of face
work given a name by Ekman
and Friesen. "Illustrators" accompany and serve to illustrate
spoken messages. You are using an illustrator when you nod
approval or shake your head in
disapproval. Like emblems, illustrators are learned by imitation and are culture specific.

Goffman describes face work as the actions taken
by a person to make whatever he or she is doing
consistent with face. "Face" is defined as an image
of self delineated in terms of approved social attributes. "Face," then, is the positive social value a
person claims for him- or herself. For each of us
maintenance of face is a condition of human social
interaction, which means that in a face-to-face encounter each face is allowed to prevail and to carry
off the role we have chosen for ourselves. This kind
of mutual acceptance seems to be a basic structural
feature of human face-to-face interaction.

Maintaining face is no small task. In everyday
life we present ourselves and our activities to others.
We discipline our faces lest they cry out messages
our minds are too careless to hide. In a face-to-face
encounter, we attempt to guide and control the
impressions we make. We constantly monitor our
own performance and adjust our faces' messages
based on what we are reading on other faces. Goffman suggested that we enact ourselves by our responses to and our readings of other people. During
our daily social encounters, which Goffman called
"face engagements," we struggle to maintain face.
To that end, we "compose" our faces, he said, "appropriately controlling through facial muscles the
shapes and expressions of the varied parts of the
instrument. Although this control may not be conscious to any extent, it is none the less exerted."
Through the face, he said, we present the public self
we share with the world. When persons sense that
they are "in face," they typically respond with feelings of confidence and assurance. They hold their
heads up and openly present themselves to others.
When face work fails, according to Goffman, one
loses face, which seems to mean "to be in the wrong
face" or "out of face" or shamefaced. In which case,
he or she is likely to feel ashamed and inferior. The
individual's manner or bearing may falter, collapse,
and crumble, according to Goffman, leaving the individual shamefaced. This feeling, warranted or not,

is perceived as a flustered state by others, which exacerbates the problem. The antidote Goffman calls "poise." Poise is an important kind of face work. It refers to the ability that enables us to suppress and conceal the tendency to be out of face or shamefaced. Goffman offered a cautionary note when he suggested that one's social face can be one's most personal possession and the center of security and pleasure, but it is only on loan to him or her from society. Face can be withdrawn unless an individual conducts him- or herself in a way that is worthy of it.

This Cro-Magnon profile is one of humankind's earliest portraits and was carved on a hard limestone plaque perhaps sixteen thousand years ago and left in a cave, La Marche, in southwestern France. The limestone walls in this cave are spongy and unfit for carving and engraving. Perhaps that is why a great many engraved blocks of varying size were brought into this small cave. It is believed that the series of faces discovered here were arranged as a frieze. Though we shall never know for sure the purpose of this portable art, undoubtedly it marks the beginning of a long tradition of portraiture.

# 10

# The Face and
# the Imagination

Faces are powerful symbols that reach deep into our past and tap into a complex network of thoughts and feelings, abilities and memories. Faces have been grist for the imagination at least since humankind first became an image maker. There is a clear line of evidence that reaches back to our earliest indisputably human ancestors, the Cro-Magnons, who left artifacts in the form of etched plaques, sculpture, paintings, and pigments in caves scattered from Spain to Russia. Significantly, eighty percent of these caves are in France and Spain, where prehistory has left a spectacular record of a profound change in human behavior wherein the face takes on new meaning and fascination.

Beginning more than thirty thousand years ago there was a burst of innovation in which Paleolithic artists of the Old Stone Age painted, etched, and carved new ideas on cave walls and on portable plaques. This artistic expression reflected a dramatic change that placed the individual in a new light. Why, after 10 million years or so of human evolution, did there occur such a profound shift in imaginative skills, in human intelligence, and in human self-awareness? How do we account for an entirely new form of human behavior in which the face would come to figure so prominently? No one knows the answer, although it appears, since behavior is a product of the brain, that something dramatic was happening to the brain's organization, to its neurological underpinnings, that led to an elaboration of skills and abilities, thoughts and feelings.

Recent studies emphasize that an elaboration of social life was driving the human brain toward self-awareness. It was during Paleolithic times that individuals were becoming less nomadic and more dependent upon one another and upon the community. Stability and security depended on balancing the needs of the individual with the needs of the group. To this end, tribal societies came into being and in this new environment no adaptation was more important than finding new ways to get along.

It has been suggested that conflict may have increased under the pressure of group living and that artistic expression may have been part of intense ceremonial occasions that reduced conflict and created an atmosphere of common beliefs and new loyalties. Group living made it increasingly important to learn the correct ways to behave. Ceremony was a way to indoctrinate individuals into the ways of the group. It was a way to pass tradition down from one generation to the next. Ceremony, then, was an effective teacher and it produced a kind of cultural "encyclopedia" wherein the rules and responsibilities of the individual were enumerated and perpetuated.

Paleolithic artists played a central role in establishing an environment in which ceremonies could take place. With a variety of materials at their disposal and an arsenal of powerful images from daily life, they transformed caves into holy places. The repertoire of images was to find its apex in the magnificent, richly rendered galleries at Lascaux in the southwestern part of France. Lascaux has been called the Sistine Chapel of the ancient world. It is a holy place where spiritual thinking has been externalized, where the drama of the imaginative life is depicted. And yet in this cave, among the hundreds of images, there is not a single example of a human face. Why? is an intriguing question.

Was the face too powerful to depict? Or had it not yet occurred to the artists that portraying a face preserves the memory of an individual? Though we shall never know for certain, the answer reaches back to the origins of the human imagination, when *Homo sapiens* first came to confront individuality and to think about preserving knowledge of it.

Though rare, there is evidence of an early fascination with the face. Much of the evidence comes from several caves near Lascaux where more than twenty thousand years ago master sculptors first confronted the notion of identity and individuality and left evidence of a desire to transmit knowledge of it.

One such group of Paleolithic faces was discovered engraved on the roof of the La Marche cave at Vienne, France. Another family of images emerged from the nearby Taillebourg cave at Angles-sur-Anglin. These include a head of a man sculptured and painted in black and red. It plainly shows in profile an individual with an upturned nose, an almond-shaped eye, a bushy beard, and longish hair.

His face strongly resembles the engraved human faces at La Marche, a contemporary site.

In another nearby cave, Font-de-Gaume, there are more than 250 painted or etched figures but only one is remotely human. To see it requires a winding journey down a dark narrow path that leads serpentine-like to a dank inner sanctum where a ghostlike face, a human head with two black dots for eyes, peers down on you as you enter. We can only wonder about the impact of those eyes on the human imagination. And we can only wonder at the ceremony in which they played a role but it suggests that, in discovering the magic and power of the human face, Paleolithic peoples sought to express in some physical and tangible way what was imagined about themselves and their world, which like our own was tense and uncertain.

In 1979, Leslie Freeman of the University of Chicago and J. Gonzales Echegaray, director of the Altamira Museum and Research Center, made an important find in a fourteen-thousand-year-old site on the northern coast of Spain called El Juyo. Here they uncovered and described a crudely worked though unmistakable human face. The proper right side of the face is that of an adult male human, with mustache and beard. The left side is a large carnivore with an oblique eye; taken as a whole, these features represent a large cat, probably a lion or leopard.

Further excavation revealed that the face had been carefully placed, wrought at such an angle that people entering the area at first saw only the right side, the human side. To see the left side, which is the feline carnivore side, required a closer look. What was the intention? Was it a message? Or an invitation? John Pfeiffer, in his book *The Creative Explosion*, underscored the notion that our analyses of this artifact "must take into account a dualism, a double theme. The face had a public and a private aspect, an esoteric meaning accessible to all who

THE LADY FROM
BRASSEMPOUY
This tiny ivory head (a reproduction) of a woman, elaborately coiffed but without a
mouth, is the earliest sculptural
evidence we have of humankind's fascination with the female face. The original is
perhaps twenty-five thousand
years old. It is obvious from
this find and another from
Dolni Vestonice, in Czechoslo-
vakia, that Ice Age sculptors
had the ability to capture the
human likeness but, for whatever reason, may not have had
the desire to do so on a regular
basis.

entered the cave and an occult, esoteric significance
known only to those who had been shown its mysteries." There are other dualisms, other mysteries
here. The face is half human and half beast, suggesting a Jekyll-Hyde version of human nature. Further, according to Pfeiffer, the face can also be
interpreted as half male, bearded and mustached,
and the other half female or feline. This habit of
dividing the world into opposites or opposing forces
may have had its birth during these distant times
when the face was becoming a metaphor in the
imagination.

Ever since Paleolithic times we humans have
been drawing attention to the face—using it as a

symbol to mine the repository of human understanding as well as to preserve the essence of individuality. As we trace the record of human fascination with the face forward, the next significant development occurs around five thousand years ago. It is a watershed moment in human history, marking a shift from a hunting and gathering way of life to a more settled agricultural existence. With these changes emerge a new fascination with the face.

Evidence found at Jericho, one of the earliest walled settlements, indicates that there was a new awareness of the face and of its power over the mind and imagination. Unearthed here were a series of skulls that had been "reconstituted" in tinted plaster and modeled into lifelike representations. Each face is distinct and strongly individual. Each is made with a purpose. That purpose was to perpetuate life beyond death by replacing the transient flesh with something more enduring.

The Jericho heads suggest that our Neolithic (meaning New Stone Age) ancestors believed that the spirit or the soul was located in the head and, therefore, it could survive the death of the body to exert power and influence over future generations. These sculptured faces were intended to be "spirit traps." They were designed to keep the ancestral spirit in its original dwelling. Evidence uncovered at the site also suggests that they were displayed above the floor of the house while the rest of the body was buried beneath it. In this way the "spirit traps" expressed in a real and tangible way a sense of individuality, of tradition, and of family continuity. Seven thousand years later these faces still serve their original purpose.

The Jericho skulls represent a profound change in the human's view of self and face and individuality. These sculptures, though artifacts of the imagination, also serve as remembrances of individuals. In so doing, they fall into a special category of art that has had an elaborate development throughout recent human history: the tradition of portraiture.

The fact is that the entire tradition of portraiture stems from this notion that an individual's identity can be preserved and that there is a possibility of participation in life when life is gone.

Over time, portraits have taken many forms and followed many fashions. They celebrate the experience of being human—though it is a celebration not of humanity but of individuality. Portraits have been executed in every conceivable medium including ivory, stone, metal, mosaics, paint, plaster, film, and videotape.

Whether they be ancestral portraits, the picture in the family album, the photograph carried in the wallet or locket, portraits hold for their possessors private meanings that lie well beyond the mere record of the likeness. They are artifacts that represent a unique concurrence of the real and the artful, the momentary and the historical. They are passed from generation to generation, century to century, connecting us to one another and to our shared past.

*A portrait is the ideal of a man, not of men in general.*

EDMUND BURKE

The reasons people have wanted images of themselves are innumerable. Originally, it was probably the belief that a likeness insured immortality and this desire to live on through one's portrait has persisted. One Egyptian word for sculptor was "He-who-keeps-alive." The Egyptian sculptor was not trying to flatter the subject nor was he trying to preserve a fleeting expression; rather, he was concerned only with the basic details and shaping a likeness in a durable material, one that ensured immortality.

By classical times, portraits indicate a trend toward individualization. The Greeks celebrated individuality and this was reflected in their portraiture but this practice of celebrating individuality would fall into disrepute with the decline of the Roman Empire. The result: European art between the fifth and thirteenth centuries contains virtually no portraiture. In fact, it wasn't until the fourteenth century that individual likenesses reappeared and then they were created with the express intention to be commemorative. Fundamental to this thinking was that the face is a proper and realistic record of the person.

Kings hold a special place in the history of portraiture. Royal portraits performed an important political function in promoting a monarch's persona. "Persona" is defined as "appearance in the eyes of the world." Most kings were aware of the value of portraits for this kind of propaganda. As a result, the best artists were appointed to official positions at court for the express purpose of creating portraits of the monarch that could be hung in public places.

Portraits were also at one time put to diplomatic use and presented to kings as gifts by visiting dignitaries. But the most important part played by portraiture in international affairs was that of conveying likenesses of prospective marriage partners. When Philip II of Spain was seeking the hand of Mary Tudor, Titian's portrait of him was shipped to her in England. In turn, the Dutch artist Anthonis Mor was commissioned to paint the queen of England for Philip's consideration.

Miniature portraits flourished between the early sixteenth and mid-nineteenth centuries. Most commonly they were worn as jewelry and incorporated into rings, brooches, bracelets, and lockets. Today, lockets are still a popular way to keep a miniature likeness of a loved one close to the heart.

The art historian E. H. Gombrich has pointed out that artists, regardless of the era, do not literally copy a face but transcribe it by means of a changing system of notation. This notation system is a code constantly learned afresh by the viewing public. A portrait, then, is a three-way collaboration between sitter, artist, and viewer.

Self-portraits are a special category of portraiture. They are the artist's attempt to discover his or her own character and personality. Sometimes they are made as a convenience by the painter, in order to keep in practice or try out some new idea. If the artist makes self-portraits regularly, as Rembrandt did, they have the additional value of being a visual diary. Few autobiographies are as searching as his self-portraits. At least twice a year he studied his face, took stock of himself, analyzed his personality, and painted a self-portrait. Today these are often read in conjunction with his life story: the arrogant and successful young man is brought by personal misfortune to a profoundly philosophical outlook later in life. (See Chapter 2 for seven Rembrandt self-portraits.)

It is not just history, archaeology, and art that bear testimony to the importance of the face in the imagination, it is also literature, language, and custom. Consider the word "face." It began in English as a noun. The first recorded use of face as a noun,

For at least fifty centuries the human face has been the starting point for works of art that have been created to capture, preserve, and celebrate the essence of identity and of individuality. At the same time, these portraits stand as cultural signatures and reveal a great deal about what role the face played in the imagination at a particular time.

Queen Hatshepsut was an unusual ruler of the Eighteenth Dynasty (c. 1485 B.C.). Egypt's most prominent reigning queen, Hatshepsut proclaimed herself king and ruled for nearly twenty-two years. Her portrait was executed in durable marble and limestone for the express purpose of achieving immortality and so it has. Despite the fact that the features are idealized, this is considered one of the most sensitive of all Egyptian portraits.

**ALEXANDER THE GREAT**
The face of Alexander the Great is featured on this silver coin. The idea of stamping metal pellets of standard weight with an identifying symbol originated in ancient Greece before 600 B.C. After Alexander, however, rulers began to circulate their portraits on coins. The idea of fame began with these portraits on coins. In fact a coin was the mass medium of its day and this is the face of political power.

**MUMMY PORTRAIT**
Excavations in the Faiyum district of Lower Egypt have yielded many mummy portraits. According to Pliny the Elder, they served an ancestor cult and were painted in a naturalistic manner and commissioned by well-to-do people. While the individual was alive, they were displayed in the atrium of the house. After death, they were taken down and shaped to the deceased's mummy and buried with the embalmed body. Though portraits like this were produced quickly and in large numbers they still have a certain immediacy, a slice-of-life reality.

**DELOS HEAD**
This face, discovered on the island of Delos, is the work of an early first century B.C. artist. Though the identity of the sitter is unknown, we get an intimate, intensely private view of him. The fellow seems sad and uncertain. His mouth and unhappy eyes reveal someone beset by doubts and anxieties. The personality irradiates the face and elicits compassion.

SASANIAN KING
Believed to be the Sasanian King Shapur II, who ruled over northwestern Iran in the fourth century A.D., this powerful image shows the extraordinary ability of Sasanian silversmiths to create true portrait sculpture out of beaten silver.

PROFILE OF A YOUNG MAN
Attributed to the Florentine Masaccio. Painted in 1425, this portrait of a young man heralded the rediscovery of classical coins and busts that featured profiles of the famous and influential. According to Pliny, the very first painting was a profile portrait made by tracing the outline of a man's shadow on a wall. This kind of portraiture became popular because people had a desire to get back to the purity of classical art. Paintings like this one stimulated a desire to perpetuate personality and ensure immortality. According to John Walker, director emeritus of the National Gallery of Art, Masaccio would have agreed with Shakespeare, who said:

*So long as men can breathe, or eyes can see,*
*So long lives this, and this gives life to thee.*

EMPEROR CONSTANTINE
Like earlier emperors, Constantine I adopted the colossal portrait to express the nature of his power. His authority was absolute. This portrait is a classic state portrait as it integrates idealism, realism, and allegory. It is idealistic in that it elevates Constantine to a superhuman level and endows him with superior qualities of leadership and character. It is realistic in that the people knew the identity of the subject immediately. It is allegorical in that it conveys a certain continuity of tradition and of the state.

## GIOVANNI EMO

Around 1475, Giovanni Bellini, a Venetian, painted Emo, a powerful and ruthless military leader. Emo is depicted as hard and resolute. Bellini painted from life and made it the fashion for anyone of prominence to be portrayed by him. Not only did he popularize portraiture, he was one of the first to start the vogue for a three-quarter view of the sitter, which he copied from painters working in the Netherlands. Portraits from this angle are called *Occhio e mezzo* (eye and a half) in Italian. Because the nose projects in space, the head takes on a more dimensional and real appearance. For this reason the mastery of the three-quarter face was a revolutionary development in the history of portraiture.

## GINEVRA DE' BENCI

In Florence a transformation brought about by Leonardo da Vinci was taking place in portraiture. Leonardo introduced the psychological portrait. To use his own words, he painted "the motions of the mind." This new concept is evident in this portrait of Ginevra de' Benci, a Florentine heiress who is depicted as withdrawn and sad. This attempt to capture mood is considered a tremendous innovation in portraiture.

**QUEEN MOTHER**
Fashioned in the early sixteenth century for the divine
king and his court at Benin, in
Nigeria, this ivory, iron, and
copper pendant mask of the
queen mother was probably
worn by the king on his hip to
honor his mother's memory.

**EDWARD VI**
Hans Holbein the Younger, a
German painter who lived
from 1497 to 1543, was an in-
cisive portraitist who strove for
objectivity and had a tremendous influence on portraiture
for hundreds of years. This
panel, which greatly pleased
Henry VIII, conveys the rank
and majesty of his child, the
future monarch of England,
and is the quintessence of
royalty.

**WILLEM COYMANS**
Frans Hals is considered a vir-
tuoso. His technique of rapidly
painting directly on the canvas
without preliminary under-
painting was well adapted to
catching the face's expressive
moments. In this 1645 portrait
he captured the essence of
youth and high spirits.

## FLORA

In the imagination of Giuseppe Arcimboldo, portraits were allegorical expressions. His 1591 composite portrait challenges our notions about what face and identity really are. Here he combines various forms of flora to create an allegorical composite portrait. *The Nymph Flora* forces you to switch back and forth from one identity to another. Flora may be the woman's name and mean woman, or it may be the flower goddess, or it may be the plant life of a specific region. The portrait is composed of a bizarre collage of images, each with its own distinct identity but collectively composing a portrait of a distinct and recognizable person, Flora. This portrait stimulated great interest among his contemporaries. About it, Arcimboldo wrote:

*Am I Flora, or am I flowers?*
*If like flowers, how then can*
  *Flora*
*Have a smiling face? And if I*
  *be Flora,*
*How can Flora be only*
  *flowers?*

*Ah! I am not flowers, nor am*
  *I Flora,*
*Yet, Flora I am, and flowers.*
*A thousand flowers, single*
  *Flora.*
*Living flowers, a living Flora.*
*But if flowers make Flora, and*
  *Flora flowers,*
*Do you know how? The flow-*
  *ers into Flora*
*The wise painter changed, and*
  *Flora into flowers.*

A great deal of portraiture is associated with the idea of family. The Romans used to display portraits of their ancestors with lines running between them, in essence illustrating the family tree. The advantage of portraits over the written word is that the legitimacy of the pedigree is proclaimed in the family resemblances that persist through the generations. Here John Singleton Copley has immortalized his family ties.

### GEORGE WASHINGTON

After the American Revolution it was the mark of a true patriot to have a portrait of the first President hanging on one's mantel or on the wall. Gilbert Stuart's George Washington is the most familiar of all these patriotic portraits. Stuart, in fact, painted many of them in hopes of profit. He told his creditors, "I hope to make a fortune by Washington alone." He did. His Washington portraits were so numerous, they came to be known as Stuart's hundred-dollar bills, his charge for a replica.

### LOUISE BRONGNIARD

Jean Antoine Houdon is considered a master of French portrait sculpture. He combined psychological perception with analytical realism in order to bring out the individual character of each sitter. Houdon made over one hundred and fifty portrait busts of the great men and women of his age but he also produced many portraits of children by commission.

UNTITLED. PHOTOG-
RAPHER UNKNOWN

The invention of the daguerreotype made portraiture all the
rage. A daguerreotype was a
permanent record of an individual on a thin, copper plate
that had a silvered, light-sensitive side. Portrait studios
sprang up in cities in Europe
and the United States and da-
guerreotypists took to the road
with their portable equipment.
For as little as twenty-five cents
or as much as five dollars, a
portrait could be made. By
1853 the New York *Herald
Tribune* estimated that 3 million American daguerreo-
types were being made an-
nually.

RED CLOUD

It wasn't long before portrait
photography became an instrument for social comment. This
portrait of Red Cloud, of the
Oglala Sioux, photographed
by Edward Curtis, captured a
terrible and tragic reality. It reveals a great chief grown sad
and old and blind and pow-
erless. This photograph speaks
powerfully of our collective
guilt. It seems to illuminate our
feelings.

## MODIGLIANI CHARACTERS

Amedeo Modigliani is considered one of the greatest portrait painters of the twentieth century. His entire life was devoted to depicting character in painted faces. Here are three Modigliani faces. Can you guess the character of each? Madame Amédée (1918) doubtless exploited women. Madame Kisling (1917) probably preferred women. The Girl in a Green Blouse (1917), one imagines, would have made an excellent wife.

## GERTRUDE STEIN

Gertrude Stein posed for Picasso more than eighty times for this portrait. Still he had great difficulty capturing a likeness. Finally he wiped out the face and repainted it months later without seeing Stein. In response to the observation that Stein bore little resemblance to the final portrait, Picasso replied, "She will." Ironically, Stein considered it to be the best portrait of her ever made.

This photograph of Gloria Swanson by Nicholas Muray epitomizes the twenties interest in "sex appeal" and "personal magnetism." Great beauties like Swanson were labeled "fascinating" and "charming." This meant they had certain properties that attracted members of the opposite sex.

FRANK

Artists of the avant-garde have continued to produce portraits but they choose their sitters rather than vice versa, and these are almost exclusively people with whom they have a special relationship, particularly friends and relatives. Such is the case with Chuck Close and his portrait of Frank, 1969. This painting is deliberately copied from an inexpensive passport-type photo. "There is no invention at all," Close has said, "I simply accept the subject matter."

*The person portrayed and the portrait are two entirely different things.*

JOSÉ ORTEGA Y GASSET

In her diary Dorothea Lange wrote that this famous photograph was created under mystical circumstances in March 1936. She was on her way home after spending the winter photographing migratory labor, when she saw a sign saying PEA-PICKERS' CAMP. She ignored it. "I didn't want to stop, and I didn't . . . but there arose an inner argument: Dorothea . . . Are you going back? Haven't you plenty of negatives on the subject already? Having well convinced myself for twenty miles that I could continue on, I did the opposite. I went back those twenty miles and turned off the highway at the sign . . . drove into that wet and soggy camp and parked my car . . . I saw and approached the hungry and desperate mother, as if drawn to her like a magnet. She said she had been living on frozen vegetables from the surrounding fields, and the birds that the children killed. She seemed to know that my pictures might help her, and so she helped me."

according to the Oxford English Dictionary, occurred in A.D. 1290. In 1440 an English grammarian noted its use as a verb, meaning "to brag or boast." In detailing our loss of face, the Oxford English Dictionary cites Thomas Jefferson as the first writer known to have used the word to mean "to look seriously and steadily at." Some linguists believe that the English noun is an offshoot of the Latin verb *facere* meaning "to make." This, of course, suggests that we make our faces to suit a variety of situations.

The face is properly the front of the head. The importance of this topmost portion of the body is everywhere celebrated. We speak of the "headmaster" and the "head of the family." We are respectful to a "head of state." We put the "head of government" in the capital, which is derived from the Latin

word for the body's head. We consider an intelligent
man to "have his head on his shoulders" and we
speak of "getting our heads straight" when we intend to reorganize our lives.

In ancient Europe, heads were prizes of battle.
The Celts collected heads and nailed them to the
walls of their houses. The ancient Scythians of central Asia fashioned the skulls of their enemies into
drinking cups. In ancient times, in many places, sev-
ered heads were used much the way a football is
used today. In fact the game was originally called
"Dane's head" in England. By the 1800s it had become institutionalized at Rugby School, hence the
name rugby.

In the past, the head was removed from a condemned individual by the stroke of a sword or ax, the severing of the head visibly symbolizing the abrogation of power and authority. Although the logic seems brutal, an execution at the block was, right up until modern times, considered a privilege of the wellborn (for heretics it was fire; for nobodies it was the hangman's rope).

The Hopi call the head the reception center for cosmic life, the very tuning fork of the universe. Africans generally center in the head both individuality and volition. "He himself" translates in many African languages to something like "he with his head."

There is another sort of evidence about our preoccupation with the power of the face over the imagination. Faces for example, are carved on the prow of a boat as symbols of intelligence and as dependable guides. In Tibet certain face paintings are made as a magical defense against the cold. People in varied cultures carve threatening faces and set these carvings up as guardians at the entrances to houses and in fields, believing that they have protective powers.

The power of the face is celebrated in figures of speech and in popular expressions. In English we say we must "face the music" or "keep a straight face." Sometimes we have to "put on our best face" or "a happy face." A prisoner learns to be "dog-faced." We have "party faces" and "funeral faces." We "face up" to a situation and do "an about-face" when we change our minds. We have a "game face," a "poker face," and sometimes we are "two-faced." We've all been known to "lose face," to have to "face facts," and to "fall flat on our face." We automatically give things a "face value," deliver a "slap in the face" when we intend to be insulting, and "interface" when we intend to interact or communicate. The list goes on, and it is a tribute to the role and to the importance of the face in negotiating our way through daily life.

In some cultures the face has sacred significance and holds magical powers. In these cultures, faces fuel the fires of the imagination and conjure up all forms of reality. Reality for the Jivaro Indians of Ecuador is making trophy heads. It is a rule that when a victory has been attained over a foreign tribe the heads of the slain are taken, cut off as close to the trunk as possible, and turned into *tsantsas*. According to the Jivaro, the making of a *tsantsa*, or shrunken head, accomplishes three things: it humiliates the victim and his group; it demonstrates the warrior's courage; it adds the victim's courage to his own.

"FACE"
is a very powerful concept to Asian peoples. "Face" is fundamentally a code of honor similar to the Western notion of a man's word. This code is based on reverence for the family over individuality. In China the ancestor cult is extremely ancient and emphasizes continuity of familial lines. Reverence for elders was strongly supported by the teachings of Confucius. "Face" developed over time to be a rigid code of behavior that has preserved the family line and promoted family solidarity. Saving face means living up to the standards set by the family. Losing face suggests that one has failed to live up to the family standards, and this has grave consequences for all concerned.

The Mayan Indians used faces as symbols in intricate glyphs. Most of these symbols have not been translated, but it is believed that high priests used them to teach ancient prophecies which contain a mixture of history and religion. The Mayans were deeply religious. They held that the head, while the command center of the body, was a source of good health and fertility. In the *Popul Vuh*, the decapitation of a great hero is described. The hero's head was placed in a barren tree by the priests and the tree was soon covered with fruit. Perhaps it was beliefs like this that led the Mayans to make faces so important to their as yet untranslated language. Many Mayan glyphs are, in fact, distorted faces.

Anthropologist Bronislaw Malinowski visited and studied the Trobriand Islanders of the western

A WORD GAME:
ABOUT FACES
The players take turns.
Mick Jagger has a *stone* face.
Tyne Daly has an *arresting* face.
Lassie has a *fetching* face.
Victor Hugo has a *miserable* face.
Cookie Monster has a *delicious* face.

*TSANTSA*
There is plenty of evidence of ancient headhunting practices in archaeological sites of the New World but it remains a living tradition for the Jivaro of the Ecuadorian highlands. When they take the head of an enemy, it receives special treatment and a ceremonial disposition. They shrink it through a process of mummification and continually shape and mold it so that it retains its human features. Ironically, from the moment of the decapitation, the Jivaro warrior believes himself to be stalked by the victim's soul and pays a heavy psychological toll for having become "lord of the head." To ensure his own safety, the victor abstains from certain foods and from his wife. He lives without comforts and will not be free from danger until he can dance with his *tsantsa* at a great feast.

Pacific, where he discovered that the face and head were held to be sacred, for the most part, and were for that reason untouchable. This was especially true in case of a person of high social rank and importance. Malinowski writes: "The sanctity of the chief's person is particularly localized in his face and head, which is surrounded by a halo of strict taboos. The forehead is especially sacred. Only equals in rank, the wives and a few particularly privileged persons, are allowed to touch the forehead, for purposes of cleaning, shaving, ornamentation and delousing."

Malinowski found that the Trobrianders devoted a lot of time and energy to decorating and elaborating their faces, especially the eyes. The eyes were the gateways of erotic desires. One source of delight and pleasure for the Trobrianders was the practice of biting off the eyelashes during lovemaking. This practice was called *Mitakuku*. Malinowski wrote that a lover would tenderly or passionately bend over his mistress's eyes and bite off the tip of her eyelashes.

This sacredness of the face in some cultures carries over into the afterlife. In some parts of the world it was the custom to preserve the face as a household treasure. The Maori of New Zealand, for example, preserved the heads of the dead because they had magical powers of protection.

Herodotus tells that in ancient times the slain heads of vanquished enemies were displayed before the conqueror's house because of their power to protect the whole house. It was also the magical power of the head and face that so fascinated the headhunters of Borneo because the adversary's spirit was believed to be contained in the head. The Indians of North and South America used to treasure and preserve the head and face of the enemy for the same reason.

There is no more convincing proof of the power of the face over the imagination than the volume and variety of folk legends involving the face. Take yawning, for example: there are some very particular rules and beliefs governing this behavior. Failure to

conceal a yawn behind a hand is considered uncouth and rude today by many different cultural groups. Why? one wonders. Does the fact that so many people feel strongly about this behavior indicate that there is a more deeply rooted significance in the custom than just good manners? Perhaps.

Our ancient human ancestors were convinced that an unguarded yawn could make all the difference between life and death. First, because man's spirit was identified with his breath, the mouth was the critical place of entry and exit. So covering the mouth while yawning was a safeguard against the soul's departing prematurely. For a long time and by many different groups it was believed that the soul actually departed via the lips, with the last breath. This is why members of some groups kiss

PRESERVED MAORI HEADS Highly decorated, tattooed faces were prized by the Maoris—on or off the owner. In the 1820s it became fashionable for Europeans to collect these decorated faces. In order to satisfy demand, the Maoris took to tattooing the faces of their slaves for the purpose of trade.

Here General Horatio Gordon Robley sits amid his tattooed Maori head collection.

JANUS

Janus symbolizes the notion that the face has two opposing sides or personalities. Janus, the Roman god of gates and entrances, kept watch in both directions. One face looked to the future, the other looked to the past.

*We are all traumatized to varying degrees about our appearance. Facial discrimination is far more overt and shameless than racial discrimination: Our culture doesn't even attempt to hide its preference for certain arrangements of facial and bodily parts over others.*

MICHAEL KINSLEY, *New Republic* columnist

the mouth of a dying person: they are trying to catch the departing spirit in order to transfer it to future generations. Others believe that it is necessary to hold the mouth and nose of a dying friend to preserve the individual's life and prevent his or her ghost from escaping.

Equally, however, a gaping mouth is an open invitation to unwelcome guests. Why invite evil spirits and demons when you don't have to? Moslems regarded the very wish to yawn as the work of the Devil, anxious to take possession of a man's body. To chase away evil ones, Hindus snapped their fingers loudly in front of their open mouths. In some parts of Spain and France, Christians make the sign of the cross for the same reason. Today good manners require that, if one cannot suppress a yawn, one must conceal it and cover up the unpleasant-looking cavern of the mouth. We still admonish a child to "cover your mouth" when yawning.

Eyes exercise great influence over the imagination. Since Neolithic times, particularly in ancient Europe and the Middle East, the eyes have been a symbol of divinity. Eyes were inscribed on potsherds and carved into stones, always watchful and disembodied. At the Mesopotamian temple at Tell Brak, dating to about 3000 B.C., excavators found countless little female effigies, all bodies surmounted by eyes rather than faces. Does this mean that Mother knew all and would provide?

The idea of the "evil eye," the eye as a malevolent influence, abounds in folklore. Eyes in this context have supernatural powers, the power of transformation. Some Greeks believe that green-eyed people are likely to be witches whether they know it or not. In some places amulets of eyes are worn as charms against evil. Some groups place them with the dead to guard the soul. Azande tribesmen consider red and inflamed eyes to hold evil power that can be exercised over others. During Elizabethan times in England the evil eye was capable of wreaking disease and death. Warrior tribesmen of New Zealand captured the power of a defeated chief by eating the dead chief's eyes, since it was known that the man's divinity rested there.

It is not just myth and magic that draw attention to the face and features and view them symbolically. We all do so each and every day as we generate images of the face in the imagination and turn these images into feelings and ideas. One crucial idea we get from these imaginings is about who we really are. In that sense, the power of the facial image over the imagination is central to our sense of self. Whether we feel good about ourselves or bad depends upon how we imagine our faces to be perceived by others. In the mind, the face and imagination join forces to create self-image.

*Was this the face that launch'd a thousand ships,*
*And burnt the topless towers of Ilium?*

CHRISTOPHER MARLOWE

One of the most fascinating and unsolved problems in biology is the evolution of our ideas as to what constitutes beauty. This complex, abstract notion that we call beauty carries with it an emotional dimension that is both difficult to describe and to define. But no matter where one lives or what the standards are in that place, a beautiful face is one that is admired.

Conceptions of beauty are varied. Even within a single society notions about face and beauty are relative, local, and highly personal. Generally speaking, your standard of beauty arises from familiarity with the person you see in the mirror. What you personally consider to be beautiful others may regard with indifference—even contempt or hostility. This indicates that the judgment of beauty is highly subjective though there is often agreement among a large number of people in any given place. Sometimes a whole community or even a nation will unite in appreciation of a certain look.

To the ancient Romans, a beautiful girl would have bright red cheeks. Her eyes would be shaded and painted saffron. Her brows would be penciled. There might be a patch or two on the cheeks. Others see beauty differently. The Kirghiz, for example, think their race, the Mongolian, offers the most finished type of beauty because the bony structure of the face resembles that of a horse—the greatest masterpiece of all creation. For the ancient Greeks, the idea of beauty was defined in terms of harmony, balance, and proportion. The perfect face was neatly divisible into thirds or "golden" proportions. The brow would be one third of the way up from the high point of the chin. The width of the face would be two thirds of its height.

Real beauty for the Victorians resided chiefly in the face and mirrored spiritual beauty. According to the French writer Cazenave, "Real beauty—the beauty which charms and seduces—resides chiefly in the visage. We are never so strongly attracted by any part of the body as by the face." Victorians favored delicate features. Fashion plates show women with oval faces, smooth, pink, rounded cheeks, fairly large eyes, small straight noses, and little rosebud mouths. A small mouth was mandatory, as it signaled refinement and freedom from strong passions.

Regardless of culture, conceptions of beauty contain a very significant sexual element. If, however, it were merely a question of sexual characteristics,

**IDEAL HEAD**
Elie Nadelman's sculptured marble faces profoundly influenced the American notion of beauty when Helena Rubinstein proposed to use this work as trademarks or symbols for the "scientific beautification of modern women."

*There is no excellent beauty that hath not some strangeness in the proportion.*
FRANCIS BACON

To give beauty a face and capture that elusive and ever
changing value that we understand as beauty, video artist
Nancy Burson created two
composites. "The First Beauty
Composite" is a combination
of the great beauties of the
1950s: Bette Davis, Audrey
Hepburn, Grace Kelly, Sophia
Loren, and Marilyn Monroe.
"The Second Beauty Composite" is a combination of Jane
Fonda, Jacqueline Bisset, Diane Keaton, Brooke Shields,
and Meryl Streep. These videographic composite portraits
capture and epitomize the differences in the ideal of the
1950s and that of the 1980s.
Note, for example, the arched
eyebrows and heavily made-
up mouth of the fifties beauty
versus the more "ge-
neric" natural look of the
eighties.

the ideal wouldn't change so much over time and
be so different in different places. To a considerable
degree beauty is an artificial construct of the mind
that is given shape and dimension by culture and
experience.

> *Beauty is not a quality in things themselves. It
> exists merely in the mind which contemplates
> them, and each mind perceives a different beauty.*
> DAVID HUME

Today we appreciate what the Scottish philosopher
David Hume realized more than two hundred years
ago: beauty is essentially a private and personal experience, a consequence of our impressions and
memories.

Even within a culture, notions about beauty are
always in a state of flux; what is beautiful to an
American in the 1980s is substantially different than
that which embodied beauty in the 1950s. And what
is beautiful to a thirteen-year-old is not the least bit
attractive to a sixty-five-year-old.

Today when we say that a man or woman is

beautiful we probably mean he or she seems healthy, pleasing to the eye, and inherently childlike. This American standard of beauty has increasingly become the world standard as fashion magazines and television conspire to reach into nearly every corner of the earth, establishing a standard and an ideal.

*'Tis not a lip, or eye, we beauty call,*
*But the joint force and full result of all.*
ALEXANDER POPE

Since an aesthetically satisfying face stimulates sexual desire, it is probably for this reason above all others that we go to so much trouble to enhance our faces' appearance. To what lengths we will go to achieve a beautiful face is clear from the billions of dollars spent every year on cosmetics.

*As a white candle*
*In a holy place,*
*So is the beauty*
*Of an aged face.*
JOSEPH CAMPBELL

*As a beauty I'm not a great star,*
*There are others more handsome by far;*
*But my face, I don't mind it*
*Because I am behind it—*
*'Tis the folks out in front that I jar.*

ANTHONY EVERS

THE ROOTS OF
ATTRACTION
An attractive face may not just
be in the eyes of the beholder,
according to psychologist Ju-
dith H. Langois of the University of Texas. She and her
colleagues reported that infants as young as two months
old, with little or no exposure
to cultural influences, show a
preference for women's faces
that have been rated as attractive by young adults.

Beauty and fame are often inextricably linked to the face, particularly in Western culture. Fame has been termed a kind of shorthand for personal recognition. Like beauty, it is in the eye of the beholder. In our modern society we often see other people, as well as ourselves, in terms of the faces of the famous. We wonder if we measure up. We judge others accordingly.

Through the explosion of the media today, certain standards of physical beauty are widely disseminated. Consider the number of Madonna look-alikes or the number of men in Congress now who still have the JFK haircuts of the early sixties. In the mass media, one kind of face shows you how to wear your makeup or cut your hair. Another tells you how to feel and how to behave. Huge numbers of people are manipulated by these images and strive to imitate them. What you are going to look like today, on some levels, is a matter of choice but the choices are often based on standards set by the society at large and by the media in particular.

Advertisers and image makers count on the fact that we are all capable of generating faces in the mind. They know that faces are powerful symbols. They use them to tap into private thoughts and feelings. For advertisers, faces are the principal source of motivational power for putting across social, political, aesthetic, and moral ideas.

Famous faces, it turns out, are particularly good motivators. They derive their power from their familiarity, from the fact that we feel as if we know these people intimately. Television creates the illusion of intimacy; it breaks down the barriers that

formerly existed between the known and the unknown. The electronic age invites you to look at faces
in new, more intimate ways. This looking exerts a
certain power over the mind's eye.

Think about the power of those larger-than-life
faces projected in dark theaters on huge motion picture screens. You see this projected face more intimately than you see the face of a lover. It is just
this intimate detail that gives us the mistaken impression that we have detailed knowledge of the person
whose face is projected on the screen. This illusion
of intimacy invests the face with power simply because we think we know the person. We want to do
what they do. These faces have the power to crys-
tallize an idea, personify an issue, embody an ideal.
These faces can sell us anything—a product, an idea,
a political candidate.

It is interesting in this connection to consider
Walter Cronkite's face, which, according to the polls
at the time of his retirement, was the most trusted
one in America. How did it come to be so described?
How did it come to be a symbol for "trust"? Is it
the fact that night in and night out television gives
people an opportunity to judge character? Or is it
a function of intimacy and familiarity? Whatever the
answer, the fact is that this public judgment emerged
from the "persona" broadcast by television, night
after night, over a very long time. It has been suggested that this same mechanism helped elect Ronald
Reagan and put him in the White House, for his
many years of motion picture and television exposure made his familiar face not only popular but
trustworthy. In politics this is a winning combination.

The power of the face over the imagination is
expressed in a myriad of ways, for faces are powerful
symbols that generate thoughts and feelings as well
as ideas and images. Most of us think a good deal
about faces—our own and others, about what they
say and what they mean, about what they look like
and what they stand for. We find faces endlessly

fascinating and share this common preoccupation with all other members of our species. Considering the biological antiquity of this ability, it seems surprising that we know so little about how we do it. We really only know that we do by the evidence that shows that faces have been grist for the imagination and a major human preoccupation for a long time.

# 11

# Changing the Face

We humans are distinct from other animals in having a special relationship with our faces and our own images. In a sense, this is problematical in that it leads the individual to want to change the face and to transform identity. Changing the face is an ancient and universal human pursuit. We change our faces to change identity and declare status. We change our faces in the pursuit of beauty and in an effort to redefine ourselves. We change our faces to be more sexually attractive. Some people change

There are many ways to change the face. Down through the ages a variety of techniques have been employed, most of them still in use somewhere.

It is custom for the Secoya tribesman who lives along the Río Santa María in Peru to wear a sprig of grass through his septum for the traditional circumcision rites.

One reason to mark the face is to announce social class or standing. The face of this Indian fortune-teller bears a caste mark that lets others know his place in the society.

Makeup alters the persona when it is painted for a performance. The earliest ancestors of the clown flourished in ancient Greece. The same baldheaded, padded buffoons appeared in Roman mime. Clowning, a change of face, facilitates jest and parody. The traditional whiteface makeup appeared in the seventeenth century and was used to relieve tension and provoke laughter.

Some groups paint their faces to be more sexually attractive. Marilyn Monroe's formula for beautiful lips in the 1950s included three shades of lipstick, plus a gloss of wax and Vaseline.

"Shades" are a common strategy for self-concealment. They produce a super poker face and obscure the optical signal transmitted by the eyes. When you converse with someone wearing silvered glasses you may experience a gnawing discomfort because nonverbal communication is interrupted. The lack of social information brings out one's uncertainties.

their faces for religious or magical reasons. Some people change them for fun. Others change them to hide from public scrutiny. In the pursuit of these objectives, faces are painted, deformed, mutilated, tattooed, scarred, made up, masked, adorned, and otherwise reshaped and reconstructed. However, whatever the reason or method, the intention is fundamentally the same: to transform identity and control the message sent by the face.

We can only speculate about the beginnings of this uniquely human activity but plenty of evidence attests to its antiquity, its universality, and its countless cultural manifestations. One of the more dramatic of the changes that have been used down the ages is to alter the face's shape and form by deforming the growing skull. This practice is both ancient and widespread. It is still practiced by some African peoples, as well as people living in Greenland and Peru. Until very recently it was popular in Brittany, Normandy, and the region around Toulouse in France. In all cases the object is to tamper with the face's natural proportions, and this is begun at birth when the head is soft and malleable. It is accomplished by applying pressure to the babies' skulls in order to make the heads round, flat, or elongated, according to the standards set by the specific cultural group. In some places elongated skulls are formed by wrapping the infant's head with bandages. In other places flattening boards are used to attain the desired shape. In still other places tight caps are stretched over the baby's skull to give it a noble shape.

Until recently it was thought that the earliest skulls shaped intentionally came from the Minoan Bronze Age, about 3500 B.C. But a recent find in the Middle East suggests that this skull-shaping practice may have more ancient roots reaching back to the time of the Neanderthals. It was an important discovery in Shanidar Cave, in Iraq, that yielded the first archaeological traces of "human nature" and evidence of human intervention in skull design.

Some people change the face to deprive it of its expressive potential. In Egypt a nomadic tribeswoman covers her face with an ornamental face cloth. Aside from masking her emotions, the ornate covering announces her status as a woman of high background.

Lip disks, sometimes called labrets, are ornaments worn in a perforation of the lip. Once a popular practice, lip disks were made of bone or silver. In some places the size of the disk indicates the rank or age of the wearer.

In many places around the world, in order to participate in religious ceremonials, individuals often have to paint and ornament their faces. In the Kavadi religious festival that takes place in Vridachalamths, devotees must paint the face white and hook coconuts to the cheeks.

Here, more than forty thousand years ago, nine chinless Neanderthalers were buried. The excavation revealed that these people nursed their wounded, cared for their aged, and, for either cultural or aesthetic reasons, deformed their skulls. Anthropologist Erik Trinkaus suggested that in at least two of the skulls there were grooves that may have resulted from head binding in infancy or from maternal pressure. What was the reason they altered the shape of the face and skull? From this point in time we can only guess and assume that these new behaviors reflected an added dimension to knowledge, to human emotions, and to individual aesthetic sensibilities.

Elongated faces are featured in the art of Egypt beginning in the fourteenth century B.C. This shape was fashionable for a time. The reason, it appears, is that King Akhenaton's head was deformed at birth into a naturally elongated shape. Because of his exalted station, his head shape set the standard for the royal court and made skull and face deformation a popular practice among the Egyptian nobility. Indeed, this royal fashion swept around the Mediterranean and penetrated Africa, where it is still practiced by some tribal groups.

Skull shaping was also widely practiced among the peoples of the Americas and reached its acme among the Mayan Indians, who long favored elongated faces and pointed heads. For the Maya, this shape distinguished the highborn members of the nobility.

The impulse to alter the face takes many forms that to us may seem both bizarre and painful. However, at the heart of the activity is the desire to alter the face according to the standards set by the community. The change stamps it with a badge of belonging and redefines the individual within the cultural order. To this end, individuals seem prepared to go through almost unbelievable suffering. It wasn't so long ago that the Botocudo girls of Brazil inserted ever larger disks into their lower lips to achieve a kind of spoonbill look. The size of the disk increased as the woman grew older, thereby announcing not only her status but her age. Among some African peoples lip disks, sometimes called labrets, are worn in pairs, one on the upper lip and one on the lower lip. The great explorer David Livingstone observed: "The women seen at a distance and in profile seem to be holding two saucers between their teeth. Eating was very difficult, and the woman was, for all practical intents, dumb. The labret was grossly uncomfortable; yet it was a mark of honor and people who so regarded it hesitated at nothing to get it and to celebrate its attainment." Lip disks used by the native peoples of the Amazon basin exaggerate the mouth and in so doing, they believe, contribute to their wisdom. In other cultures male lips are pierced and disks inserted when they are expected to behave like men. Sometimes they are painted fiery red as a symbol of aggressiveness.

Piercing the nose, the lip, and the ear is common in many places. The Papuans of New Guinea put a sharpened stick through the septum of the nose as a mark of virility and fierceness. A Jivaro girl announces her readiness for marriage when she pierces her lip. Captain Cook reported that New Zealanders pierced huge holes, the diameter of a man's finger, in the lobes of their ears through which they threaded bone, colored cloth, twigs, and feathers. In South American a fierce Amazon tribe called the Cobeus made large holes in their ears for the purpose of holding arrows. In the South Pacific feathers, knives, and heavy rings hang from perforated ears. For the Bella Coola of the Pacific Northwest, not to pierce a baby's ear is to ensure that it does not live long. The Suya of South America punch large holes in their lower earlobes in order to insert ever larger disks until ultimately the ears hang down to the shoulder. The ornamented disks, after they are outgrown, are considered among a man's most prized possessions. Such practices as these are intended to

Piercing the nose can send a message of fierceness or beauty or wealth.

By 1360 B.C. all Egyptian royal
heads were characterized by an
elongated face and skull. This
was a mark of sophistication
and elegance. The style is
clearly reflected in this profile
view of the famous Princess
Nefertiti.

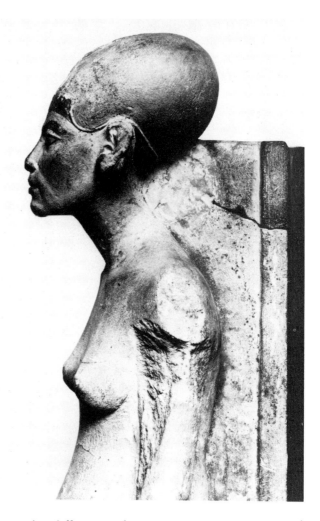

assert the differences between one community and
another, and to establish the differences between
individuals within a community.

Depilating the face is another common and widespread method for changing its appearance and the
message it displays. In ancient Egypt both men and
women depilated their faces, as a matter of attractiveness and status. During the fourteenth century
European women first plucked their eyebrows and
hairlines to accentuate the height of the forehead.
This also had the effect of flattering the features by
reducing their apparent size. Raising the hairline created a youthful, gentle, and innocent impression.
Konrad Lorenz demonstrated that a large forehead
reminds us of the tenderness of young babies, whose

foreheads are proportionately very large. Depilating the face is still a common practice in many places for the express purpose of signaling youthfulness.

Among the many ways to change the face's appearance is to alter the teeth. In some cases the point is to create a threatening appearance. To this end, many groups exaggerate the canines by knocking out the incisors, which leaves the canines framing the gap and produces a kind of Dracula face. This technique, called ablation, has been practiced since prehistoric times in places ranging from Spain to Japan and from Florida to Alaska. Filing the teeth to a point is still another method. This one is practiced widely in Africa, Southeast Asia, and the Americas as well as by the pygmies in the Philippines.

## PIERCING PRACTICES

A decorative lip ornament is worn by the men of Bume in Ethiopia.

The Hindus say that a girl with a pierced left nostril is married.

Perforated earlobes serve as a centerpiece for beadwork. This is a common custom in much of East Africa.

The native women of Papua, New Guinea, pierce their septum to announce their status as women. The two girls on the right have yet to be initiated.

FACT Pirates put holes in their ears and wore earrings because they thought it helped them see better.

In other cultures beauty is associated with tooth deemphasis. One method is to dye the teeth black; another is to chew betel nuts, which has the same effect. In both cases the point is to return the face to a baby-like appearance. This practice is most common among women.

Many painful changes made to the face are often an intrinsic part of puberty rites, in which young people are welcomed into the privileges of adulthood. The indigenous peoples of Australia and New Guinea used to celebrate their ascendancy to adulthood by having their two top front teeth knocked out. The Ibans of Borneo had holes drilled through the six front teeth, into which they inserted plugs of brass. Then they filed the teeth to sharp points.

The practice of scarring the face in order to mark and change it dates back to Paleolithic times and has continued to the present. Many female statues found in Crete and on Cyprus bear specific incised markings that are believed to have been ritually inscribed. The indelibility of scarring gives it a special place among methods used to change the face. When a tribal initiate receives the ritual markings, he or she is committed forever to membership in the tribe. In turn, tribal identity confers certain privileges and obligations.

Scarring requires deliberate incisions on the skin which leave scars that form a significant and meaningful pattern. This is a painful process. First the design is marked out on the skin. Then a needle or

PORTRAIT OF A LADY
Down through the ages depilation has been a popular way to change the face. During the fourteenth century it was common and fashionable for women to pluck both their eyebrows and their foreheads, as it was believed that the added height enhanced the charm and innocence of the female face.

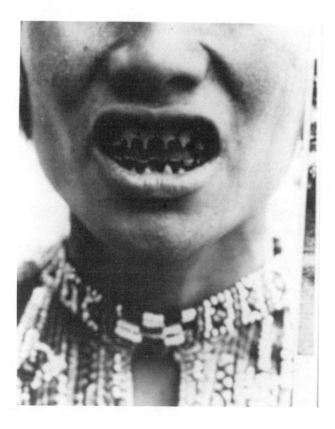

Filing the teeth to points is a common practice among the Negrito pygmies of the Philippines.

This drawing was made by the eminent French archaeologist Léon Pales from the original plaque (see illustration page 186), which he discovered. Pales made the drawing to clarify the nature of the markings on the face. Though there is no way to know the purpose of the markings (nor even to know whether they are scars, tattoos, or paint), they were deliberately made and suggest that our ancient ancestors were aware of the power of the face as a message center and were already involved in altering its message.

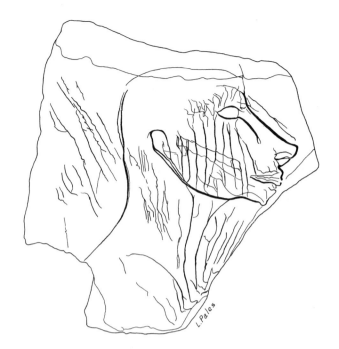

thorn is driven under the epidermis and the wound is filled with an irritant that produces a keloid scar. The aesthetic effect of this procedure was discovered in Africa at least as long as eight thousand years ago, for figures painted on Saharan cliff walls bear scars not too different from those to be seen today in West Africa. Africans, and to a lesser extent the people of Australia, New Guinea, and Melanesia, scar enthusiastically and for numerous reasons. There are tribal scars, there are clan scars, there are maturity scars gained through initiation ordeals, and there are the scars of personal adornment. All tribal societies that practice scarification carry it out in the course of a ceremony attended by the whole community. It is an ordeal in which the person undergoing the procedure is expected to repudiate his or her previous identity. Although each group has its own rationale, the Bafia of the Cameroon, a country in Africa, put it this way: a man who is not scarred looks like a pig or a chimpanzee.

Tattooing is another way to permanently change the face's appearance and its message. While scarification is practiced by dark-skinned people and prevails in Africa, tattooing is generally practiced by people with lighter skin and is popular in the Americas, Asia, and Oceania. Tattoos are made by puncturing the skin and inserting dark pigments with needles or pointed pegs. These prickings, when clustered densely, assume the appearance of patterns or paintings and have social, religious, or magical significance depending upon the time, the place, and the people who apply them. Like scarification, the process is painful and principally serves to dedicate an individual to a group. Permanence fits the purpose.

By Neolithic times, when the world's people were adopting farming ways, tattooing was in vogue in many places. One ancient facial design, favored in the Middle East, was an inverted blue trident. This tattoo can still be seen adorning the chins of the Berber women of North Africa.

The practice of tattooing is attested to in the fifth millennium B.C. in Egypt, where it appears to have been reserved for women and in particular for prostitutes, dancers, and singers.

Tattooing seems to have been on the wane in the Near East with the introduction of modern religions. Religious law proscribed such activity: "ye shall not make any cuttings in your flesh . . . nor print any marks upon you." Scarring and tattooing had been practiced by the ancient Jews but had been expressly outlawed by Moses. We are told that "the Lord set a mark upon Cain" (Genesis 4:15), probably on his brow as a brand or stigma. The Christian Church formally banned tattooing at the second Council of Nicaea in 787.

Like Christianity, Islam proscribed tattooing out of respect for the divine creation. The Koran explicitly censured any alteration of the body's appearance. Some Muslims have, however, held out against this religious ordinance as the practice of tattooing has endured throughout the Maghreb and also in Yemen, chiefly among the desert nomads. Here women still tattoo the lower part of the face between lower lip and chin. These tattooings consist

The face of a Meru girl from Kenya has been ritually ornamented by the painful process of scarification. The pattern marks her as having passed through the early stages of womanhood. When she dies, this permanent badge of belonging will admit her into the afterlife.

DUELING SCARS
Many of the dueling scars sported by German university students were produced by self-inflicted wounds in which a hair was inserted to produce a keloid scar. This identified a student as a member of the aristocratic and academic elite.

of a vocabulary of signs inherited from the pre-Islamic period and perhaps going back to Neolithic times. The effect of the Koranic prohibition was simply to change the ritual significance of the tattoo marks into a therapeutic or curative function. Tattooing around the eye, for example, now guards against eye disease.

For Ainu women of the northernmost Japanese islands, the tattoo was like a wedding band applied after marriage to the brow, the lips, and the hands. A dutiful woman, so marked, proclaimed that she lived for her husband and spoke only for him. The lip tattoo enlarges the mouth and curls the lips in a permanent smile.

The word "tattoo" may have been formed by onomatopoeia from the blow of the mallet on the

TATTOOED
A New Zealand Maori chief is elaborately tattooed with marks that speak of his rank and identify his achievements. Claude Lévi-Strauss reports that in Brazil a Caduveo woman's tattoos speak of her biologic functions, her blood, her menstruation, her pain.

pointed instrument; or it may come from the Tahitian word *tatau*, which means "to strike." The word was introduced into Europe in the 1770s by Captain Cook, who in his journal for July 1769 wrote of the natives of Tahiti: "Both sexes paint their bodies. Tattoo as it is called in their language, this is done by inlaying the color of black under their skins in such a manner as to be indelible."

An elaborate tattoo technique called *moko* was perfected by the Maori of New Zealand. Maori face tattoos artistically conformed to an individual's facial structure and were generally made by specialized artists, who were skilled carvers of ivory, bone, and stone and only went to work on the human skin after a long apprenticeship with a master. The operation nearly always took on the character of a rite and was

*An unpainted body is a stupid body.*

A CADUVEO INDIAN

practiced by males and females. Though a painful ordeal, the results were always beautiful and highly prized. One traveler described a tribal chief who prided himself on having spared no visible part of his body: even his lips, tongue, gums, and palate were completely tattooed.

Eskimos tattoo a whale's tail on their foreheads for each whale they kill. The Naga of Assam in northeastern India believe that tattoo marks are useful as identification in the spirit world. Not only will the gods recognize chosen people, but husband and wife will recognize each other by their tattoos. In some cultures, for the warrior, tattoos serve as a permanent equivalent of service ribbons.

A less painful but equally dramatic way to alter one's appearance is to paint the face. Painting one's face enlarges the self, idealizes it, enhances it, transforms it. Colors decompose the face, single out its orifices and protuberances or, on the contrary, ignore them and break up its symmetry. In short, paint undermines the subject's unity and wholeness and transforms the subject into someone else. "We lead an excessively facial life," said the French poet Henri Michaux, meaning that we invest in the face a unified focus of our personality. It is precisely this frail façade that face painting acts upon and demolishes. Face painting is a way to make a person unlike him or herself and allows individuals to play the roles assigned by myth, ritual, and society. In paint, a community displays its collective values and an individual demonstrates participation and belief in a common identity.

The face is painted for many reasons. It can be painted to go to war and in this way serves like a uniform, to distinguish factions and announce rank. With respect to this property, one Fijian chief made it a practice to change the face's painted design every two or three days in order to avoid ruses on the part of the enemy.

The Indians of North America apply paint for

religious reasons, for its curative and protective powers, for good luck in war, and to mark the transition to an afterlife. Some tribes paint black circles around the eyes as protection against snow or sun blindness. Some rub red paint on the face to protect the skin from the cold. Others paint a red band across a chief's forehead to invoke the spirit of the clouds. Arapaho Indians of the North American plains painted a semicircle on the forehead to signify rapidity. The Pawnee Indians painted an archlike line from the cheeks over the brow and then a straight line down the nose to symbolize the path by which life ascends from above. The Moqui Indians of Southern North America painted vertical lines over the whole face to call down rain. They also painted slanting lines to call for a change in the direction of the wind. The Jicarilla Apache, who had a segregated

**THE POWER OF THE PAINTED FACE**
Face painting is common in circumcision rites around the world. These three Tanzanian boys are painted for their traditional circumcision rites. In this case the power of the paint is the power of transformation. The paint obliterates the old identity, changes the personality, and binds these initiates to the society, making them full-fledged members of the tribe.

clan society, smeared their faces with white clay and then etched four black bars for magical protection.

The Yanomamo of the Orinoco Basin paint black on their faces to appear ferocious. The native people of New Guinea use black against red to celebrate victory in battle or to promote success in trading and commerce. Black symbolizes male aggressiveness while red stands for fertility and the feminine mystique. For the Australian aborigines, yellow is the color of peace. When they mourn the death of a loved one, they smear their faces and bodies with white paint.

The southeastern Nuba of Kordofan Province in the Sudan are an isolated group that have evolved an unusual tradition of paint on the face. With them, the medium is the message and the primary purpose of applying paint to the face is an artistic one. Lines of the jaw, contours of the chin, nose, and forehead are integrated into geometrical patterns that celebrate and enhance a healthy face. The color and shapes vary with different age groups and can be analyzed like a visual grammar, revealing something about each man's role in the community.

Anthropologist Roland Dixon reported that face paint plays a key role in Shasta Indian puberty ceremonies for girls. The ceremony begins on the night after the girl attains puberty, when she goes to her mother's menstrual hut or to a special hut built for her. The young girl's face is painted with a number of vertical stripes in red, running from the forehead to the chin. Once painted, she assumes the status of a woman.

Charles M. Doughty first described the practice of painting the whites of the eyes blue after encountering Bedouin tribesmen in 1876: "In all Arabia men and women paint the whites of their eyes blue with kohl or antimony."

There is no question but that painting the face makes a philosophical statement but just how long humankind has felt the urge to change the face in this way can only be guessed. Prehistorians suspect that painting the face was probably the first ritualized method for altering appearance and that our ancient ancestors were engaging in this practice by about four hundred thousand years ago when the Old World was populated by *Homo erectus*. That *Homo erectus* had a fascination with paint is clear from the quantitites of ochers, in the form of crayons, that have been found in various camps and habitations. One of the ocher sites, located in Nice, France, was apparently a summer home for many generations of hunters. Here were preserved many well-rounded and well-worn crayons. Since there are no cave paintings here or nearby, the experts believe that the crayons were used to paint the face and body.

In those dim and distant times, what ideas could possibly have required graphic expression on the face? What messages were conveyed by color? We don't know, of course, but we do know something about the colors that they used. In the beginning it was a simple palette—the red and yellow ochers, earth colors. These iron oxides were ground into powder and mixed with an emollient such as animal fat or vegetable oil. The reds were heated to intensify the color and formed into crayons. Crayons were also made of yellow ocher, of black manganese oxide, and of white clay. Some crayons appear to have been rubbed, as if applied to the skin; others are scratched, as if they were used to prepare a powder. The archaeologist François Bordes has uncovered in the cave of Pech de l'Aze, in southern France, a limestone palette on which paints of this kind were ground and prepared for use on the first canvas, the human body.

We also know that it was a Neanderthal custom to paint the bones of the dead with red ocher, and presumably also the body of the living. Among the so-called primitive tribes still in existence, red ocher, as the blood color and symbol of vitality and fertility, is used ritually for face and body painting and is also used more frequently than any other color.

If the face and body were the original surface

for ritual inscription one can understand why the human face and figure are so rarely depicted on the cave walls. Perhaps there was no need to duplicate the magic on cave walls. Perhaps that is the reason that the human face and figure account for only five percent of Paleolithic art.

Using cosmetics to paint the face is an age-old practice. In some cultures it is believed to be one's duty to retouch the human likeness, to improve upon it, to, in effect, amend reality. Women from the days of King Tutankhamen to the present have used makeup to draw attention to the messages sent by their faces. The eyes, in particular, are often show-cased. The ancient Egyptians enhanced the beauty of their eyes by outlining them with a dark paint called kohl. They also applied powdered green copper ore below the eyes and gray lead ore above them. In addition, Egyptian women reddened their cheeks and lips with red ocher and darkened their eyebrows with crushed ant eggs.

The Greeks by and large rejected such methods of enhancement, believing in the ideal of a pure and elegant natural state. The Greek physician Galen noted that "the art of the toilet, which is part of medicine, differs from the art of makeup. The purpose of makeup is to achieve an alien beauty; the purpose of the toilet is to preserve the body's natural state, from which arises a natural beauty."

During Roman times makeup was popular and used to excess according to the poet Ovid, whose advice to women was that such enhancements should be "unsuspected."

The Crusades had a profound effect on the use of cosmetics during the Middle Ages. The returning crusaders brought back from the East a variety of cosmetic substances including dyes for the lips and eyes and pastes to whiten the face. As a result, European women began to use makeup to create a pale and wan appearance that was considered the ideal of feminine beauty. These new products contrib-

**EGYPTIAN MAKEUP**
Women have used makeup as long as recorded history. None of our modern cosmetics are new. They were applied in like manner in ancient Egypt, Babylonia, and China. The purpose: to enhance beauty and sexual attractiveness.

uted to a new concern for personal appearance and this was probably intensified by the introduction of metal mirrors, which had just become available.

By the time of Elizabeth I many of the popular cosmetics were made of highly dangerous and poisonous substances. The face, for example, was whitened with ceruse, which contained lead oxide, hydroxide, and carbonate. Kohl, largely composed of lead and antimony sulphides, was widely used for darkening the eyelids, lashes, and eyebrows. Colored eye shadows were prepared from powdered green malachite, and a strong and dangerous mercuric dye was used on the lips. Because of these poisonous "beauty aids," untold numbers of women suffered and died at an early age, many before reaching their thirtieth year.

During the seventeenth century it was popular to put drops of the drug belladonna into the eyes to increase their brilliance. Belladonna literally means "beautiful woman." This drug achieved its effect by dilating the pupils, which robbed the eye, for a time, of its natural reflexive ability to close down the iris and limit the amount of bright light falling on the retina, hastening the onset of glaucoma.

By the eighteenth century both men and women in England were wearing makeup on a daily basis but by 1770 the English Parliament passed an act imposing stiff penalties on women who used makeup "to entrap men into marriage" by deception or artifice. Though the law was unenforceable it did discourage the use of cosmetics and by 1784 a women's magazine reported that "white paint is now looked on as disgraceful and dangerous."

Across the channel, at this time, the French were reaching a peak of artificiality. Such ladies as Mesdames Pompadour and Du Barry and Queen Marie Antoinette used cosmetics freely and with dramatic effect. Casanova noted, in commenting on his mistress's makeup: "I liked it because she had put it on the way that ladies do at Versailles. The pleasing

Kabuki theater arose in the seventeenth century at Kyoto, Japan. Kabuki actors put on extremely elaborate makeup, which is designed to emphasize the character and type of person being portrayed. The face is first whitened to obliterate the natural face. The designs all come from a strictly codified repertory of motifs and colors but the actor improvises with the elements as he applies them.

thing about this painting lies in the negligence with which it is applied to the cheeks. She does not want her rouge to seem natural: she puts it on to please the eyes that see in it the tokens of an intoxication fraught with the promise of entrancing frenzies and excitements."

A century later Baudelaire took up where Casanova left off: "Makeup need not be subtle, need not try and keep its presence from being guessed at. It may on the contrary show itself off, if not with affectation, anyhow with a certain candor." Baudelaire based his essay, "In Praise of Makeup," on the idea that nature is immoral and that beauty, like virtue, can only be artificial.

By the time of Queen Victoria's reign the use of cosmetics had almost disappeared in England. Rouge and face paint of any kind were judged improper. Most women of substance avoided the daylight and covered their heads with hats and their faces with veils. The ideal was to be pale and without color.

Twentieth-century women no longer use drops of belladonna to enlarge their pupils, but a majority do use a variety of other ancient beauty aids: eye shadow, eyeliner, eyebrow pencil, and mascara. In using these cosmetics, a woman modifies her real appearance according to some generally accepted image and according to continually changing fashions and conventions.

Through facial makeup the jawline can be exaggerated, the cheekbones made more prominent, and the texture of the face can be modeled to reflect a more childlike appearance. In a sense, makeup exploits the face's potential for change and transformation. Yet, in Western society, the change must not be too obvious. Makeup is supposed to have an illusionistic function. It is not supposed to be apparent. When it breaks away from this standard and becomes obvious and overdone, we call the individual "a painted woman" and the remark is not a compliment.

Reconstructive surgery has expanded the limits of what can be done to change the face's appearance. The origin of reconstructive surgery probably lies somewhere in the Stone Age when men and women first sought to repair disfigurements caused by accident and warfare.

Sanskrit writings, including the famous *Rig Veda*, dating back fifteen hundred years, refer to methods used to restore and repair the nose. Sustra Samhita, a great Hindu surgeon and teacher, describes an operation for the restoration of a lost nose that used a technique that is the basis of a method still used today. Even at that early date the method was so well developed, it must have already had a long history. Briefly, the operation involved cutting and raising a flap of skin and tissue on the forehead immediately above the missing nose. This flap was then raised and brought down to cover the area of the nose and sutured into position. Large ants with heavy mandibles were caused to bite through the edges of the wound, and their bodies were cut off, leaving the jaws still strongly closed.

The Hindus were not the only early people who left records of plastic surgery techniques used to correct disfigurements. The ancient Egyptians applied their knowledge to reparative and military surgery: evidence comes from the *Papyrus Ebers,* named after the German Egyptologist who discovered and deciphered it, that can claim to be the first textbook of plastic surgery. Operations were described in some detail for the replacement of missing ears and noses and for the repair of same when they had been mutilated in battle.

An early Roman writer, Aulus Cornelius Celsus, wrote *De medicina,* one of the landmarks in the early history of plastic surgery. In this work Celsus gave detailed descriptions of operations on the nose, lips, eyelids, and ears. Gentleness, he insisted, was essential, and fine judgments must determine the placing of stitches. Perhaps his greatest claim to fame is that he was the first to give complete details of an operation for correcting the defect in which the eyelid is everted, revealing the red mucous lining. Celsus also detailed operations for the correction of nasal defects, using flaps raised from the cheek.

> *We restore, repair and make whole those parts of the face which Nature has given but which Fortune has taken away, not so much that they may delight the eye but that they may buoy up the spirit and help the mind of the afflicted.*
>
> GASPARO TAGLIACOZZI

The next great figure in plastic surgery is Gasparo Tagliacozzi, a professor at the University of Bologna, who is frequently called the Father of Plastic Surgery, perhaps because he wrote a seminal textbook on the subject, *De curtorum chirurgia*. This book, published in 1597, gives detailed instructions for performing the arm-flap method of grafting for the reconstruction of the nose and the ear. Tagliacozzi's instructions are accompanied by twenty-two detailed woodcuts which illustrate the surgical procedure. Though Tagliacozzi was a successful cosmetic surgeon, he was ruthlessly denounced as a sorcerer by the Church, which regarded his efforts as inherently sinful since they sought to meddle with the work of God.

Since Tagliacozzi's time, reconstructive surgery techniques have improved enormously—more than early practitioners ever imagined. The First and Second World Wars created a pressing need for plastic surgery and attracted original minds out of whose work sprang a multitude of new techniques. These have enabled modern practitioners to raise the practice of reconstructive surgery to an art form. Today it is possible to correct most congenital anomalies, such as cleft palates and jaws that won't close, as well as disfigurements that affect muscle, tissue, and skin and which may be caused by disease, auto accidents, cancer, or burns.

In addition, another factor serves to improve the surgeon's ability to rebuild and redesign the human face and that is the quest for beauty, which continues to drive technology to produce new tools that further refine the art, so that today painstaking resculpting of the face is possible in order to achieve aesthetic improvement.

New imaging techniques now make it possible for a patient to see a lifelike picture of the postsurgical outcome well in advance of entering the operating room. This technology emerged from a three-way collaboration among artist, computer scientist, and plastic surgeon. The electronic device can simulate almost any corrective or reconstructive procedure and give both doctor and patient control over

These illustrations from Tagliacozzi's textbook, *De curtorum chirurgia*, published in
1597, show how remarkably sophisticated the techniques
were for cosmetic surgery as
early as the sixteenth century.

the final outcome of any elective procedure, whether
it is reshaping the nose, making a cheekbone or chin
more prominent, changing the jawline, or removing
wrinkles. For every operation there is a plethora of
techniques: different anatomies call for different approaches, different surgeons favor different procedures.

Today in the United States there is a cosmetic
surgery boom that has seen the number of cosmetic
operations double from three hundred thousand to
more than six hundred thousand since the beginning

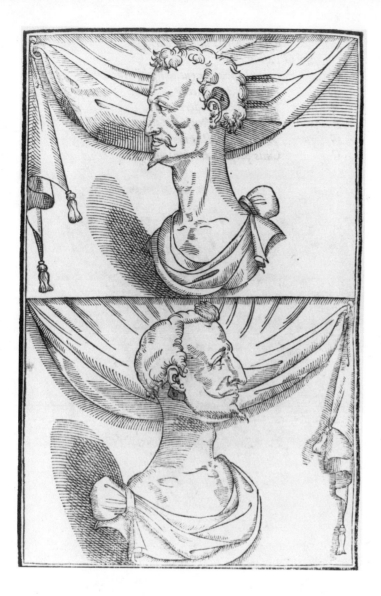

of the 1980s. Almost ninety percent of cosmetic surgery patients are women. At issue is the way people
feel about themselves; specifically, about how their
looks impact their position in society. To forestall a
loss of status due to the physical ramifications of
aging, more and more people are electing to change
the face in order to maintain the social status that
is correlated with youth.

For some, the urge to retain the bounce and
gleam of youth becomes an obsession and self-
scrutiny becomes a way of life. Sometimes called

Michael Jackson's ongoing and purposeful surgical reshaping of his face is possible because of today's highly sophisticated medical imaging tools, which have made it possible for him and his physician to redesign his face, from the inside out.

"scalpel slaves," these individuals are vulnerable to the face-saving appeal of plastic surgery and have themselves done and redone to forestall the signs of aging and to be free from what they consider distressing flaws. Plastic surgery junkies are in many ways akin to the anorexic or bulimic. According to the experts, this incessant self-corrective behavior is part of an identity disorder about which we know very little.

On the other hand, there are others who are sensible and realistic and for whom the emotional benefits of plastic surgery can be enormous. For them, though cosmetic surgery is a luxury, elective, and expensive, it is possible to recontour necklines, chins, cheekbones, to lengthen and contour lips, to

According to doctors from the U.S. Air Force Medical Center in San Antonio, breathing pure oxygen under pressure improves the success rate of facial-reconstructive surgery. In this new approach, patients breathe pure oxygen in a special hyperbaric chamber for ninety minutes at a time for a total of thirty hours before and fifteen additional hours after surgery. This stimulates the facial tissue to form the blood vessels and cells necessary to sustain the graft. Michael Jackson has used this technique to facilitate healing in his ongoing efforts to redefine his image.

## FACE LIFT BEFORE AND AFTER

Called a rhytidectomy, a face lift is performed to rid the face of lined and sagging skin. Usually the incision begins inside the hairline at the temples. It continues downward just in front of the ear, curves snugly back up around the earlobe, and trails upward into the hair in back. Lifting the freed skin, the surgeon removes excess underlying fat from the cheeks and jowls. The surgeon may probe deeper and tighten slack jowl and neck muscles. With the skin pulled gently upward and back, the surgeon snips away excess flesh and secures the edges with sutures, exerting just enough pull to prevent a taut look.

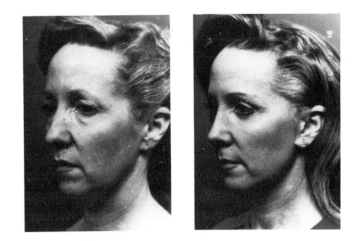

smooth out the forehead, change ear size, correct baggy upper lids or puffy pouches beneath the eyes—all of which contribute to improved self-esteem. The crucial issue here is not "self-improvement" but self-acceptance, and self-acceptance, regardless of culture, is fundamental to human happiness. Self-acceptance within a cultural context is at the heart of any elective change made to the face.

*Whether ritual, funerary or for any spectacle, the mask is an instrument of ecstasy. He who wears one is no longer himself.... He becomes "other" even when the mask is his own portrait.*

MIRCIA ELIADE

## BLEPHAROPLASTY BEFORE AND AFTER

Blepharoplasty is the operation to remove excess skin that causes droopy folds above the eye and bags below. The surgery is very common in the United States and Western Europe.

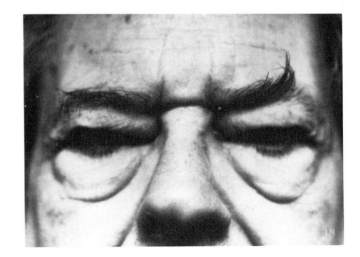

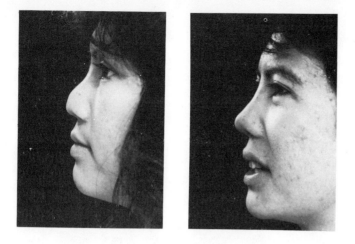

The nose operation is the most
frequent request made of cosmetic surgeons. During the
procedure the surgeon usually
works to modify the nose by
trimming down the cartilage
and bone in the bridge. To
build up a nose, cartilage from
the nasal septum or ear is
added.

Face masks are another powerful way to change
the face and its message. Simply defined, a mask is
a form of disguise, a way to transform identity. By
its own features, a mask transforms the individual
and establishes another being. The wearer becomes
anonymous and denies us access to the signals we
are accustomed to, or sends us new messages to
interpret. This essential characteristic of hiding one's
personality and revealing another is common to all
masks used in all cultures.

The manner of wearing masks varies greatly.
Some masks cover only the face. Others cover the
entire head. Some rest on the shoulders, some are
worn above the head, attached to a headdress.

More and more men are turning to cosmetic surgery, according to Dr. Mary Ruth
Wright of the Baylor College
of Medicine in Houston, but
apparently having cosmetic
surgery can be far more trau-
matic emotionally for men than
for women. Male patients, especially those who have nose
operations, tend to more complex expectations of and reactions to rhinoplasty than
women have. For many men,
the nose can be a symbol of
masculine identity; for others,
it can be an excuse for failure.
When surgery alters the nose
significantly, the experience
can be psychologically disturb-
ing, says Dr. Wright, who has
reviewed a number of cases.
She has discovered that men
often can't communicate as effectively as women exactly
what they want their surgeon
to do. A man generally wants
his nose to look better but not
different, says Dr. Wright.

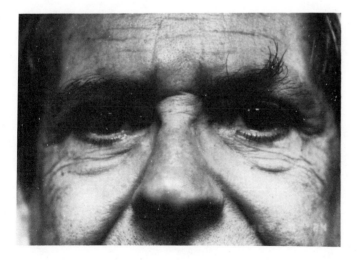

## PINOCCHIO

We usually think about computers generating an image of a new nose, a new ideal for patients to preview. However, Gerard Holzmann of Bell Laboratories has played with this notion of transformation by designing software that stretches the nose to Pinocchio proportions. The original nose appears upper left. He created this image of his department head, Doug McIlroy, just for fun.

Some masks are associated with religious or social ceremonies that concern funerary customs, rites of passage, and curing the sick; these are usually prescribed by tradition. Other masks are used on festive occasions or to portray a character in a drama or to reenact mythological events. Masks are used for warfare and as protective devices in certain sports and occupations. Some masks are made purely for aesthetic purposes, others are made for the purpose of disciplining children. In some places throughout the world, a judge wears a mask to protect him from future recriminations.

Wearing masks dates back to prehistoric times as cave paintings depict their use as early as thirty thousand years ago. A famous ancient masked face can be found in France, in the Trois Frères cave, where a human believed to be a sorcerer is represented. It wears a stag's head topped with immense antlers, an owl's face, ears like a wolf's, and a long goat's beard. Other early masked faces are found on cave walls in Tassili, in southern Algeria, and in Spain.

As early as 2000 B.C. the Egyptians used burial masks, modeled to the face of the deceased. The masks were made of layers of linen pressed together and covered with a thin stucco upon which the features were painted.

Ancient death masks of Mycenae, Peru, Manchuria, Korea, and Egypt were made of plaster, gold, silver, bronze, and terra cotta. Because these masks, especially the gold ones, were made of an incorruptible material, they still preserve the facial features erased by death and serve their original purpose.

When you look at the face of a mask, you confront the power of the face as a symbol, as an idea. Masks can be beautiful objects in their own right. They can perform duties in religion, magic, and war. They are versatile. They demand attention. Masks can entertain. They can amuse. They can preserve life and cure ills. Masks can generate intense emotion. Masks can release inhibitions to do terrible things, as when Ku Klux Klanners don hooded masks and set out in the night to torment and terrify.

A mask can save face and give face. It can confer rank and identity larger and grander than is rightly one's own. At the same time, masks provide anonymity. It is for this reason that executioners of all times and all places have worn masks.

Masks and drama are closely allied and have been since Paleolithic times. The psychological effect produced on both the masked person and the audience is undeniable. It has been demonstrated that when one dons a mask and starts to interpret the character the face unconsciously imitates the expression of the mask.

*The mask is the only right medium of portraying the expressions of the soul as shown through the expressions of the face.*
EDWARD GORDON CRAIG

Masking is a way to fundamentally change the face, disguise it, conceal it, establish another being. As cultural objects, masks have been employed throughout the world in all periods since the Stone Age and are varied in appearance, in use, and in symbolism. The origin of masking is lost but this practice may have come about out of the hunt as a means of controlling game, or it may have originated as a means of ancestor worship. Whatever the origin, the practice serves a variety of purposes when it expresses group ideas, terrifies enemies, or wards off demons.

In classical Greece the actor's mask was neutral, without expression: it was intended to depersonalize and perhaps bewilder. In Hellenistic times, however, the actor's mask evolved toward expressiveness and pathos. Masks were used in tragedies, comedies, and satirical plays. Sophocles and Euripides wrote elaborate plays in which several characters could be impersonated by one actor changing masks.

In large Greek theaters it was hard to communicate moods and feelings to distant spectators, so masks were used to create a larger-than-life appearance. Today, though masks are uncommon in the theater, makeup is used to achieve a similar effect.

In Chinese drama masks are highly conventionalized, a red mask signifies the god of war or a famous soldier; a black mask signifies an honest man; a white mask denotes cunning; a golden mask stands for a god.

In traditional Japanese theater, as in early Greek drama, the characters are identified by their masks, which enable the actors to enact and project intense emotions. *Noh* drama (*noh* means "talent") is about five hundred years old. It has been compared to Greek drama because of its use of masks, a chorus, poetry, and song. *Noh* masks are smaller than the actor's face and are always worn by men. The mask-maker follows an exact procedure established long

Masks worn during hunting festivals often represent the spirit of an animal in a combination of symbolic and realistic form. These Alaskan masks were worn at a ceremony related to hunting. Sometimes the face's design incorporates recognizable parts of the prey. In this case wearing the mask empowers the wearer with the spirit of the hunted.

In cultures in which burial customs are important, masks are used to depict the dead and the departing spirit. Funerary masks were used to cover the face of the dead. Through the mask a relationship is established with the spirit world. Perhaps the most famous of all death masks is known as the "Mask of Agamemnon," though it is not Agamemnon. This gold funeral mask of an unknown Mycenean ruler dates from about the thirteenth century B.C. Upon discovering this particular mask in 1887, the famous archaeologist Heinrich Schliemann wrote to the king of Greece, "I have gazed on the face of Agamemnon."

From a necropolis dating to the tenth century in Peru comes this large golden "death mask" painted and ornamented in such a way that almost the entire golden surface, except the outline of the eyes, the nose, and an area of the chin, is hidden. The significance of this is unknown.

This Malaggani funerary mask comes from New Ireland, Melanesia. It is a mask of opposites: life and death; day and night.

This shell mask was found in an Indian burial mound in Tennessee. It is between four hundred and a thousand years old. According to art historian H. W. Janson, shell masks such as this one seem to have been placed in graves for the purpose of providing the dead with a second, permanent face, one that would trap the person's spirit underground.

In many places masks are central to initiation rites. Boys of the Bayaka tribe, in what used to be known as the Belgian Congo, don wooden masks like this (left) for their puberty rite ceremonials. At Gungu near Kikwit, also in the Congo, young initiates wear this mask (right) to enact the same rite of passage.

In Mexico masking is an ancient practice primarily associated with religious beliefs and ceremonies related to curing, hunting, and warfare and the impersonation of deities.

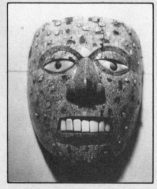

Masks, the most widely distributed art form of the northwest coast Indians, are for the most part dominated by one overriding shamanistic theme: transformation. Shamans are religious specialists who, by virtue of their unique powers, have access to the supernatural. This Tlingit mask must have come to life with electrifying effect.

The Iroquois of the northeastern United States carved and painted wooden "false face" masks for use in curing rites. Wearing these masks, professional healers performed violent pantomimes to exorcise demons that they believed were responsible for sickness. One can imagine the dancing firelight heightening the effect of these threatening faces.

Playing with identity is the motivation behind the masked ball or masquerade. Classically, a masked ball invites guests to release inhibitions as the mask protects one's identity. We all experience this when we dress up for Halloween or Mardi Gras. The disguise is designed to create a momentary confusion and anonymity.

ago. Once the mask is finished, the actor who wears it gives it life. Through nuances of movements and subtle changes in the tilt of the actor's head, the masked face becomes radiant one moment, grief-stricken the next. Tragic masks of the *noh* drama deal mainly with somber themes such as the transitory nature of life and the grim pranks of nemesis.

In Korea masks are used primarily in religious rites, for dispelling evil spirits, curing illness, and promoting a good harvest. Color symbolism and the shape of the features show the character of each person represented. Black means evil, red signifies power.

In Bali wooden masks, *tupeng*, are used in theatrical dance dramas that are performed both as amusement and as a safeguard against calamities. Every activity associated with the mask, from carving

through performance to the masks's storage and preservation, is treated with respect.

Masks have been important in African culture. African masks very in size and material. Some are used in initiation ceremonies and cult rituals. Some celebrate the harvest or are worn in judging the guilt or innocence of prisoners. Some are used in the exorcism of evil spirits. Some are used for entertainment.

By the end of the sixteenth century masks were popular among European noblewomen. They were worn to the theater to avoid recognition and outdoors to protect the complexion. By the seventeenth and eighteenth centuries, masks were used for disguise, coquetry, and as protection in bad weather. We still wear festive masks when we dress up for Halloween or Mardi Gras. In wearing such a dis-

The Kwakiutl Indians of the northwest coast created complicated transformation masks that combined human and animal attributes. Believing that the human spirit could take animal form and vice versa, the mask fused man and bird into one. During the winter months masks like this one came to life in the firelight ceremonials and worked their magic, part of which was to bind the individual to the group.

In *Noh* theater performers are storytellers who use their visual appearances and movements to suggest the essence of the tale rather than the action.

guise, we create a momentary confusion of identity and relish the brief anonymity.

Masks, whether used in meditative silence or to the persistent drumming of instruments, whether simply hung or intricately lit, conceal and reveal. In so doing, they awaken in the individual a sense of belonging, a sense of participation in the inscrutable mystery of being a social animal. That is what changing the face is all about.

All in all, there are a bewildering number of ways to change the face. They are as varied in appearance, significance, and use as the lives of the men and women who employ them. Whether high tech or low, dramatic or subtle, the desire for transformation seems to be inherited, passed down the genetic line, for today there are individuals in all human groups who change the face in order to find a place in the cultural order and to become part and parcel of the group's effort to go about the important business of daily living.

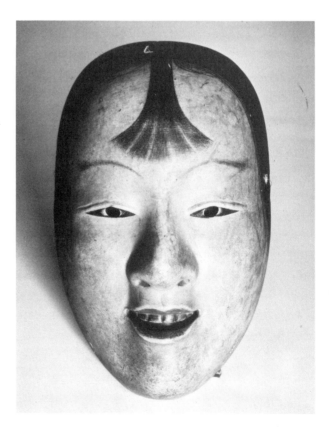

# 12

# The Face and
# the Future

*Believing as I do that man in the distant future
will be a far more perfect creature than he now
is, it is an intolerable thought that he and all other
sentient beings are doomed to complete annihi-
lation after such long-continued slow progress.*

CHARLES DARWIN

What does the future hold for the human face? Some scientists think that neoteny, the biological effect that produces a more "youthful" version of the face (and body), is still at work. The evidence includes the fact that our teeth, which are responsible in part for our faces' appearance, continue to decrease in size. Anthropologists at the University of Michigan, in fact, have demonstrated that in the last ten thousand years tooth size has been shrinking twice as fast as it did during the previous ninety thousand years. This shrinking will continue as long as our teeth are not challenged to work hard in order to process edible materials for digestion. There is also the fact that our wisdom teeth appear to be on their way out. Even today, many people are born without these powerful grinders.

Another clue is our apparent tendency toward hairlessness, a neotenic characteristic that has the effect of making the face smoother and more child-like. One of the social advantages of hairlessness is that it projects appeasing, nonthreatening qualities. Could it be that hairlessness was brought neoteni-cally into the adult stage of development to create a more appealing face and body wherein babylike skin and a baby face become treasured attributes contributing significantly to one's courtship poten-tial and hence one's social status?

As we learned earlier, the neotenized face came along with a change in the tool chest, a change in manual dexterity, a change in the species' self-concept, a change in the individual's notions about self. All these new perceptions coalesced and found expression on the face—in its shape and structure as well as its message and meaning. A more childlike face figured prominently in developing social bonds and may now be reflected in the genetic code.

From this perspective, the most important social force in human neoteny has been the role played by a more youthful face in one's social status, sexual attraction, and courtship. One's status can be trans-lated into courtship potential, and age is a critical factor in courtship. This may be why youth has be-come more and more revered, the standard by which we measure attractiveness and desirability. Crow's-feet, gray streaks, and bald spots are dreaded not so much for their implications about aging as that they signal reduced courtship appeal and, therefore, a lower social status.

The fact is that, regardless of age, a juvenile-looking man or woman is more likely to receive courtship invitations than, say, an older-looking man or woman of the same age. This phenomenon has been an important selection pressure in that those who look young naturally leave more young-looking progeny.

Will the face continue to evolve in this more "youthful" direction? There is every reason to believe that some of these trends may continue and no reason to assume that the process has stopped. In the last several hundred years, for example, our reliance on courtship potential as a reinforcement of our social status seems to have grown way out of proportion and there appear to have been some detrimental emotional consequences of judging everyone at face value. This overemphasis on the face's appearance is a heavy burden on both the unattractive and the attractive alike. The unattractive live in a world where their inner selves rarely get a proper showing and are immediately dismissed on the basis of their faces' appearance. The beautiful people, on the other hand, live in a world where the emphasis on appearance has created a preoccupation with the mirror, with makeup and plastic surgery. The very attractive are often riddled with self-doubt and uncertain about who they really are and why people are attracted to them.

Moved by instinct and motivated by the mysterious and unknowable, we humans do not ordinarily choose our mates by any cognitive design. Rather, that electric feeling called lust washes over us and we are in love. We mate and give birth to creatures much like ourselves. Of all the many things we know about being human, we probably know least about the biology of these feelings as they pertain to appearance and face. And yet they are of great consequence. In fact, most of the important things that will happen to us socially are in large measure dependent on them, at least for the present.

In terms of humankind's collective future, there are those who suggest that there are forces no human face can affect, such as the forces of the galaxies, or the solar system, or even the forces of the earth that will ultimately determine the face's fate. Any of these, it has been suggested, will at some point influence and determine the face's future. On the other hand, there is the opposite view that from day to day we have everything to do with our face's future and even now have set in motion circumstances that will fundamentally change the way faces look and behave.

Millions of years hence, some experts speculate, our eyes and ears could increase in size to accommodate the ever increasing amounts of information those sense organs are required to absorb. In this scenario, our noses decrease in size because the hairs of the nostrils will lose their function of having to scent prey and warm incoming currents of cool air while we live in an atmosphere of constant air conditioning. Our jaws and teeth will get smaller because we won't have to grasp and tear food. The palate, larynx, and tongue will get bigger to accommodate speed in conversing as it becomes increasingly crucial to exchange huge blocks of information.

Experts disagree on what our cranial size will be in the near future. Some say that humankind will develop much larger heads than we presently have so we can retain much more information than now. On the other hand it is believed that head size is severely limited by the female pelvic profile. A greatly increased skull size would make birth as we know it impossible but would not preclude birth by a caesarean section. The more likely direction is that, rather than the brain becoming significantly larger, changes will occur in its organization.

Looking back, it took about 12 million years for humans to double in height from that of *Ramapithecus*. Does that mean that at the end of another 12 million years humans will be thirteen feet tall? The accepted view is that humankind will reach optimum height, perhaps seven or eight feet for men, in the next 2 million years.

There are other prognosticators, from a wide

*We know what we are, but know not what we may be.*
SHAKESPEARE

variety of disciplines, who dismiss these kinds of evolutionary changes by natural selection and posit that we humans have a new future in which we are in charge. In this future, the possibilities are endless and humankind transcends evolutionary contraints. Until now the human face represents a series of evolutionary solutions to a series of biological problems. Bone and muscles as well as behavior interaction have been modeled by evolution. But the distant future portends something completely different. According to the futurist F. M. Esfandiary, extensive mapping of genes may put the human face's appearance in the hands of genetic engineers. Head-to-head communication may result from implanted microtransceivers. Procreation via ova and sperm selection from sex cell banks may put a different light on the face's physical appearance, as will fertilization and gestation entirely outside the body. This may make gender differences increasingly irrelevant. The improvement of humanity's gene pool will have a significant impact on human intelligence. Indefinite life expectancy and a significant slowdown in aging, due to far-reaching advances in biochemistry and microbiology, are bound to change our perception of the face. Esfandiary predicts that abundant resources, ultraintelligent machines, a global life, and accelerated space colonization will lead to the emergence of a whole new species, which he calls posthumans. These posthumans will arise from the coalescence of humans and ultraintelligent machines. Sound farfetched? The fact is that many of these projections are based on models designed by scientists and scholars in an attempt to extrapolate the future based on what is known about the present. They may seem farfetched today but will they in fifty years? Probably not.

Take the anti-aging revolution that has just begun to change the nature and meaning of the face. In A.D. 1 life expectancy was 22 years of age. By 1800 it was 35 years. By 1900 it was 49.2 years. In 1980 the average face lived to see 74 years. By the year 2000 the average face will see 85 years. By 2030 the average life expectancy will be 120 years, and by 2050 or 2060 we may well come face-to-face with immortality.

All this will be made possible by human cloning, which will provide genetically identical organs, tissue, and cells for aged persons. Anti-aging drugs will be available by prescription to arrest and reverse the aging process in humans. By 2030, it is projected, computerized analysis of human chromosomes, followed by artificial construction and their subsequent introduction into human egg cells that have been removed from the body, will allow for the creation of human faces and bodies according to any desired genetic program. Advanced techniques of neurosurgery may allow the consumer to trade in his or her original face for a new, custom-built, improved model. The ramifications of such changes are multitudinous, though little understood, and will undoubtedly have a profound impact on family life (including courtship and procreation), on education, employment, international affairs, and concerns of the spirit.

Events in the interim will also affect our day-to-day social encounters. In the very near future population pressures will put the face to work in new ways as face-to-face interaction is increasingly characterized by stressful encounters. Our whole sense of ourselves, our faces, and society arose when a few people had to get together, depend upon one another, and share in order to survive. Times have changed. During our brief history we have multiplied our numbers and improved communication until society now reaches over the whole habitable area of the earth. Increasingly, we crowd one another. Increasingly, we impinge on one another's space. In so doing, our aggressive tendencies come to the fore, and this has important psychological ramifications.

Excessive crowding distorts behavior. Fighting

increases. The normal processes of reproduction are interfered with. There is increasing frustration and irritation. The resulting tension erupts into outbreaks of violence and antisocial behavior. Overcrowding is going to challenge us to behave in more conciliatory ways.

It appears that a major factor in the control of aggression is personal acquaintance. Being anonymous makes aggressiveness much easier. If you know your adversary, just know his or her face, you find it more difficult to attack and easier to control your own aggressive propensities. Consider again what happens in traffic when you are isolated in your car. The dangerous thing is that you don't see the other driver's face. You see a Chevy or BMW or a Toyota. Without a face, the occupants of the other cars aren't even people. Yet they arouse in you feelings of anger, hostility, and aggression. These ancient feelings—in fact the whole repertoire of human emotions which find expression on the face—will likely be managed by the pharmacology of the future. It is predicted that by the turn of the century there will be drugs to control aggression, drugs for a deeper consciousness of beauty, drugs for retarding adolescence, drugs for suppressing or developing maternal behavior, and drugs for controlling sociability. All of these drugs are bound to have a radical effect on the face's behavior and its role as a multisignal, multimessage medium of communication.

It has been claimed that today's modern anonymous mass society, with all that it entails, is far from ideal for the healthy social development of children and social groups. This reality seems to have permanently disrupted our traditional sources of emotional support. Yet we seem to have in part adapted to this new reality by creating "in-groups" within the framework of large cities. We have developed friendship ties around occupational ties. In so doing, we have developed strong bonds and created extended families with whom we have regular and intimate contact. This, as we have seen, has been fundamental to our development and our success as a species. We continue to carry our evolutionary past with us in our genetic code. In that code is programmed the need for intimate bonds, for face-to-face communication. The irony of modern forms of communication is that, though they link people together, they effectively keep them apart. What will this mean long term as more and more people effectively telecommunicate? No one really knows for sure. The only thing certain about the face's future is that it will continue to be challenged by an ever changing reality and that we will respond accordingly. For example, we may diffuse the problems of crowding by widespread colonization of desert lands and of space.

**ZERO GRAVITY**
When television images of the astronauts are beamed down to earth from orbit, they usually show the effects of zero gravity. In a weightless environment, astronauts float and move about easily and do their jobs. But the absence of gravity has an effect. Since most activities are easy to perform and require little work, the body adapts by atrophying, actually losing bone and muscle mass. To counteract these deleterious effects, astronauts exercise on treadmills while on board.

If humankind's future is in space, which many long-term forecasters predict, surely that will have a significant impact on both the face's appearance and its behavior. Work by NASA has already demonstrated that at least two crucial physical changes occur as a result of zero gravity: the first involves the bone; the second involves the muscles.

In space no one gets enough exercise, according to astronaut Pete Conrad, who once estimated that it would be necessary to work out five hours a day just to make up for the lack of expended energy in zero gravity. Living in gravity requires the body to work. Living in weightlessness puts fewer physical demands on the body. To adjust, the body atrophies and loses bone mass and density. Bones lose a half to one percent of their calcium content each month in a weightless environment. The result is that prolonged space travel will cause the face to shrink, altering its proportions.

Another significant change resulting from weightlessness is the redistribution of blood and fluid to the head. In fact the physical appearance of the face changes so much that space travelers may not even recognize themselves in the mirror. The face becomes extremely puffy, the eyes bloodshot, and bags appear under the eyes. Veins tend to swell in the neck and forehead. Facial tissue shifts upward. Finally, the puffed and distended face loses it ability to produce distinctive expressions and communicate subtle kinds of nonverbal information. Indeed, these changes are obvious after living only a few days in zero gravity. Imagine what the long-term effect might be.

To keep matters under control, space travelers will probably be equipped with body suction machines, aluminum barrels that look as if they have been fabricated from four-foot lengths of oil pipeline, with tight rubber seals that fit around the waist. At the front of each barrel is a set of valves and tubes, as well as a backrest resembling part of a hospital gurney. The object is to sit in the suction

## THE FACE IN SPACE

Zero gravity refashions the face. It becomes puffy, the eyes bloodshot, bags develop under the eyes, veins tend to swell in the neck and forehead. Facial tissue shifts upward. The face loses its ability to produce distinctive expressions. Compare the faces of the crew members of the space shuttle when on earth and in space while in orbit aboard the shuttle.

machine until the vital body fluids have been pulled down into the body.

Still another feature of weightlessness that affects the human face is the fact that weightlessness carries with it the continual feeling of a stuffed-up nose. With the blood that would ordinarily be in the legs now redistributed to the head, the feeling of congestion is hard to avoid. This stuffiness cuts off many of the sensations of taste and smell.

Living in space poses another problem for the face. Space colonies, large space missions, even enclaves set up on other planets, may demand new forms of social order because men and women living so close together in isolated situations are likely to survive only when the rules governing social behavior and face work are extremely clear. In communities on earth, stability and balance are emphasized in permanent human relationships. Frustrations and aggravations can be released through various channels in the wide society. But in a space colony there would be little room for releasing hostile emotions. In space it will be essential that every person be able to adapt swiftly to changes and that these adaptations do not interfere with cooperative activities, for a breakdown of the social order in space would be a disaster.

According to George Robinson, expert in space law, the dependence of space inhabitants upon technology for their survival, together with a synthetic and alien life-support environment, will foster values and behavior that are quite different from those of human living on earth. He predicts that the majority of people leaving the earth for permanent or long-term habitation in space may be female, that the social order in space communities will be primarily matriarchal, which may be advantageous because women are generally less aggressive than men. In space, audiovisual technology will play an important role in bringing individuals together.

Based on today's rapidly advancing technology, there are some givens about the face's near future. Faces will increasingly be rebuilt with new parts, including artificial eyes, ears, noses, tongues, larynxes, not to mention skin and bone. These artificial face parts will owe their existence largely to advances in biomechanics, electronics, and microsurgery. Most forecasters foresee a future when we humans will be able to completely redesign our faces to predetermined specification. It won't be long, perhaps by the second decade of the twenty-first century, before artificial skin will enable anyone to put on a brand-new face. Indeed, artificial skin is likely to revolutionize plastic surgery.

Right now research is being conducted at the Massachusetts Institute of Technology to perfect

Map point 4: Move arrow to
corner of your eye as shown
on icon. Press SELECT

Move arrow to choose a face.
Press SELECT

Choose: Mix oc Blend
Press SELECT

Choose: Mix or Blend
Press SELECT

Move arrow to choose a face.
Press SELECT

## MIX AND BLEND

Mix and Blend is an interactive video exhibit created by Nancy Burson and David Kramlich for the "About Faces" traveling exhibition. They made it possible for the museum visitor to create an entirely new kind of self-portrait in which the subject can either exchange features or totally blend his or her face with another well-known face from the exhibit's data base. The exhibit holds twelve images in its data base: Jane Fonda, Andy Warhol, Paul McCartney, Marilyn Monroe, Oprah Winfrey, Ronald Reagan, Pat Morita, Frankenstein, Princess Diana, a witch, Ted Lange, and the visitor. The results are both fascinating and fun.

computer-based machines that will scan and recognize faces. These devices will probably be used as part of a surveillance system in airports, bus terminals, and other public places. They will be used to validate security clearances, among other uses, and so tend to raise the concern of civil libertarians, who see in them a threat to personal privacy.

In the future there will continue to be a number of ways to change the face, though it seems likely that the world will continue to prefer the Hollywood-Madison Avenue image that is now ubiquitous the world over.

Today, because of the work of a variety of scientists, artists, and engineers, computers offer all of us new ways to look at faces. Traveling exhibitions,

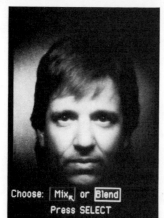

Choose: [Mix] or [Blend]
Press SELECT

Move arrow to choose a face.
Press SELECT

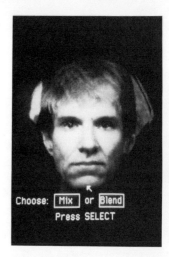

Choose: [Mix] or [Blend]
Press SELECT

Choose: [Mix] or [Blend]
Press SELECT

such as "About Faces" (which was the original inspiration for this book), will invite the public to use the face as an object of study. Interactive video technology will enable you to look at your own face as a strange landscape and to explore it, much like a tourist, bit by bit, feature by feature, in order to better understand how it works, what it says, and how it reveals human needs and desires.

Indeed, the marriage of art and science is producing new ways to think about the face and to explore its symbolic potential. In the vanguard are a group of video artists and scientists. One such artist, Nancy Burson, is experimenting with conceptions of face. Her portraits of the imagination give face to abstract ideas. They challenge us to think

The exhibit works like this:
* The computer is given the coordinates of the visitor's face, in this case, Paul Avery's. The computer then lines up the eyes, nose, and mouth.
* Paul selects a face from the menu, in this case, Ronald Reagan's face.
* He instructs the computer to blend the two faces to produce a composite personality.
* Paul enters his face into the computer's data base again.
* He selects Andy Warhol's face from the possibilities and instructs the computer to make a composite of the two faces.
* Another exhibit visitor, Lori Landeck, enters her face into the computer's data base.
* She selects Jane Fonda's face for the composite and instructs the computer to create a new portrait.

  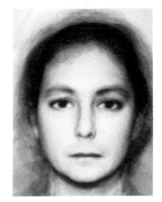

## PORTRAITS OF THE IMAGINATION

Portraiture has taken a distinctly different turn as the human imagination finds a new way to conceptualize ideas and turn them into faces.

EVERYONE AND NO ONE    In this composite portrait Nancy Burson has given a face to universal man. The portrait is a racial composite weighted according to population statistics for the three major racial groups: Oriental, Caucasian, and Black.

WARHEAD IV    gives a face to the threat of nuclear war. Burson combined the images of Reagan and Gorbachev and weighted them according to the number of nuclear warheads in each man's arsenal: Reagan (52%) and Gorbachev (48%).

ANDROGYNY    This face is actually a composite photo of six men and six women. Interestingly, it is the female qualities that seem to predominate in the composite.

about faces in terms of both their messages and their meaning.

In the very near future we can expect the face to carry on traditions that are extremely old and tribal in nature: the nurturing of human beings, educating them, refining their behavior and skills so that each new face can enter the circle of humanity as a fully contributing member. For the time being the face will remain one of the most compelling structures in the known universe. It will continue to be an instrument on which we play the melody of our individuality against the harmony of our shared humanity. But the face's future is uncertain as the possibilities for change increase exponentially with advances in technology and genetic engineering. Undoubtedly, future discoveries will propel us to new thresholds of understanding about this structure that has for so long mirrored the mind, defined us as individuals and expressed the wonderfully sentient nature of being human.

### SYM-LATIONS

This interactive video exhibit was created by Ed Tannenbaum for the "About Faces" exhibition primarily as a device for encouraging the visitor to explore the face's asymmetry. But, as you can see, Tannenbaum's program also makes it possible to play with the very notion of face.

### MAX HEADROOM

Max Headroom is a computer-generated altered face, a disembodied head that lives only on a TV screen but has the uncanny appearance of being a real, though different, person. He functions as a kind of robotic Clark Kent designed and manufactured for the video generation. Max's face was picked up by Coca-Cola and used in commercials. After the first run of commercials, seventy-six percent of all teenagers in the United States recognized Max Headroom. This suggests just how effective the talking head is in reaching into the minds and imaginations of real humans. We can only guess at what this portends for the future.

# Bibliography

ANGELOGLOU, MAGGIE, *A History of Make-up*, Macmillan, New York, 1970.

BELL, C., *Essays on the Anatomy of Expression*, Longman, Hurst, Rees, and Orme, London, 1806.

BERNHEIMER, RICHARD, *The Nature of Representation*, New York University Press, 1961.

BINFORD, LEWIS R., *In Pursuit of the Past*, Thames & Hudson, New York, 1983.

BIRDWHISTELL, RAY, *Introduction to Kinesics*, University of Louisville, Kentucky, 1952.

———, *Kinesics and Context*, University of Pennsylvania Press, Philadelphia, Pennsylvania, 1970.

BRADSHAW, JOHN L., and NORMAN C. NETTLETON, *Human Cerebral Asymmetry*, Prentice-Hall, Englewood Cliffs, New Jersey, 1983.

BRAIN, C. K., "A Hominid Skull's Revealing Holes," *Natural History 83* (10): 44–45, 1984.

BREGER, LOUIS, *From Instinct to Identity*, Prentice-Hall, Englewood Cliffs, New Jersey, 1974.

BRENNAN, SUSAN E., "Caricature Generator: The Dynamic Exaggeration of Faces by Computer," *Leonardo*, vol 18, No. 3, pp. 170–78, 1985.

———, GILLIAN RHODES, and SUSAN CAREY, "Identification and Ratings of Caricatures: Implications for Mental Representations of Faces," *Cognitive Psychology 19*, pp. 473–97 (1987).

BRONOWSKI, JACOB, *The Ascent of Man*, Futura Macdonald, London, 1981.

BURSON, NANCY, RICHARD CARLING, and DAVID KRAMLICH, *Composites*, Morrow, New York, 1986.

CHEVALIER-SKOLNIKOFF, S., *Darwin and Facial Expression*, P. Ekman, ed., Academic Press, New York, 1973, pp. 11–89.

CIRILLO, DENNIS P., and M. RUBENSTEIN, *The Complete Book of Cosmetic Facial Surgery: A Step-by-Step Guide to the Physical and Psychological Experience by a Plastic Surgeon and Psychiatrist*, Simon & Schuster, New York, 1984.

CORBALLIS, MICHAEL C., *Human Laterality*, Academic Press, New York, 1983.

CORSON, RICHARD, *Fashions in Makeup*, Universe Books, New York, 1972.

DARWIN, CHARLES, *The Expression of the Emotions in Man and Animals*, John Murray, London, 1872.

DAVIES, G., H. ELLIS, and J. SHEPERD, "Wanted—Faces That Fit the Bill," *New Scientist*, (106): 26–29, May 16, 1985.

DEWDNEY, A. K., "Computer Creations," *Scientific American*, vol. 255, October 1986, p. 20.

DIAMOND, JARED, "I Want a Girl Just Like the Girl . . ." *Discover*, November 1986.

————, "Survival of the Sexiest," *Discover*, May 1988.

DOBZHANSKY, THEODOSIUS, *Science and the Concept of Race*, Ethel Tobach and Robert E. Light, eds., Columbia University Press, New York, 1968.

EIBL-EIBESFELDT, I., *Love and Hate*, Holt, Rinehart & Winston, New York, 1971.

EKMAN, PAUL, "Facial Signs: Facts, Fantasies, and Possibilities," *Sight, Sound and Sense*, T. Sebeok, ed., Indiana University Press, Bloomington, Indiana, 1978.

————, *The Face of Man: Expressions of Universal Emotions in a New Guinea Village*, Garland STPM Press, New York.

————, *Telling Lies*, Berkley Books, New York, 1986.

————, and WALLACE V. FRIESEN, *Unmasking the Face*, Prentice-Hall, Englewood Cliffs, New Jersey, 1975.

————, W. V. FRIESEN, and P. ELLSWORTH, *Emotions in the Human Face*, Pergamon Press, New York, 1972.

ERIKSON, ERIK, *Childhood and Society*, Norton, New York, 1950.

————, *A Way of Looking at Things: Selected Papers*, Norton, New York, 1987.

FAST, JULIUS, *Body Language*, Evans, New York, 1970.

FIELD, T. M., "Discrimination and Imitation of Facial Expressions by Neonates," *Science*, October 1982.

GERASIMOV, MIKHAIL, *The Face Finder*, Hutchinson, London, 1971.

GESCHWIND, NORMAN, "Specializations of the Human Brain," *The Brain, Scientific American Book*, Freeman, San Francisco, 1979.

GHALIOUNGUI, PAUL, *Magic and Medical Science in Ancient Egypt*, Barnes & Noble, New York, 1963.

GILBERT, C., and P. BAKEN, "Visual Asymmetry in Perception of Faces," *Neuropsychologia*, 1973.

GOFFMAN, ERVING, *Interaction Ritual*, Pantheon Books, New York, 1967.

————, *The Presentation of Self in Everyday Life*, Doubleday, Garden City, New York, 1959.

GOMBRICH, ERNEST H., *Art and Illusion*, Pantheon Books, New York, 1960.

GREGORY, R. L., and E. H. GOMBRICH, eds., *Illusion in Nature and Art*, Scribner's, New York, 1973.

HALL, EDWARD T., *The Silent Language*, Doubleday, Garden City, New York, 1959.

HARMON, LEON, "The Recognition of Faces," *Scientific American*, November 1983.

————, and KEN KNOWLTON, "Picture Processing by Computer," *Science*, April 1969, vol. 163, pp. 19–29.

HEILMAN, K. M., and E. VALENSTEIN, eds., *Clinical Neuropsychology*, Oxford University Press, 1979.

HESS, ECKHARD H., *The Tell-Tale Eye*, Van Nostrand Reinhold, New York, 1975.

HIBBARD, HOWARD, *The Metropolitan Museum of Art*, Harper & Row, New York, 1980.

HOWELLS, WILLIAM, ed., *Ideas on Human Evolution: Selected Essays, 1949–61*, Harvard University Press, Cambridge, Massachusetts, 1962.

HU, HSIEN CHIN, "The Chinese Concepts of 'Face'," *American Anthropologist*, January–March, vol. 1, pp. 45–65, 1944.

HUBER, E., *Evolution of Facial Musculature and Facial Expressions*, Johns Hopkins Press, Baltimore, 1931.

IZARD, CARROLL, *The Face of Emotion*, Meredith, New York, 1971.

————, *Human Emotions*, Plenum Press, New York, 1977.

JASTROW, ROBERT, *The Enchanted Loom: The Mind in the Universe*, Simon & Schuster, New York, 1981.

JAYNES, JULIAN, *The Origin of Consciousness in the Bicameral Mind*, Houghton Mifflin, Boston, 1976.

KNOWLTON, KEN, "Computer-Produced Grey Scales," *Computer Graphics and Image Processing*, vol. 1, April 1972.

KONNER, MELVIN, *The Tangled Wing*, Harper & Row, New York, 1982.

LEAKEY, LOUIS, *Olduvai Gorge, 1951–61*, 3 vols., Cambridge University Press, 1965–71.

LEAKEY, RICHARD, "Evidence for an Advanced Plio-Pleistocene Hominid from East Rudolf, Kenya," *Nature*, 242, pp. 447–50, April 13, 1973.

———, *The Making of Mankind*, Dutton, New York, 1981.

———, *People of the Lake*, Anchor Press/Doubleday, Garden City, New York, 1978.

———, and ROGER LEWIN, *Origins*, Dutton, New York, 1977.

LEE, RICHARD, and IRVEN DeVORE, eds., *Man the Hunter*, Aldine Publishing, Chicago, 1968.

LEFAS, JEAN, *Physiognomy: The Art of Reading Faces*, Ariane Books, 1975.

LEWONTIN, RICHARD, *Human Diversity*, Scientific American Books, New York, 1982.

LIGGETT, JOHN, *The Human Face*, Stein & Day, New York, 1974.

LUMSDEN, CHARLES, and EDWARD O. WILSON, *Promethean Fire*, Harvard University Press, Cambridge, Massachusetts, 1983.

MALINOWSKI, BRONISLAW, *Sex, Culture, and Myth*, Harcourt, Brace, and World, New York, 1962.

MALPASS, ROY S., "Enhancing Eyewitness Memory," in G. Koehnken and S. L. Sporer, eds., *Eyewitness Identification: Psychological Knowledge, Problems and Perspectives*, May 1988.

———, "A Cross-Cultural Face Recognition Field Manual: Description and a Validation Study," in L. H. Eckensberger, W. J. Lonner, and Y. H. Poortinga, eds., *Cross-cultural Contributions to Psychology*. Swets and Zeitlinger, Lisse, The Netherlands, 1979.

———, and JOHN BRIGHAM, "The Role of Experience and Contact in the Recognition of Faces of Own and Other Race Persons," *Journal of Social Issues*, vol. 41, no. 3, 1985, pp. 139–55.

———, and K. D. HUGHES, "Formation of Facial Prototypes," in H. D. Ellis, M. A. Jeeves, F. Newcombe, and A. W. Young, eds., *Aspects of Face Processing* (NATO ISI Series), Martinus Nijhoff, Dordrecht, The Netherlands.

———, HENRY LAVIGUEUR, and DAVID WELSON, "Verbal and Visual Training in Face Recognition," *Perception & Psychophysics*, vol. 14, no. 2, pp. 285–92, 1973.

McDERMOTT, JEANNE, "Making Faces Just Comes Naturally," *Smithsonian*, vol. 16, no. 12, March 1986, pp. 112–23.

MONTAGNA, WM., *The Structure and Function of Skin*, 2nd ed., Academic Press, New York, 1962.

MONTAGU, ASHLEY, *Human Heredity* and *Touching: The Human Significance of the Skin*, Columbia University Press, New York, 1971.

————, *The Concept of Race*, Free Press, New York, 1964.

MORRIS, DESMOND, *Bodywatching*, Crown, New York, 1985.

————, *Manwatching*, Harry Abrams, New York, 1977.

OAKLEY, KENNETH P., *Man the Tool-Maker*, 6th ed., University of Chicago Press, 1976.

PENRY, JACQUES, *How to Judge Character from the Face*, Hutchinson, London, 1939.

PFEIFFER, JOHN, *The Emergence of Man*, Harper & Row, New York, 1978.

PILBEAM, DAVID, and STEPHEN JAY GOULD, "Size and Scaling in Human Evolution," *Science*, December 6, 1974.

PORA, CLARE, and STANLEY COREN, *Lateral Preferences and Human Behavior*, Springer-Verlag, New York, 1981.

READ, SIR HERBERT E., *Art and Society*, Faber & Faber, London, 1950.

ROOK, A. J., D. S. WILKINSON, and F. EBBLING, *Textbook in Dermatology*, 1968.

SACKEIM, H. A., and R. C. GUR, "Lateral Asymmetry in Intensity of Emotional Expression," *Neuropsychologia*, 1978.

SACKEIM, H., R. GOR, and M. SAUCY, "Emotions Are Expressed More Intensely on the Left Side of the Face," *Science*, 202, pp. 434–36, 1978.

SCHWARTZ, LILLIAN, "Leonardo's Mona Lisa," *Art and Antiques*, January 1987.

STERN, MADELEINE B., *Heads & Headlines*, University of Oklahoma Press, Norman, Oklahoma, 1971.

TANNER, NANCY MAKEPEACE, *On Becoming Human*, Cambridge University Press, 1981.

THEVOZ, MICHEL, *The Painted Body*, Rizzoli, New York, 1984.

TRINKAUS, ERIK, *The Shanidar Neanderthals*, Academic Press, New York, 1983.

VARGAS, MARJORIE FINK, *Louder Than Words*, Iowa University Press, Ames, Iowa, 1986.

VON BOEHN, MAX, *Modes and Manners*, Benjamin Blom, New York, 1932.

WALKER, JOHN, *National Gallery of Art*, Harry Abrams, New York, 1984.

WASHBURN, SHERWOOD, *The Study of Human Evolution*, University of Oregon Press, 1968.

ZAJONC, ROBERT, "Emotion and Facial Efference: A Theory Reclaimed," *Science*, vol. 228, April 5, 1985.

# Acknowledgments

I am indebted first to Jeffrey Kirsch, Executive Director of the Reuben H. Fleet Space Theater and Science Center in San Diego, California, who first invited me to think about faces and to participate in the development of the "About Faces" exhibition for the Exhibit Research Collaborative. The exhibition was created by a team of scientists, designers, educators, and artists. To all of them I owe a debt of gratitude. In particular I wish to acknowledge the help and expertise of Elsa Feher, project director; Paul Avery, project designer; Paul Ekman, content adviser; and Shab Levy, exhibition consultant. In addition I am grateful to Ed Tannenbaum, Nancy Burson, David Kramlich, Ken Knowlton, and Lou Katz for inspired discussions, guidance, and their generosity in allowing me to include their work in my book.

Others who contributed graphic material and provided valuable assistance during the writing of this book include Joel Gotler, Ed Manning, Michael Anderson, François Robert, Hiroko Hoshikawa, H.J. amd Anne Brown, Susan Brennan, Diane Franklin, Laura van Dorn Schneider, Geri Baur, Susan Stribling, Norman Seeff, Bob Klewitz, Carroll Fitzhugh, Jamie Stobie, Blandine Pelessier, Dr. Peter Andrews, Dr. Roger Shepard, Dr. Bela Julesz, the California Society of Plastic Surgeons, and the Doremus Company.

I want to thank Barbara Lowenstein, my agent, for her strong encouragement and representation, and my editor, Loretta A. Barrett, for her enthusiasm and for asking the right questions. I am indebted to family and friends. Special thanks to Robin Snelson, Jesse Salb, Linda Scarf, the Corbins, the Goldfarbs, the Quealys, and especially to my husband Richard and my daughter Marika for their support and understanding.

Writing a book of this kind, one draws on the work of many experts in a variety of fields (see Bibliography). In this way, many have contributed to this study, though ultimately its deficiencies are mine alone.

# Index

# Photo Credits

Page 36    Top left: Fogg Art Museum, Harvard University; top right: Norton Simon Foundation; middle left, bottom left: National Gallery of Art, Washington, D.C.; middle right: Frick Collection; bottom right: Metropolitan Museum of Art, New York.

Page 37    Metropolitan Museum of Art, New York.

Page 38    Norton Simon Collection.

Page 39    Kunsthistorisches Museum, Vienna.

Page 40    Lillian Felman Schwartz.

Page 41    Top, bottom left: Wide World; bottom right: Department of the Army.

Page 44    Cincinnati Art Museum.

Pages 46–47    Susan Brennan.

Page 49    Scotland Yard, London, England.

Page 50    Wide World.

Page 51    Nancy Burson.

Page 52    Wide World.

Page 56    Top: Diane Franklin; bottom: Leon Harmon.

Page 57    Blocpix®/Watson-Manning.

Page 58    Ken Knowlton, Lou Katz, and Metron Studios.

Page 59    Marlows.

Page 60    Ken Knowlton.

Page 62    Clockwise from top left: Hiroko Hoshikawa, Hiroko Hoshikawa, François Robert, Hiroko Hoshikawa, H. J. Brown, Hiroko Hoshikawa.

Page 63    Clockwise from top left: François Robert, Hiroko Hoshikawa, Hiroko Hoshikawa, François Robert, François Robert, François Robert, François Robert.

Page 64    Top: Salvador Dali Foundation; bottom: Roger Shepard.

Page 65    Top: Bela Julesz; bottom: Kaiser Porcelain Ltd.

Pages 66–67    Robin Snelson.

Page 68    UNICEF.

Pages 70–71    Reuben H. Fleet Space Theater and Science Center/Software by Ed Tannenbaum.

Page 73    Julian Jaynes.

Pages 76–77    *Games* magazine/Rick Tulka.

Page 80    National Library of Medicine, Maryland.

Pages 84–85    Diane Franklin.

Page 86    Top: Diane Franklin; bottom: Marlows.

Page 87    Diane Franklin.

Page 89    National Library of Medicine, Maryland.

Page 160   National Library of Medicine, Maryland.

Page 164   United Nations.

Page 173   Wide World.

Pages 182–83   Norman Seeff.

Page 186   Musée Nationale de St.-Germain-en-Laye/L. Pales

Page 191   Richard Wells.

Page 193   Jericho, Jordan.

Page 195   Metropolitan Museum of Art, New York.

Page 196   Left, center: J. Paul Getty Museum; right: National Museum, Athens.

Page 197   Left, center: Metropolitan Museum of Art, New York; right: National Gallery of Art, Washington, D.C.

Page 198   National Gallery of Art, Washington, D.C.

Page 199   Left: Metropolitan Museum of Art, New York; center, right: National Gallery of Art, Washington, D.C.

Page 200   SCALA/Art Resources.

Page 201   National Gallery of Art, Washington, D.C.

Page 202   Top: George Eastman House; bottom: Pierpont Morgan Library.

Page 203   Top, middle left and right: National Gallery of Art, Washington, D.C.; bottom: Metropolitan Museum of Art, New York.

Page 204   Top: George Eastman House; bottom: Chuck Close/ Minneapolis Institute of Art.

Page 205   Library of Congress.

Page 206   Metropolitan Museum of Art, New York.

Page 207   Louvre Museum, Paris.

Page 209   American Museum of Natural History.

Page 211   Bishop Museum, Hawaii.

Page 212   SCALA/Art Resources.

Page 215   Rhode Island School of Design.

Pages 216–17   Nancy Burson.

Page 222   Top left: United Nations/P. S. Sudhakaran; top center: Circus World; top right: Peabody Museum; bottom left: Marlows, bottom right: Laura van Dorn Schneider.

Page 223   Top: UNICEF/George Hamilton; bottom: American Museum of Natural History/Captain Frank Hurley.

Page 224   United Nations/P. S. Sudhakaran.

Page 225   Top: American Museum of Natural History/E. T. Gilliard; bottom, United Nations.

Page 226   Staatliche Museen zu Berlin.

# About the Author

Terry Landau is an educator, television writer/producer/director whose productions include *Who's in Charge?* (PBS, 1987), *The Two Brains* (PBS, 1983–84), *In Search of Mayan Mysteries* (Alan Landsburg Productions, 1977), and *The Diet Jungle* (KABC, 1987), for which she won an Emmy Award. Ms. Landau is one of the creators of the "About Faces" traveling exhibit for the Reuben H. Fleet Space Theater and Science Center, 1987–88. Born in Chicago in 1942, she graduated from UCLA in 1966. Ms. Landau lives in Los Angeles with her husband and daughter.